A Program for Renewed Partnership

MEMBERS OF THE SLOAN COMMISSION

A Program For Renewed Partnership

The Report of the Sloan Commission on
Government and Higher Education

Ballinger Publishing Company ● Cambridge, Massachusetts
A Subsidiary of Harper & Row, Publishers, Inc.

International Standard Book Number: 0−88410−193−2

Library of Congress Catalog Card Number: 80−14347

Printed in the United States of America

Library of Congress Cataloging in Publication Data

Sloan Commission on Government and Higher Education.
  A program for renewed partnership.

  1. Higher education and state—United States. 2. Education, Higher—Research—United States. 3. Sloan Commission on Government and Higher Education. I. Title.
  LC173.S57 1980   378.73   80−14347
  ISBN 0−88410−193−2

Contents of Report

✳

Foreword

At their meeting of February 1, 1977, the Trustees of the Alfred P. Sloan Foundation approved the formation of what was then called the Sloan Commission on the Regulation of Higher Education and appropriated the funds to begin its work. The agenda for that meeting defined the questions to be addressed and the approach to them in part as follows:

—How does the country strike the balance between institutional freedom and government authority?

—To what extent is the academic institution to be responsive to what may be perceived as social needs?

—What both the regulators and the regulated find themselves in need of is a detailed, comprehensive analysis of the regulatory process by a distinguished but disinterested body whose recommendations would define and protect—and would be seen to define and protect—the public interest.

The Sloan Commission on Government and Higher Education has been precisely this kind of body. It has adhered closely to the agenda and the timetable set forth originally.

As in the previous cases in which the Foundation has established independent commissions, the role of the Foundation has been restricted to selecting the Commissioners and providing the funding for their work. Foundation officers have attended the meetings of the Commission as observers, but the recommendations are those of the Commission and not those of the Foundation or its Trustees.

We are deeply indebted to the members of the Commission, described briefly on page 305, for their conscientious efforts over many months and for the knowledge and insight they brought to their task. We are also indebted to the able staff of the Commission for the substantial body of research that lies behind the Commission's findings and recommendations. Perhaps our greatest debt is to Mr. Louis Cabot, the Chairman, and Dr. Carl Kaysen, the Vice Chairman and Director of Research. It is not an easy task to achieve a high degree of consensus among Commissioners of diverse backgrounds and points of view while still retaining substance and avoiding platitudes. They have achieved this with unfailing skill and tact, and the Report is testimony to their accomplishment.

Albert Rees, President
Alfred P. Sloan Foundation.

✳

Preface

Our Commission worked for more than two years. During this time, the public interest in the need for government and the academic world to resolve their differences became clearer as the adversarial posture stiffened on both sides. We present our recommendations early in a presidential election year when the urgency of other national and international issues can easily overshadow those we address. Nevertheless, we believe that the health of higher education is of great importance to the future of the country. If our report can stimulate public discussion and our recommendations find a place on the national agenda, its timing will prove fortunate.

From the first, we recognized that the key to the problems cannot be found in the concerns of any single set of institutions within the huge and diverse enterprise called "higher education." The balance between private and public institutions was an issue we discussed long and hard. The standards and needs of the elite research universities—our group had highly articulate spokesmen for them—are just one part of the dilemma facing higher education in its relation to government. There was no danger that we might ignore the viewpoints of women or of Blacks since they were particularly eloquently presented by members of the Commission. Those from the academic world were gently, if repeatedly, reminded by those from the business world of their own struggles with government regulation.

Our meetings were searching, spirited, and occasionally heated. The issues are complex. They also are controversial. Except in the few specific cases noted in the Overview, our recommendations reflect a natural resolution of our differences.

Our work could not have been done without the information assembled and analyzed by our excellent professional staff: Dr. Kenneth M. Deitch, Edward S. Gruson, Crystal C. Lloyd-Campbell, Esq., and Geoffrey White. Together with outside consultants, they kept us supplied with what we needed to know and highlighted the issues for us continuously over the period of our work. Finally, our logistic needs, both in Cambridge and in many other meeting places, were attended to with far more than logistic skill by Kathleen Fox.

We think we have given the country something to think about.

Louis W. Cabot
Chairman

Carl Kaysen
Vice Chairman and
Director of Research

A Program for
Renewed
Partnership

Chapter 1

An Overview

A new drama opened on the college campus in the seventies. Though not much in the headlines, it distracts the faculty off-stage and keeps a large audience absorbed. A growing number of lawyers and administrators are in the cast needed by colleges and universities to deal with a growing number of federal agents and investigators. Their dialogue of the deaf about affirmative action and financial accountability leads to little more than bad feeling on all sides. The struggle centers on how much right the government has to tell higher education what to do.

The academic world is traditionally autonomous, and its history offers considerable justification for its proud belief that it is able to change with the times. Over the past decade, the government steadily increased its output of laws and regulations affecting the campus, and moved aggressively in many places to get the compliance with them that it must have. This is what spawns the tension.

The discord comes at a time when American higher education is suffering the pangs of entering a new age, one of uncertainty and growing pessimism. A time of unprecedented expansion, change, and buoyancy has given way to a time of retrenchment. The growth came from the explosion of the college age population after World War II and from all the other changes that produced a rising percentage of those who chose college over work following high school. But now, the stark fact is that there are many fewer eighteen-year-olds to go to college and that this will continue at least until 1995. Even though many students today are not in the traditional age group, the Commission is confident that their numbers will not begin to make up for the enrollment losses caused by demographic changes.

This declining demand coincides with a period of severe financial stress for higher education, when inflation is driving up operating costs dramatically and hitting hard at all of its sources of income.

Government was a powerful and generous ally during the expansion. It could not have been otherwise since it understood well how our colleges and universities could fill the existing extraordinary demands for education and research. Its nose barely poked on to the campus. But today, there is less understanding, and sometimes it seems that the entire camel is bumping and thumping around inside the higher education tent.

The conflict has persisted for some years and our Commission was created to examine the reasons for it. We are convinced that although there are real problems that will not go away, much can be done to improve the ways in which the government and colleges and universities get along. This was our limited objective. We did not set out to present a vision of the ideal structure and to call for drastic change. Still, some of our proposals are bold and suggest a new order of priorities. Not everyone, on or off the campus, will like what we have to say. Without opposition, we would be left in doubt that it was worth saying at all.

Although our report is detailed and its recommendations highly specific, we mean it for the concerned citizen as well as the expert. Some of what we recommend is addressed to colleges and universities. Some of what we recommend needs action in state legislatures, in government agencies, and in Congress. All of what we recommend deserves wide public discussion. Every American is involved—as parent, as student, or as taxpayer.

Higher education is now a big business. It involves many people and much money. There are 11 million students in our colleges and universities and they employ 1 million faculty, administration, and staff. Total revenues are currently about $45 billion each year: $11 to $12 billion come from students and their families while $3 billion come from gifts, non-government grants and contracts, and endowment income. All the rest is provided by governments.

Large sums of public money are involved. In the fiscal year 1979–80, state legislatures invested $19 billion, and the federal government spent $14 billion, most of which went directly or indirectly to institutions.

These figures point up the importance of higher education to each of us as taxpayers. If it is to survive in something resembling its present form, public funds of this magnitude will be needed for as far ahead as we can see. Each of us has a large stake in making sure that the money is well used.

There are no easy answers to the questions we had to consider. Many are deeply philosophical ones that divide the public, and involve a conflict between two conceptions of fairness in how American society distributes opportunities and rewards. One view emphasizes individual effort and would reserve rewards for those who earn them. The other view stresses our obligations to meet the needs and claims of disadvantaged groups. As we, ourselves, examined the specific problems of public policy in higher education, we tried to arrive at a proper balance between these two philosophies.

The Commission's recommendations are shaped by the following broad convictions:

—It is of first importance to preserve the diversity of higher education. The response to new conditions, here as elsewhere, should be directed by the pluralistic choices of students and their parents, rather than by centralized decision-making.

—The social goals of equal opportunity legislation must be maintained, but a better way to reach them is needed. The initiative and responsibility must be kept primarily with the colleges and universities.

—Retrenchment is a new and difficult task. Reduction of capacity must be managed in a way that maintains quality and variety. The whole burden should not fall on private institutions.

—Federal financial aid should continue to be used primarily for helping students, so that no high school graduate who wants further education is denied it because of financial need. Yet, self-help should also be an element in every aid program. The federal government should also enable students to have wider choice among institutions by making its borrowing power available to all students and their families.

—Present mechanisms of federal support for research and scholarship at colleges and universities are fundamentally sound. Steadier funding and long-run growth in real terms are nevertheless needed to maintain America's preeminence in science and scholarship.

—The heavy involvement of the federal government in medical education, with its tendency toward manpower planning and direction, point to future dangers for higher education as a whole.

We call on our congressmen, on our state legislators, on our government officials, and on our political leaders to recognize that there has been an alarming loss of perspective on what higher education is all about, what it can do and must do, and what it should not be asked to do. More and more, the government is raising questions about faculty appointments and promotions through agents who simply do not know enough about higher education. More and more, problems are in the hands of administrators and legal advisors rather than in the hands of faculties who are responsible for the results. More and more, student admissions policies are under attack, and present procedures shift the attack to the courtroom. More and more, the government is expressing views on curriculum. More and more, scientists and scholars working with federal grants feel they are being treated like suppliers of office equipment or builders of dams. More and more, decisions on who shall teach, what they shall teach, and whom they shall teach are passing from colleges and universities to government agencies and the courts.

What we are saying is that present procedures—causing increasing bitterness and pessimism on both sides—ignore the vital interests of higher education. All too often, the standards are incomprehensible and inconsistent. Most of the procedures evolved in other contexts—secondary school or business. Many of the mechanisms are clumsy, duplicative, insensitive, time-consuming, ineffective and expensive. The remedies we recommend are ones we believe to balance fairly all the complex values at stake. If accepted, we think they will make a difference for the coming generation.

We call on the colleges and universities to recognize that some governmental oversight is inevitable. While we deplore the government's present lack of perspective, we also emphasize that it is unreasonable and unfair for higher education to accept billions in public money annually without being ready to account for its use, and without meeting the social goals toward which so much of the resented oversight is directed. What is needed now is simple acceptance of some of the government's demands as minimal and proper, even if onerous and sometimes expensive.

Our recommendations for improvement call for much self-regulation, and more is needed. We urge our colleges and universities to take a new hard look at themselves. Academics have been pioneers in calling for change in other social institutions, but have not always been ahead of society in changing their own. Many of the current demands resented by academic spokesmen are neither extraordinary nor illegitimate. The academy claims special status as the disinterested custodian of truth. But some of the advertising by 'academic' institutions is as extravagant as any in the commercial sector.

Both sides must work to restore the good will and feeling of partnership they enjoyed for so long. The prevailing adversarial mood is dangerous, particularly in the coming period when the dependence on the government as a patron will be so great. Those in higher education must anticipate problems, must educate the regulators, and, above all, must themselves make the changes that are needed. They are in the best position to decide how to change and keep their capacity to do what society needs them to do.

The pluralism of America is reflected in the forms and purposes assumed by colleges and universities, particularly in the last generation. This immense diversity embodies to a remarkable degree the values of our society. It is unique to this country and one of our greatest strengths. Ours is the only country in the world that makes it possible for all high school graduates to find the kind of further education that suits their talents and desires. Present trends could well end in the substitution of a table d'hôte for an à la carte offering.

Some of our colleges and universities are predominantly Catholic, some Baptist, some Jewish. Some serve only women. Some serve small local communities; many draw students from all sections of the nation and from abroad. Some are public and almost tuition free; others are private, charging high tuitions. Some have large endowments and depend heavily on the generosity of their graduates. In the last two decades, much of the growth in enrollment was in new wide-access public institutions requiring only a high school diploma for admission. There was a phenomenal increase in the numbers of two-year community colleges, most of which offer vocational training along with the traditional liberal arts, as well as in new four-year comprehensive colleges.

Not every college of every type can survive, or should survive, the coming enrollment decline and competition for students. But we can be sure that every college of every type will fight hard to keep open. The pressures on the public and the legislatures for support will be formidable. Anticipating this, we were led to think about how to guard quality. What the states do in the next fifteen years will have a profound influence on both the quality and variety of higher education.

We want to emphasize that we see great risks of federal intervention in the retrenchment process. Our Commission concluded that the federal government should strongly resist pressures to shape its financial aid or other policies to bolster an otherwise declining demand.

Most college students today are in institutions that are not nationally known. We think this fact is not widely appreciated, and that is why we stress it. If too many institutions of a particular type are forced to close their doors in a particular locale, it would be a great loss not only to the students who would have elected to go to them, but to our society. Homogenization of viewpoint and form is a threat to our deepest values. Public support must continue to be distributed broadly. We offer recommendations that we believe will safeguard diversity while encouraging the survival of the fittest.

We asked these questions, and answered yes to all of them:

—Is it important to keep successful comprehensive and community colleges alive? Yes, because they are a major new channel of social mobility.

—Is it important to continue to have a significant number of small private liberal arts colleges? Yes, because they preserve our intellectual inheritance and provide a sanctuary for moral and social criticism.

—Is it important to keep our great research universities, both public and private, strong? Yes, because they make our world leadership in science and technology possible by maintaining and enlarging our knowledge through scholarship, research, and teaching.

—Is it important to continue supporting some colleges that are predominantly for Blacks, or for Hispanic-Americans, or for women? Yes, because historically, these institutions have been the seedbed where people with talents for leadership were first awakened to their possibilities.

Of course, no one type of institution serves only one purpose, nor has every type of institution been mentioned. But all share the job of educating and training our young men and women. We believe that only if we continue to encourage a mix as varied as the present one will higher education still be able to accomplish all its tasks so vital to the nations's health.

Summary of Recommendations

Our full report has many recommendations, described and analyzed in detail. In the following summary, we highlight the major ones. Of those, two are particularly important: (1) the creation of a single enforcement agency for equal opportunity laws and regulations in higher education; and (2) reform of the federal financial aid program to insure that grants are reserved for poor students, while loans are used to widen choice of institutions by students and families of all incomes.

At first glance, these, and some of our other recommendations as well, appear to add to bureaucracy. Our purpose is just the opposite. We believe that the consolidation we recommend will bring together sprawling and conflicting procedures so that higher education and government can get along more amicably and more effectively.

At the outset, we decided that our report would be incomplete if it focused on federal regulation alone, although the academic reaction to its growth was the immediate stimulus for the creation of the Sloan Commission. Therefore, we covered all the major federal policies of importance to higher education. In addition to regulation, these are financial aid to students, support for academic research, and medical education. Our discussions were organized around these topics and the full report contains chapters on each. We treat all colleges and universities as part of one system, as does federal policy.

It was also clear that we could not make detailed recommendations for each of the fifty states. On the other hand, there are a few important questions most states face and we have a chapter on these.

At the beginning of the full report, we present the context in which the wide expression of protest at governmental intrusiveness must be heard: the structure of higher education and how the states and federal government are involved in all parts of it. We also describe the economic situation of colleges and universities today and show why their financial outlook is gloomy.

Federal Regulation

Enforcement of laws on non-discrimination and equal opportunity create many difficult problems for colleges and universities, where the impact is peculiarly important. Most of the academic community accepts, by now, the broad substantive aims of these laws, or, at least, the obligation to comply with them. Moreover, since our colleges and universities have an actual, as well as symbolic, role as a major channel for social mobility, the need for effective application of the laws in higher education is clear and compelling. The Commission strongly reaffirms these goals, and believes that regulation continues to be needed to achieve them.

But difficult questions remain. What constitutes discrimination? Who should decide when it exists? On the basis of what standards? What should be done if it does exist? Who decides that? We concluded that the current machinery is not producing the answers that are needed, and is unlikely to do so without modification.

We have already discussed the vital interests of higher education in choosing faculty, students and curriculum. In the coming decades, compliance with the equal opportunity laws will be even more difficult for colleges and universities because of their poor growth prospects. There will be severe competition for academic jobs so that both hiring and promotion of faculty will be constantly challenged for discriminatory practices. Issues involving fairness of student admissions and maintenance of academic standards will intensify as enrollments go down and competition for students goes up.

There are now seventeen federal laws and executive orders relating to equal opportunity to be enforced. There are eight different agencies, with many regional offices, responsible for enforcement. The federal courts, of course, have ultimate jurisdiction. This diffusion of responsibility is one major source of confusion. Another is that Congressional legislation never spelled out clear standards or powers for any of these agencies. Compliance standards and enforcement procedures vary among them, and even within them, as officials are replaced or succeeded. Also, there is considerable duplication of effort on all sides, making the process expensive for both government and higher education. Field representatives are typically young, relatively low paid, with little experience or knowledge of colleges and universities. There is high turnover.

In addition, many aggrieved individuals and groups feel that the agencies do not protect their rights adequately and turn to the courts. The judicial, rather than the administrative mode, in fact, now prevails for enforcing equal opportunity statutes. The courts have become the principal forum for hearing complaints, and now shape the substantive content of equal opportunity policy.

The Commission views the reliance on litigation as counterproductive since it reinforces adversary relations. It is also expensive and time-consuming. Though it has produced some results that might not otherwise have been realized, the question must be asked whether they justify the conflict, the cost, and the frequent failures not only for higher education and the government, but even for those the litigation seeks to protect.

On the whole, financial incentives, widely discussed today as an effective and equitable way to achieve the goals of regulation, are not easy to apply to equal opportunity enforcement. However, the Commission has two recommendations that do use such incentives in addressing two specific problems. Both involve federal matching funds for institutional investment. First, **we recommend that large investments made by colleges and universities to provide better facilities for the handicapped be matched by the federal government.** Second, **we recommend the strengthening of an existing fellowship program for Black and other minority graduate and professional students by providing for federal matching of university contributions.** Since colleges and universities often find themselves with too small a pool of qualified minority candidates for faculty appointments, it is in their own interest to enlarge the supply. A further advantage of requiring matching contributions from the institutions is that it could increase congressional willingness to fund the government half of this program fully.

But a basic reform of procedures is needed over the whole range of problems of achieving equal opportunity in higher education. The present process, as we have seen, gets people into court too often and too soon. We believe that useful results can be produced at more bearable costs.

We set about designing a procedure that puts more of the responsibility on the institutions for doing the job themselves. In particular, we focus on the proposition that academic institutions are collegial and not hierarchical. If affirmative action is to have lasting impact on our colleges and universities, it must be managed by the people who make the decisions. In these institutions, all of the really important decisions must involve faculty as well as administration. We looked for a procedure, then, to get the faculties seriously involved. But sanctions and controls must be retained; more than good intentions on their part is essential. Above all, each institution must check on its progress through criticism by its own community—the faculty.

Council for Equal Opportunity in Higher Education. Accordingly, **we recommend the creation of a single consolidated agency for the enforcement of all equal opportunity laws in higher education,** which we call the *Council for Equal Opportunity in Higher Education.* It would be an independent regulatory agency within the new Department of Education, under the Secretary; it would provide incentives for effective self-regulation; and, as much as possible, it would unify standards and consolidate enforcement.*

The key feature of the new Council's procedures would be an assessment report required of every college and university, filed with the Council on a regular basis, and published. Each institution would develop its assessment procedures in a way that realistically reflects its own structure and decision processes. At present, affirmative action plans are typically produced by the central administration. A collegial process, involving those responsible in detail for decisions on students and faculty, would encourage genuine change and probe its limits. Publication of the assessment report would be very important as a further prod toward institutional initiative. Suggested procedures for the regulatory agency's handling of the reports are spelled out in the body of our full document.

All complaints would be initially investigated by the Council and it would be responsible for their resolution. The Council would have the power to issue rules and regulations, and to provide policy guidance on issues that bear on compliance problems, such as confidentiality and privacy. It would have the power to impose sanctions, including: cease-and-desist orders, provision of back-pay or salary equalization, and ordering 'targeted' fund terminations limited to offending programs, departments or schools. It would also have the ultimate power to order termination of all federal funds to the institution. This threat, as now used, is a hollow one.

The Council should rely heavily on mediation and other informal, non-adversarial techniques, especially in cases initiated by individuals. The services of the regional offices of the Federal Mediation and Conciliation Service, as well as those of private groups, such as the higher education associations them-

---

*Peter Clark and A. Leon Higginbotham dissent from this recommendation. See comments, pp. 89-93.

selves, could be drawn on for this purpose. Only if all these efforts failed, would the Council proceed to formal hearings.

The Council should be required to meet a procedural time-table. So long as it kept within that calendar, only its final orders could be appealed to the courts. On the other hand, if the Council failed to act in the required time, the parties would be entitled to take their complaints to court.

Creation of the new Council we recommend requires new leg-islation. We recognize the difficulty of securing it, and the im-portant obstacles to be overcome. Protected groups—such as women, ethnic minorities including Blacks, the handicapped—must be persuaded, as we are, that the new procedures will be more effective in representing their interests. From the per-spective of those who have been denied opportunity, the gains they have won to date have come about as a result of their own determined efforts to get the courts to enforce the laws. The Commission believes that there are now enough forceful and articulate spokesmen in place in the academic world to monitor effectively the work of the recommended Council.

Our recommendation may be dismissed by many as adding just another intrusive bureaucracy. Actually, the structure we propose would replace many other far more complex ones with little real power. We believe that a special agency is justified because present procedures are ineffective and enforcement problems are particularly delicate. Other areas of American life with similar problems, such as upper-echelon executive and pro-fessional employment, may find that the Council provides a successful model.

Any change leading to more effective enforcement would, in itself, be a considerable step toward realizing the goals of the equal opportunity laws since it would diminish the adversarial attitudes that now dominate the relations between regulators and regulated. In the final analysis, the academic community itself must act. Until it accepts this obligation, more govern-ment intervention, not less, will result, and the threat to aca-demic integrity and independence will increase.

Other Federal Regulations. There are two other kinds of federal regulation about which many in higher education com-plain. First, are all the laws relating to social security, work-men's compensation, occupational health, and the like, many of them only recently extended to colleges and universities. These regulations add costs, and their impact is magnified by higher education's current financial problems. Small, private institutions are particularly burdened, often needing to add administrative staff, while large ones, with their high visibility, are scrutinized regularly and thoroughly. Appropriations for public institutions, on the other hand, typically take these additional costs into account. Although some of the academic community asks for exemption from these measures, the Commission concluded that they are here to stay for all society, in substance if not in detail, and that it is neither fair nor realistic for higher education to expect special treatment.

The second resented set of federal regulations involve financial accountability and are attached primarily to the student aid and research support programs. Accountability for public money is inescapable. However, the present auditing processes for research grants do have enough adverse substantive impact on scientists and scholars for the Commission to propose some modification in our section on research support.

All of these regulations, as well as others, are discussed more fully in the complete report. While the Commission does not mean to minimize any problems created by regulation, we believe we accurately reflect the assessment of the academic world that non-discrimination and affirmative action confront higher education with the most painful and important problems. Higher education must show the way in purging itself of all forms of discrimination.

Role of the States

Today, most students are in colleges financed and governed by the states, which contribute more to the total higher education budget than either the federal government or students and their families.

The share of total state budgets devoted to higher education has already levelled off, and in a number of states, begun to decline. With college enrollments falling and competing demands for state services increasing, public higher education will find it difficult to get the appropriations it seeks. The decisions the states must make in the impending period of retrenchment will be crucial to the quality and variety of higher education offered the next generation.

Appropriation formulas now used by most states pay a substantial premium for each additional student enrolled. They effectively promoted expansion during the enrollment boom. As enrollments go down, however, the same formulas pose a double threat to academic quality. They erode the financial base of public institutions because funds needed to maintain the quality of academic programs are not granted. They also increase the incentive for institutions to compete for students by lowering academic standards.

Even though many public institutions may be operating below capacity and, in order to attract students the academic standards at some may decline, few will close on their own volition. Indeed, since the Great Depression, only one state-supported four-year public college or university has been closed. Private institutions must attract a relatively full complement of tuition-paying students to remain solvent and stay open. Public institutions can stay open as long as legislatures supply the minimum appropriations needed. Since most public colleges and universities have strong constituencies within their states, legislatures reduce capacity only reluctantly, prolonging the pressures on enrollments and finances for all.

If the states use their financial resources to maintain the capacity of the public sector at present levels despite the decline in demand, the burden of contraction will fall disproportionately on private colleges and universities. Students at these institutions receive some support from the states, but, of course, it costs the states more when the same students attend public colleges and universities. Therefore, a disproportionate contraction of the private sector increases the cost to the tax-paying public of providing higher education to state residents. It also weakens the variety of institutions in a state. There is a clear interest, then, for each state to see that the burden of contraction is shared fairly by the public and private sectors.

As a matter of social philosophy, we believe that the necessary adjustments to declining enrollments are best made by the institutions themselves, public or private, rather than imposed by state governments not always attuned to, or sophisticated in, educational matters. That, after all, is the prime responsibility of the institutions' administrations and trustees. Yet the incentives built into the present system, the limitations of the market as an instrument of discipline for publicly funded institutions, and the consequent one-sidedness of the public-private competition, all demand a more self-conscious, systematic, and widely applied process of quality control than now exists.

Composition of Higher Education Boards. Higher education boards now vary widely among the states in their degree of influence. The decisions the Boards face in the years ahead must be made by people who fully understand the purposes and problems of higher education. We believe that the best way to strengthen the boards is by strengthening their composition, not their powers. Members must command such respect that it is impossible for political figures to ignore their recommendations without drawing considerable public criticism. **The Commission recommends that each board have a majority of respected lay members, that no more than one-third should be representatives from higher education, and that the voice of the private sector be included.**

Reviews of Program Quality. **The Commission recommends that each state arrange for a periodic review of the quality of educational programs at every public college and university within the state. The reviews should be conducted by academic peer groups, not by state employees.** To the greatest extent possible, existing accrediting mechanisms, such as the regional and professional accrediting associations, should be drawn on to organize and conduct the reviews.

Any governmental effort, whether state or federal, to evaluate the quality of education arouses profound uneasiness throughout the higher education community. It is seen as a threat to institutional autonomy and academic freedom. In our judgment, the impending enrollment decline justifies so radical a step. Candid evaluations of program quality, made by competent and disinterested reviewers, would be particularly valuable during a period of retrenchment. They can both provide warnings to the administrators in a particular institution and help institutions as a group resist the temptation to compete for students by lowering academic standards. Further, independent judgments of program quality should be an important consideration when a state agency redefines the mission of an institution and changes its role, or even recommends closing it.

Publication of the reviews is an essential part of the process. Only broad dissemination of the results is likely to create a climate of opinion that would support change. Without publication, the institutions and other responsible actors would find it too easy to suppress or ignore unfavorable evaluations. The reviews should be made public after a one-year delay to allow time to act on recommendations.

Should private colleges and universities be included in the review process? On balance, inclusion of the private as well as public sector is probably desirable. With coordination between the two, it is more likely that wasteful duplication of programs could be avoided, and that contraction of capacity would proceed as equitably as possible. All would benefit if the voice of private higher education were made a deliberate part of the state-wide coordinating and planning process, as is now the case in nine states. But, because the private institutions will look at the review process as an undesirable intrusion into their autonomy and may see it as a first step on the slippery slope to public control, we believe states should invite, but not require, them to participate.*

Changes in Appropriation Formulas. The Commission believes that the new retrenchment situation requires an adaptation of the basic appropriation formulas now used. The states could, for example, alter their formulas to combine a flat basic grant that covers a substantial part—perhaps one-third—of each institution's overall budget at current enrollment levels, with a per-student allowance that provides the remainder. This would reduce somewhat the incentive to compete for students by lowering standards. Also, by putting a clear price—the amount of the flat base grant—on keeping an institution open, a formula of this type would focus legislators' attention on the costs of failing to reduce capacity. Searching questions on possible mergers of institutions, changes in scope, and the like would be inescapable.

No change in an appropriation formula can itself resolve the underlying problems of declining demand. Public authorities

*William Friday and James Killian dissent from this recommendation. See comments, pp. 119–121.

must face their responsibility for adapting capacity to demand in a way that perceives quality, and recognizes the risks of forcing the whole burden of adjustment on the private institutions.

Minimum Standards. The problem of maintaining quality has another side, the maintenance of those minimum standards that entitle an institution to call itself a college or university. Competition for students appears to have engendered an increase in questionable recruiting practices. A few colleges and universities have gone beyond aggressive recruiting techniques and begun to engage in practices that seriously detract from the educational quality of their programs. Instances of extramural curricular programs close to fraudulent are not unknown. These practices will probably become more widespread as enrollment declines and competition for students becomes fiercer. **Each state should empower its higher education agency to license all institutions for operation within the state, and should establish and enforce minimum standards of academic conduct as a condition of licensing in order to prevent fraudulent and deceptive practices.** No institution of higher education should be exempt from this licensing process.*

Financial Aid to Students

The number of high school graduates able to further their education increased tremendously in the last generation. This was made possible by government programs. State governments took the initial and most important step years ago when they greatly expanded the capacity of their low tuition institutions in which high school graduation is the only entrance requirement. The federal government, through its programs of grants and loans begun with the Higher Education Act of 1965, also played an important role in promoting wide access to higher education. Because there are now so many wide-access institutions, widely distributed throughout the country, almost every high school graduate can find a low-cost college to attend, and can have federal financial aid if needed.

Yet family income remains an important factor in determining which high school graduates go on to college. A far larger proportion of young people from families at the top of the eco-

*Peter Clark comments on this recommendation, see p. 121.

nomic spectrum attend than do the rest. If equal opportunity is truly a national goal, and we believe it is, more needs to be done.

The Commission recommends that the central purpose of direct federal aid to students should continue to be what it has been since 1965—to lower financial barriers to post-secondary education. Our recommendations incorporate certain elements of alternative views we weighed. Several general principles guided our thinking on federal policy:

—That access should continue to be the central theme.

—That student financial aid should be designed to assist the student, not necessarily to assist the institution.

—That no student should be fully supported through public grants. Self-help should become one of the fundamental elements of any student aid package.

—That parents should contribute as much as possible to pay for their children's education.

—That the states make their greatest contribution by maintaining low tuitions in the first two years of open-access institutions, and that this role will be increasingly important.

—That academic achievement should also be rewarded, at least symbolically.

—That the most appropriate federal role in relation to "choice" of institution is offering a rational and equitable program of widely available loans.

The coming enrollment decline will intensify competition among institutions for aid-bearing students because of the revenues they bring in tuition, fees, and room-and-board charges. Congress will surely feel conflicting pressures to define aid mechanisms and allocation formulas so that they favor one or another type of institution. If the central purpose of financial aid continues to be helping students, this must remain the key criterion in designing federal programs.

Limitations of Present Programs. The many federal programs of grants and loans, those now in existence as well as those under immediate consideration by Congress, lack coherence. There has been little attempt by the legislators to see or manage the various programs as interlocking although, in fact, they are. Their combined effect has an enormous influence on who goes to college, to which college, and who pays for it. The Commission believes that the right way to achieve overall coherence is through a clear separation of loans and grants to serve different needs. What are now called loans are actually an untidy intermingling of grants and loans. Our recommendations are directed towards achieving major improvements in equity without increasing total federal expenditure.

The Commission believes that grants should be reserved for those who need them most—the poor. Help for the children of higher income families is already provided by the states in the form of low tuitions in public sector institutions. This is a substantial subsidy. Also, we recommend a new loan program, whose features we describe below, that would provide essentially unsubsidized loans to help middle income families overcome short-run cash flow problems. By contrast, the present Middle Income Assistance Act (1978) makes the children of the middle-class eligible for outright grants, and the children of those at the very top of the income distribution eligible for heavily subsidized loans. These features enhance neither access to higher education nor choice of institution even though serving these two purposes is the reason for offering federal grants and loans.

Changes in the Basic Educational Opportunity Grant Program. The Basic Educational Opportunity Grant program (BEOG, 1972), is the most revolutionary contribution of federal policy in influencing who goes on to college. It promises to continue to achieve more as a major channel of social mobility than any other single federal program in higher education. Yet there are ways in which the Commission believes the program should be improved.

We recommend, first, that appropriations for the program be large enough so that every eligible student can receive the full amount of the award. Supplemental appropriations, if required, should be forthcoming.* **We recommend, second, that every**

*Peter Clark dissents from this recommendation. See comments, p. 162.

Congress adjust the maximum award so that it reflects changes in the consumer price index. On this basis, the 1980 maximum should be $2,400.

These two recommendations protect the integrity of the program as it now stands while ensuring that the language of the law and the practice of its administration coincide. Congress's past behavior on appropriations for BEOG—both in level and timing—made it impossible for students to know what amount of aid they could count on. A reasonable degree of certainty is important in providing effective access. With the recommended changes, each applicant could make a reasonably accurate estimate of how much aid to expect and plan accordingly. This is especially important for entering students. Further, there are now serious inequities since students with the same need can be treated differently in different years.

Third, **we recommend that the present half-cost rule be rescinded and a self-help requirement applied instead.** To support the renewed emphasis on self-help, spending on College Work-Study programs should be increased by $100 million, or roughly 20 percent. The half-cost limitation now operates to reduce the awards of students from the poorest families attending the least expensive institutions. The alternate procedures we recommend retain the principle that no one should go to college simply because there is public money to do so. We believe that every student should contribute at least $500 a year toward higher education.

These changes would substantially increase the cost of the Basic Grant program. As a counter-balance, **we recommend the elimination of social security education benefits for college students as no longer necessary.** This would save more.

Public understanding of financial aid programs would be strengthened if there were a single schedule of Expected Parental Contributions, rather than the two different major ones that now exist. **We recommend consolidating the two.** This would also help reinforce the principle that parents should continue to contribute as much as possible to their children's education. So would a stricter definition of the "independent student." We are in favor of both.

Low Tuitions at Open-Access State Institutions. The Commission believes it is vitally important to keep tuitions relatively low in community colleges and in the first two years of other open-access institutions. This recommendation is central to the purpose of broadening access. Even if the Basic Grant program is improved in the important ways we propose, it still will not be able to provide enough help for the students most in need if tuitions are raised at the institutions most of them attend. The only qualification for entrance in most of these colleges is high school graduation.

It must be recognized that the first two years of college for such students are an important personal testing time. Some try it out, discover they can profit, and go on; others drop out. The sorting once accomplished, those who stay can reasonably expect tangible personal benefits. This is the case for charging them a larger proportion of the costs of their education after they complete two years.

The role of the states in promoting broader access to higher education remains critical, and the aim of our recommendation is to establish priorities for the states in responding to emerging pressures for tuition increases.

Modification of Title III. The Commission has one further recommendation closely related to access and tied to the Basic Grant program. 'Wide access' can become an empty rallying cry. It has another side that should receive more attention: once admitted, do students stay on and graduate? All too many colleges take students in and turn them over frequently. The drop-out rate is high.

As a group, the historically Black colleges have had notable success in keeping students who are both particularly underprepared and particularly disadvantaged. Their graduation rates are high and the later achievements of their alumni are outstanding. These colleges represent a national treasure that should be maintained.

The Commission recommends that all four-year institutions making the same kind of contribution should receive special awards, both as an incentive and as support for their efforts. Recipients should be chosen by the Secretary of Education on the basis of the institution's proportion of students from exceptionally poor families, its rate of retention for students who enter as freshmen, and the success of its graduates in going beyond the B.A. degree. The award would be an unrestricted grant matching the aggregate BEOG awards of the students enrolled during the year it was made. Nor are only private institutions in question: the program should continue to be open to all four-year institutions.

We offer this recommendation as a modification of the present Title III program, "Aid to Developing Institutions." The program was originally conceived to help colleges out of the mainstream, especially the Black colleges. The continuing need for their efforts in the years ahead is clear. Other institutions are equally deserving of special support on the same grounds. Some colleges in Appalachia have done as well for white students with poor preparation coming from poor families as the traditionally Black colleges have for their students.

We believe that federal assistance in maintaining the capacity of such institutions to meet these goals is highly desirable. Title III should be continued and will achieve its purpose better with the proposed modifications that give emphasis to retention as well as access. This judgment, made from today's perspective on race relations is, of course, subject to reconsideration in the future. The program should be reexamined from time to time.

Our sense of the order of magnitude of the proposed program is that about 150-200 institutions could qualify, at a cost of about $150 million each year.

National Educational Loan Bank. The Commission believes that there is a federal role in helping students have a wider choice of institutions, including the opportunity to attend more expensive private ones. Further, we concluded that a fundamental reform of the federal loan programs is needed in order to reduce the element of subsidy in loans to students, as well as to begin government sponsored lending to parents. Borrowing for higher education should be insulated from the cyclical ups and downs of credit availability, as well as from local variations in them. We believe this is an appropriate role for the federal government to assume.

We propose that Congress establish a National Education Loan Bank to make essentially unsubsidized loans to undergraduate and graduate students alike. The Bank should also make it possible for parents to borrow in a way that makes credit widely available to them on more uniform terms, with limits set on combined loans to parents and their children. The

Bank would be allowed to borrow without limit from the Federal Financing Bank, and its obligations would be guaranteed by the Secretary of Education.

The major features of the proposed National Educational Loan Bank are as follows:

1. It would lend to students at the average cost of capital to the government for terms of up to twenty years.
2. Borrowers would have the option of graduated repayment programs.
3. Its operating costs, including defaults, would be borne by the federal government.
4. National Educational Loan Bank loans would be available to form part of each financial aid package, as loans do now. However, they would also be available to students who do not receive any financial aid, regardless of family income.
5. Any undergraduate (except freshmen) could borrow up to 25 percent of the cost of education; any graduate or professional student up to 50 percent.
6. Parents of students could borrow up to 50 percent of the cost of education. However, the combined parent and student borrowing should not exceed 50 percent of the cost of education for undergraduates, and 75 percent for those in graduate and professional schools. Thus, a loan directly to a student would diminish, dollar-for-dollar, the amount that the parents could borrow.
7. Parents would have ten years to repay, and would pay somewhat higher interest rates than students.

Despite a far wider reach and the inclusion of parents as well as students as eligible borrowers, this program would be much less expensive than the several present lending programs it replaces, in which interest rates are far below any realistic measure of the government's cost of capital. The Bank would rationalize a lending system whose working has become haphazard, and whose costs are high in relation to its purposes.

Merit Grants. Finally, **we recommend that the federal government establish a modest program of grants based on academic merit and achievement.** This would emphasize and honor values that, in recent years, have taken a back seat to society's intense efforts to encourage and help those previously outside the mainstream of intellectual achievement and economic reward.

We recommend the annual award of 3,000 scholarships at the undergraduate level for four years at the institution of the student's choice. One-half would be awarded by national competition, while the remaining 1,500 would be allocated among the states on the basis of their population of eighteen-year-olds, and awarded by state competition. Each scholar would receive a minimum of $1,000 per year, but the rest to be determined by need.

We recommend another 3,000 awards to college seniors to cover the full cost of education at the graduate or professional school of the student's choice. Qualities of leadership, enterprise, and character that promise professional achievement would be considered as well as academic record. By emphasizing other aspects of achievement, the program would recognize that qualities not necessarily reflected in scholastic success are also socially valuable.

Every four-year institution in a state would be entitled to nominate a fixed number of candidates for the state-wide competition. A panel of experienced and objective citizens would select the winners on the basis of college records, recommendations and interviews, similar to the way in which Rhodes Scholarships and Rockefeller Public Service Awards are made. Since graduates of each four-year college would have a chance to compete, the proposed program would counter-balance to some degree the cumulative advantages of those beginning the competition in an advantageous position.

The National Merit Scholarship Corporation (NMSC) already has an admirable program broadly similar in conception. A plan to permit the government to match NMSC funds in order to expand its program along the lines we suggest would be a further development of this recommendation in keeping with its spirit.

Both the undergraduate and graduate programs we propose are modest in scale. But they would have considerable symbolic importance in influencing aspirations, conveying a sense of opportunity, and encouraging achievement.

The Total Program. Separate programs of financial aid interrelate. From the point of view of students in the aggregate and of institutions, they form a single whole. The Commission believes its recommendations give a coherence now lacking to federal financial aid programs.

The following table compares the costs of present programs in fiscal year 1979 with the estimated costs under the proposed changes we recommend. These estimates are based on 1979 enrollments, income distributions, price levels, and so forth. They include several existing programs not mentioned above for which no significant change is proposed. Altogether the changes would save nearly $900 million.

Table 1.   Comparison of Actual Costs (Rounded) and Estimated Costs Under Major Recommendations, Department of Education Programs, and Selected Other Existing and Proposed Programs.

	Actual Fiscal Year 1979 (in millions of dollars)	Estimated Under Proposed Changes, Fiscal Year 1979 (in millions of dollars)	Change (in millions of dollars)
Basic Grants (BEOG)	2,600	3,800	+ 1,200
Supplemental Grants (SEOG)	340	340	0
Federal Matching Grants to States (SSIG)	80	80	0
College Work-Study (CWS)	550	650	+ 100
National Educational Loan Bank (NELB)	0	250	+ 250
Federal Direct Lending (NDSL)	310	0	− 310
Insured Lending (GSL)	970	0	− 970
Title III, Strengthening Developing Institutions	120	150	+ 30
Special Remedial Programs (TRIO)	140	200	+ 60
Federal Merit Scholarship Programs	0	80	+ 80
Sub-total Department of Education Programs	5,110	5,550	+ 440
Social Security Education Benefits for Students in College	1,300	0	− 1,300
Veteran's Education Benefits	2,400	2,400	0
Sub-total (other Programs)	3,700	2,400	− 1,300
TOTAL	8,810	7,950	− 860

Financial aid policies and recommendations are difficult to summarize adequately. Our full report provides additional detail.

Research Support

The partnership between government and higher education for the performance of basic research has made enormous contributions to the nation's health, prosperity, and security. In the last forty years federal dollars helped transform the leading American universities into centers of scientific discovery, and enabled the United States to attain a position of unquestioned world leadership in science. Great public respect for scientists led to a high level of public support; from the end of World War II to 1969 the compound annual rate of growth of real funding for academic research averaged 15 percent.

In the last ten years, however, public and congressional attitudes toward science and scientists have become more critical, and the notion that every advance of scientific understanding produces social benefits is no longer accepted without question.

Growth of the science budget faltered in the late 1960s and came to a halt in 1969. In 1979, federal spending was nearly $4 billion in current dollars, but only slightly higher in real terms than the $2.3 billion (1969 dollars) spent a decade earlier. Through the 1981 fiscal year at least, pressure to hold down the federal budget and continuing inflation are likely to produce a modest decline in real expenditures on federal research or, at best, no growth.

Now university administrators and researchers fear that excessive regulation and financial oversight, together with an unwillingness of the funding agencies to bear the full cost of federally sponsored projects, threaten to undermine academic research. Congress questions the need for still more growth and increasingly wants to be sure that federal expenditures actually serve social goals rather than simply satisfy the curiosity of scientists at the taxpayers' expense.

We believe that the system of federal support for academic research that evolved in the years following the end of World War II is fundamentally sound. It is a pluralistic system. Basic research is funded chiefly on a project basis. The most promising among the unsolicited proposals submitted by investigators are chosen by their peers on grounds of scientific merit. More than one federal agency usually provides funds for most types of research, so that no single set of decisions shapes the entire program. This system has withstood careful and repeated scrutiny, and no alternative system has been proposed that promises an equally effective, much less a better performance.

The present system concentrates research support in a small number of institutions, and rightly so. A relatively small number of highly talented individuals can make important contributions and, in each discipline, tend to assemble in a few departments so that they can work together. The distribution of funds thus reflects the distribution of scientific and scholarly talent and is in turn a consequence of the way research is naturally carried on.

The Need for Modest Real Growth and Stability of Funding. We recommend that funding for academic research incorporate a modest degree of long-term real growth, and that procedures protect the research enterprise from fluctuations in funding levels from year to year.

Some growth makes it more likely that adequate resources will be allocated to new ideas, on which much of the vitality of the scientific enterprise depends. The real cost of performing a particular experiment does not rise from year to year. Research, however, does not involve the same experiment year after year. The next step, because it probes more deeply, almost always requires more sophisticated equipment than the last. As a result, the cost of research escalates more rapidly than the cost of most other activities.

Basic research maintains the stock of knowledge on which our economy is founded. The United States depends increasingly on sophisticated technology for growth. If the share of gross national product invested in basic research diminishes, then the role of basic research in supporting the economy also diminishes. The cost to the country of failing to maintain an adequate science base is likely to be greater than the cost of paying for more research than can be demonstrated to be absolutely necessary. Some shading to the side of too much rather than too little funding for research is desirable. If our investment in basic research is to keep pace with the long-term rate of real growth of the economy, it should grow in real terms at about 2 percent annually—roughly equal to its growth over the past five years.

It is important that federal support for research in humanities and humanistic social sciences also continues to grow modestly. There is a deeper unity in all research and scholarship that transcends disciplinary boundaries and methodological differences. The university is an ideal place for basic research precisely because knowledge in all fields is pursued for its own sake more than for practical results. A narrow focus on natural science based on practical considerations, even if it is self-imposed, will ultimately dampen the intellectual curiosity that sustains research and higher education as a whole.

A smooth slow-down in growth would have created less financial trouble for academic science than the sudden end of growth in funding in 1969 and the fluctuations in levels since then. Congress, the funding agencies, and the scientific community should find mechanisms for agreeing on long-term targets for funding levels and adhere to them over a period of several years. Whatever the ultimate targets, the gain in certainty for researchers would be beneficial.

Stability of funding is also important at the level of individual research projects. It could be improved by more use of step funding, and we recommend widespread adoption of this system which provides funds for a number of years, but at declining levels. At every periodic review, the project is either extended and the lower funding step pushed forward in time or the investigator is assured of funds for an orderly phase out if the project is terminated.

Reallocations: Fellowships, Laboratories, Libraries, Discretionary Money. Now that rapid growth has ended, certain reallocations away from project funds to other needs which were well served in the earlier period are in order: scientific manpower, laboratory instruments and equipment, academic libraries, and the needs of research universities for some discretionary research money.

The vitality of the scientific enterprise requires a continual flow of talented young people into graduate study and postdoctoral research. Job opportunities clearly play some role in influencing the career choices of young scientists. The possibility of finding rewarding research careers in government, industry, and non-profit institutions outside higher education can partially substitute for the sharp decline in academic jobs in the next decade. Providing short-term support for the new

Ph.D.'s in academia can provide further help. We recommend that about $100 million per year be spent on two kinds of new fellowships for this purpose: 1,000 competitive National Post-Doctoral Fellowships per year, fully portable, carrying two years of support and renewable for two further years; 300 National Research Fellowships, carrying five years of support for research on university campuses, in federally funded research centers, and intramural federal laboratories. The successful competitors would have the prospect of nine years of research activity. While they would still face a depressed academic market at the end, their experience and achievements would give them a preferred position in finding continuing research employment.

Many universities have fallen far behind in maintaining up-to-date facilities, and for the first time since before World War II, American scientists speak enviously of the laboratories and instrumentation in Europe. We, therefore, recommend that a total of $50 million be divided between the National Science Foundation and the National Institutes of Health in each of the next five years for a program of grants to upgrade research laboratories and equipment at universities and colleges. Funds for these purposes have almost totally disappeared.

Academic libraries are the basic resource for research and scholarship in the humanities and many of the social sciences. They are rapidly becoming more costly and complex; the annual expense of maintaining a major research library is now about $10 million and increasing. Rising costs mean that only a very few libraries will have the resources to continue to maintain strong, self-contained collections in every discipline. Collection development and management and the preservation of physically deteriorating books will have to become increasingly a cooperative venture with each library concentrating on areas of particular strength. We recommend help to research libraries for speeding up these activities.

The productive capacity of the research universities would be greatly helped if discretionary research funds were made available. Resources are needed to support promising juniors who have not yet established their reputations, to assist in building new research projects to the point where they can attract federal support, and to fill in the gaps left by federal grants that do not cover the full cost of research. To this end, we recommend that every research grant and contract carry with it an additional 7 percent of the project's direct costs, to be used in support of research, and so accounted for. These funds should come from the current budgets of the funding agencies with no increase in overall appropriations. Universities should not be allowed to spend general research funds on indirect costs of research, or on unrelated costs.

Financial Oversight. In addition to these concrete steps, a change in attitude of both governmental agencies and research universities from their present rancorous tone to one of mutual respect is needed. Federal agencies increasingly treat the funding of academic research as if it were another kind of procurement. One result has been an excessive increase in the extent and detail of financial oversight. An investigator's work on a particular research project is not perfectly separable from work on other projects, on teaching, or on faculty committees, and auditors cannot distinguish between costs that are allocable to research and those that are not with perfect precision. In trying to do so, they lose sight of the fact that the government is engaged in supporting a socially necessary activity, not merely purchasing a product. The auditors may also fail to recognize that the investigator's scientific curiosity and desire to establish a reputation among peers create powerful incentives for productive use of research funds.

Excessive oversight creates a costly burden of paperwork. Its greatest cost, however, is not financial but its potential effect on the research process itself. If close financial oversight requires the investigator who has a novel idea to interrupt research to get approval for budget changes, or to lay down a trail of documentation and, later, to justify the change in plans to auditors, it can mean that new leads are not followed while the now less fruitful, original plan is. This result is entirely self-defeating.

Academic administrators and researchers must recognize, for their part, that as recipients of public funds they are accountable for their use. The fact that financial oversight may sometimes interfere with the researcher's desire for flexibility or the university's desire for autonomy does not alter its legitimacy.

We recommend the development of a corps of federal auditors, sophisticated about scientific research and how research universities operate. This will make financial oversight less burdensome and improve its efficiency as well. At present, most federal research in colleges and universities is audited by the Department of Health and Human Services, whose representatives often have little experience in dealing with research institutions, receive limited training, and typically stay on the assignment only briefly. Because sponsored research is such a small part of HHS's oversight responsibilities, the special problems involved are neglected.

The natural location for a new audit agency would be in the National Science Foundation, in a new Inspector General's office reporting directly to the National Science Board. As the only federal agency devoted entirely to research, NSF understands the process best and is most competent to conduct financial oversight. Its total scale of activity is small enough to ensure sufficient attention to auditing responsibilities. To maintain a clear separation between the award and administration of research grants by the Foundation, and the financial oversight of these and other agencies' grants by the new office, the two should operate as independent bodies, each reporting directly to the National Science Board.

Medical Education

Medical schools and their affiliated hospitals are the only producers of physicians and major centers for biomedical research. They also are important providers of health care in the United States. For these reasons, the federal government has been centrally involved in the medical schools of our universities for a long time.

Government engagement on a large scale began after World War II with research support growing more rapidly in biomedical and clinical research than in other fields. In the two decades following the war, government research funds in the medical area grew from less than $100 million a year to nearly $2 billion.

The next major federal initiative in academic medicine was the effort begun in the early 1960s to stimulate an increase in the output of M.D.'s through the use of federal subsidies and incentives to medical schools. These policies produced a great expansion in the number of doctors between the middle 1960s and the present. By 1978, the size of the first year medical school class reached 16,000, double its 1962 number.

Shifts in Federal Concerns. Rising costs of medical education and doubts about the need for more physicians brought an end to expansionary federal policies in the mid-seventies. The focus of federal concern shifted from the total number of M.D.'s produced to their distribution, more particularly to underserved inner-city neighborhoods and rural areas, and to the growing concentration in specialty practice. The Health Professions Act of 1976 mandated that to continue to receive federal 'capitation' payments (cost of education supplements tied to enrollment), which had been instituted as incentives to medical schools to increase enrollments, the schools had to train a certain proportion of their graduates for primary care.

Most of what the government sought to do in the medical schools was part of a broader effort to control the cost of medical care and, at the same time, make it more widely available. Therefore, though much of the government involvement with medical schools parallels that with the university at large—in support of research and training of manpower—there is a striking difference. Government has been more ready to apply to medical schools the kinds of direct controls used in other parts of the health care system, but not in other areas of higher education.

Since government seems to have chosen the instruments of planning and direct controls to deal with the problems of the health care system, academic medical centers can expect even deeper involvement by the government in its further attempts to solve the problems. For example, government may well make additional efforts to affect the specialty distribution of physicians by reaching more deeply into the medical curriculum, affecting programs for the M.D. degree as well as for residency training. And medical schools in public universities may increasingly be required to tie admission to a commitment to practice within the state for a period of time, a requirement some already have.

The cost of medical education is likely to become a matter of greater policy concern and be subjected to even closer scrutiny. Cross-subsidization—the extent to which research grants and revenues from patient care are used to support the cost of instruction—is a chronic issue being pressed with new vigor by government. Its desire to constrain the rising costs of hospital care will lead to further stringencies, as will efforts to enforce conformity to accounting rules aimed at complete segregation of research from other institutional costs.

These developments, and the planned end of capitation, are putting further pressure on medical schools to increase tuition. The complete withdrawal of federal support for undergraduate medical education, and an effort to prevent indirect support through research funds and reimbursement for patient care, would put all medical schools in a difficult position and might force the private schools to increase tuition by staggering amounts or to close their doors.

Minority Admissions. Another persistent problem in the relations between government and medical schools is minority admissions. More than a decade ago, the schools recognized that their admission practices had discriminated against Blacks and other minority candidates and they began to make a substantial effort to increase minority enrollment. This effort was reinforced by affirmative action requirements in civil rights legislation. The proportion of Black students among all freshmen rose sharply from about 2.5 percent in the 1950s and 1960s to 7.5 percent in 1975. Whereas in the 1950s, three-quarters of all Black students were enrolled in two Black medical schools, Howard and Meharry, by 1975 more than 80 percent of the much larger total number were spread throughout predominantly white schools.

After 1975, however, the momentum of affirmative action slackened and Black enrollment fell slightly in proportion to the total; in 1978—79 the figure was 6.4 percent. The proportion of Black applicants selected no longer exceeded substantially their share of the total applicant pool as it had during the period of rapid expansion of minority enrollment. The reasons for the change are not clear. The Bakke case, which challenged the affirmative action program of the University of California, Davis medical school, and in which the California Supreme Court found for the plaintiff in 1976, may have tempered the willingness of admission committees to select minority candidates according to some affirmative action programs.

What is clear, however, is that the end of growth in the number of medical school students will sharpen the problem. The situation will be even more difficult if enrollments begin to decline. The puzzles and conflicts that affirmative action generates will increase, and the counter-pressures from those in the majority who feel it is discriminatory will become sharper.

Limitations of Places in Medical Schools. The limited number of places in medical schools is likely to become a focus of controversy in the near future. At the moment, both federal officials responsible for health care and academic physicians agree that the medical schools are training enough, if not too many, physicians. The evidence supporting this view is disputable, and an evaluation of it involves difficult and controversial questions of the supply, organization, and financing of health care that lie far beyond our Commissions's mandate.

There are many capable applicants to medical schools who could become well-qualified physicians—currently about two for every opening. Some of those who are turned away go to costly foreign medical schools for training, many of which are of admittedly inferior quality. Yet these foreign-trained graduates are accepted for residencies in U.S. hospitals and, in due course, join the corps of practicing physicians. Most of the disappointed applicants are simply denied the opportunity of training for and entry into a lucrative and prestigious profession.

Some undesirable results of limitation are already visible. As the number of qualified applicants has increased, the admission decisions at the margin become more and more difficult. Small differences in grade point averages and test scores are accorded a significance that cannot be justified in terms of outcomes. The fierce competition for grades and narrow focus on "appropriate" courses among many undergraduates planning to study medicine constrict their experience in college, depriving them of the opportunity for experimentation and inquiry that should be an important part of their education.

Rising tuitions, tending to limit the opportunities for entry into medicine more and more to children of well-to-do families, will further sharpen the issues of fairness raised by the present situation.

If larger considerations of health care planning really do require that the annual flow of newly trained physicians be limited to far fewer than the number of capable candidates who seek training, both the fairness of selection processes and who controls them will become issues. Federal and state governments will be increasingly ready to question medical schools on both points, and the large numbers of those who feel aggrieved by their exclusion will stimulate that process.

Recommendation. The intimate connection between medical education and the provision of medical care that intensifies the difficulties of relations between government and academic medical centers makes it hard for our Commission to recommend ways of ameliorating these difficulties. Any proposals for changes in government policies toward medical education must be made with full attention to their probable effects on the health care system. Analysis of the problems of the whole health care system is beyond our scope. **What we learned, however, leads us to recommend strongly the creation of a national commission on medical education and its relation to health care.** It should include on its agenda a thorough consideration of the complex problems of access to and financing of medical education.*

Concluding Remarks

A period of profound change in the size and shape of higher education and its place in American life followed World War II. The federal government and the states were partners and patrons to our colleges and universities during a dramatic boom period filled with optimism and expansion.

A new period of retrenchment has begun. The tide of eighteen-year-olds that produced the growth has turned; striking demographic shifts are already bringing lower enrollments in some kinds of colleges. Public higher education must compete with other claims on the tightening supply of public funds, while private colleges and universities find revenues from tuition, gifts, and endowment funds failing to keep up with inflation.

Now the governments look less like helpful partners and more like unfriendly policemen. With the growth of student aid, the federal government has become more important as a patron, and our colleges and universities are widely dependent on it for their operating budgets. It has also become more intrusive as a regulator. Government enforcement of laws and regulations

*William Roth, with whom Ralph Dungan and Robert Ingersoll join, would add a further recommendation. See comments, p. 209.

encroaches on decisions held to be central to the traditional autonomy of the academic world, and imposes increased costs. To many in higher education, the government is at once indispensable and intolerable.

Our recommendations aim to help the institutions adapt to their new situation. All of them are what we believe to be workable improvements on present practice. The specific policy changes we recommend are important not only in themselves but also, taken as a whole, for their effect on the tone of relations between government and higher education. We believe that they can help change it from the present harsh wrangling to the more cooperative note it had earlier. All parties would benefit from such a change.

In the end, it is the colleges and universities themselves that must lead the way in adapting to the new circumstances of the next fifteen years. A central belief of the Commission, shaping many of our recommendations, is that higher education must have the largest possible scope for autonomy. But it cannot consistently call for less government and more money at the same time.

Chapter 2

The Context of the Problems

Government's involvement in academic affairs is not new. It evolved over our history as higher education itself evolved to serve all the purposes it now does in American life. The problems considered by this Commission are best understood in the context of the structure of higher education and how its diverse institutions function as a system. This chapter provides that context, and describes the development of the different roles played by state governments—which actually finance and govern public colleges and universities—and by the federal government—which has come to support and regulate all of them, public and private. Finally, we describe how higher education's financial situation makes a close dependence on government essential.

STRUCTURE OF HIGHER EDUCATION

There are about 3,000 colleges and universities spread all over the United States. They vary widely in scope, size, control, location, age, and cost. There are two-year vocationally oriented community colleges, and research universities with a full array of graduate and professional schools. There are small liberal arts colleges with fewer than 500 students, and giant university complexes with over 50,000. There are public institutions and private ones, and of the latter some are controlled by churches while others are termed independent. Locations are urban, suburban, or rural in every state in the union. Some colleges were established within the last five years, and some can celebrate bicentennials and even greater age. Some public institutions have virtually no tuition and a commuting student body, while expensive Ivy League universities have many dormitories and a preponderance of students in residence. In its most important policies, the federal government makes no distinction among all these widely diverse institutions. Similarly, the Commission's report deals as one with the whole collegiate sector—what has come to be known as "higher education."

1. Every institution is very much the child of its history. The visions inspiring its founders and the circumstances shaping its development remain important to each one. A great strength of this variety is that it serves a student body equally diverse in preparation, interest, and aspiration. Also, the way in which the system developed reflects the way in which most of American society responds to changed conditions—not by centralized decision-making, but through competition and pluralism. It is a system that adapts rapidly to a changing world, that provides many independent loci for potentially useful innovations, and allows a natural trial-and-error process to govern their spread.

All of higher education articulates loosely, rather than neatly, with a structure of secondary schools that is almost as varied. Local finance and school boards play a central role in determining the character of these schools, so that the full diversity of both local economics and local politics is reflected in secondary education today.

A central theme of the Commission's work is that this diversity is in itself an important strength of higher education. It is good for the system and it is good for the country. It should be protected, and our recommendations always keep this goal in mind.

2. When all of its purposes are considered, the system can be seen as made up of functionally differentiated parts. Even the

institutions with the widest scope vary greatly in their emphasis. Research, scholarship, and advanced professional training are the particular concerns of the universities but this is not their exclusive focus, nor do they have a monopoly. The last generation brought an immense number of open-access institutions into existence that are now the most significant initial channels of social mobility. But traditional liberal arts colleges also make an important contribution in this way, and, in fact, so does every other type of college.

Strong strands tie the system together. They all compete for the same pool of students. Although institutions vary dramatically in what they look for in students, every high school graduate usually has some choice of type as well as particular college to attend. Students move among institutions, both laterally as they transfer, and vertically as they progress from two-year to four-year programs and on. In fact, routes from community colleges to distinguished professional schools are open. Most of the faculty are products of the universities. Their similar education and training is, of course, centrally important to the content and quality of what is taught.

3. Many voices speak for higher education today. The public interest in the enterprise as a whole becomes less easy to discern as it multiplies and as more is heard from the many interests within it. No single institution can speak for the whole system.

Intellectual leadership for the system is provided by a small elite group of institutions to which talent, energy, and money flowed naturally together over the years. Not all of them are old, however, and they are both public and private, and colleges as well as universities. Because of the achievements of their graduates and faculty, they speak with authority on many matters, both within the system and to the country.

Spokesmen for the rest of higher education are now of equal importance, and increasingly effective in the political arena. There has been a rapid growth in the number of associations formed within the academic community for mutual help and to represent it outside, particularly in dealings with the government. These groups will give our recommendations careful scrutiny, can help to get them adopted and can help to make them work. Some of the associations are limited to particular types of institutions and are based on a sense of common problems and missions. Some are umbrella organizations, staffed by professional educators with wide experience, and address the interests of the whole system.

THE ROLE OF THE GOVERNMENT

Until the last half of the nineteenth century, higher education was chiefly a private enterprise in the United States. Colleges were set up at the initiative of particular groups, most of them religious in the beginning, with money they raised and standards for students, faculty, and curriculum they set for themselves. Ultimate responsibility for policies and decisions was given to non-academic boards of trustees made up of people with close ties to the institutions who knew them well and cared for them deeply. Autonomy was possible because they were financially independent. This model was used by the early public universities as well. It continues to be the way all private institutions are governed. The big difference is that now they must have money from the government to survive.

The last generation saw a dramatic change in the balance between public and privately controlled institutions. As recently as 1950, higher education was evenly divided. Now 80 percent of all enrollments is in institutions financed and governed by the states. This shift puts strains on the system, both financial and political, that probably would have become apparent even without the immediate problems. We are moving closer to the situation in the rest of the Western world from which our structure of higher education has been fundamentally different in this respect for most of its history.

1. The states have ultimate responsibility and control over every public college and university. Most states have a higher education board, variously named, with authority for statewide coordination, responsibility for submitting budgets to legislatures as well as for academic programs. In many states, the private model is still followed in that each institution, or group of similar institutions, continues to have a board of trustees through which the higher state board carries out its decisions. But, in each state, a complicated interplay of the legislators, the governor, the members of the boards, and the administrators of the colleges and universities determines the fate of policies and programs. This changes as elected and

appointed officials change, but on the whole it has been surprisingly little affected by the changes in administration.

State government is, in theory, responsible for education at all levels and at all places where it is carried on within its boundaries. But, in fact, few states make any serious effort to include private institutions in their responsibilities. And, if they were to try to do so, the private sector would strenuously assert its right to autonomy. The chief way in which most private institutions must deal with the state government is in respect to funds that are appropriated by legislatures, mostly for student aid. Thus, the overall planning of most states tends to focus on the public institutions, rather than to look at the whole system.

2. The role of the federal government in higher education is entirely different. Our constitutional tradition implicitly forbids a role like that of the states. In fact, of course, the federal government is now centrally involved in the academic world. Its involvement came in the wake of various support programs for higher education, each with its own history, purpose, clientele, and political base. Also, in the last fifteen years, the federal regulatory role grew in importance, and it, too, is the product of diverse processes involving various sets of actors with different ends in view.

Support of academic science on a large scale is the oldest program, but even this is new, given the age of higher education. It dates back to the immediate post-war period when, through various makeshift arrangements, the government tried to insure that academic science would continue to serve national needs as it did during the second World War. The partnership was institutionalized with the creation of the National Science Foundation in 1950. A modest effort to support humanistic scholarship came in 1965 with the establishment of the National Endowment for the Humanities. In the interim, expenditures by the National Institutes of Health grew to the leading position they now occupy, with their consequent effects on medical schools and on research in life sciences generally.

Broad scale student aid had a precedent in the G.I. Bill at the height of the second World War. At the time, this was seen in the context of post-war compensation for veterans rather than as a new departure in federal policy for higher education. The Higher Education Act of 1965 first embodied the present purpose of student aid and was part of President Johnson's Great Society program, a broad movement to legislate greater equality that dominated Congress in 1964–65. By 1972, the proposition that federal aid should go to students rather than to institutions, and should be distributed according to financial need, was firmly established.

Almost every institution in the country, private as well as public, is affected by student aid programs. In fact, federal policy makes no formal distinction between the public and private sectors. Although policies often vary greatly in their effects on the two groups, formal neutrality in respect to the public/ private difference has been one of the major political premises for all federal actions affecting higher education.

The newest regulations to be enforced on higher education had their chief targets and goals elsewhere, and their application to the academic world was partly incidental and partly afterthought. The most important set of regulations—equal opportunity—dates to the civil rights legislation of 1964. Much of the other regulation imposed on colleges and universities stems from the general increase in legislation in the late 1960s intended to protect the health and safety of workers and the environment and the extension of earlier legislation to higher education. Like the civil rights legislation, the focus was not specifically on higher education but on nearly all organized activity in the country.

There is a wide division of responsibility among federal agencies when it comes to dealing with colleges and universities. Those responsible for regulation have little or no connection with those providing support, and all are widely dispersed. The complexities of higher education and the intimate connection of its research, scholarship, and teaching functions are best understood by those in government who fund research. The agencies responsible for student aid and for enforcement of equal opportunity legislation show less understanding of these interrelations.

Congress through its committee system separates research support, student aid, matters concerning medical schools, and enforcement of federal regulations into distinct concerns. The wide influence that separate policies in each of these areas has on higher education as a whole is rarely taken into account. The new Department of Education will do little to change this situation because its jurisdiction and programs are substantially the same as those of the Office of Education it replaces.

THE FINANCIAL PROBLEMS OF
COLLEGES AND UNIVERSITIES

Introduction

Economic pressures on higher education are becoming increasingly severe and are an important contributing factor to its present pessimism, and to the attitude with which it responds to the government's demands. Resentment increases with dependency.

However, there is a sense in which colleges and universities are always in precarious financial balance. They regularly operate at the margin. There is a tendency for costs to grow more rapidly than revenues, and there is little room for cost reduction. Any expansion is difficult to reverse. Inflation is a constant challenge. Any academic institution usually needs more money than it has.

1. Colleges and universities, as non-profit institutions, rarely aim to achieve anything more than balanced budgets. Institutions regularly are under great pressure to spend all the money they can get and a little more. Every one has a large and seductive inventory of programs to improve its quality and dispatch any surplus: to increase the range and variety of course offerings, to reduce class size, to expand the library, to improve athletic facilities, to add to and improve laboratory space and equipment, to raise faculty salaries. The list is endless.

2. Higher education, by its nature, can benefit little from economies of scale, or technological advance, or cheaper labor. Even at constant price levels, there is a tendency for revenues not to keep up with costs. Some very important resources, such as libraries, seem to suffer from significant diseconomies of scale. Yet large and growing, and thus more expensive, libraries are essential for research and advanced training in many disciplines. Higher education depends on costly skilled labor—it is essentially a handicraft technology. Faculty and staff salaries are broadly determined by competitive forces, both within and outside the academy. But in other sectors of the economy, the rise of incomes reflects technological progress and increasing

productivity per person. Even though they do not benefit from these advances, colleges and universities must increase their pay scales in a roughly parallel way—there is a long-run upward trend in unit costs.

Academic salaries account for the largest part of academic budgets. Because of the high proportion of tenured faculty, the adaptation of other sectors of the economy to financial stress—reducing employment—is one that is difficult for higher education to use.

3. Whenever a college or university expands, the legacy tends to be permanent. Buildings are added and teachers are added. Administrative, clerical, maintenance, and housekeeping staffs grow. Higher costs become difficult to reduce without making drastic other changes to the institution.

4. Inflation in the country at large is, of course, immediately reflected in the cost of operation. This affects public and private institutions in different ways, but all suffer. The heavier burden falls on private ones, which usually respond by raising tuition since this is the major source of revenue for most of them.

Rapid Expansion of the System
After World War II

There was a steady growth of higher education in the postwar period. It reached its peak fifteen years ago.

1. Between 1950 and 1965, enrollments grew at an average annual rate of over 9 percent: nearly 400,000 students were added each year. Part of this growth came from the fact that eighteen-year-olds were an increasing proportion of the population, and the other part came from a steady increase in the fraction of the college-age population that enrolled. The proportion of high school graduates who entered college rose from 43 percent in 1950 to the historic high of 62 percent in 1970.

Increased enrollments demanded more teachers, and supply expanded slowly and with a lag. Competition for faculty was keen, especially for those with established reputations and special promise. There was a rapid increase in academic salaries, greatest for natural scientists but not confined to them. Faculty members in the humanities and some of the social sciences were also helped by equity considerations within institutions to get increases that rising demand alone might not have produced. Extension of the coverage of minimum wage laws, social security and unemployment insurance, increasing unionization, as well as general economic forces, also led to higher costs of supporting operations.

Close to one-half the colleges in the U.S. today were established between 1950 and 1975. Year after year, the states increased their investment; new colleges, and branches springing from established campuses, were created in large numbers; many teachers' colleges were transformed into comprehensive institutions with a wide variety of programs. By 1975, almost 1,200 new institutions had been added, and two-thirds of them were in the public sector.

2. Federal support in the form of aid to students also came to be very important to the budgets of colleges and universities. By 1978, the federal government was distributing $8.5 billion to students through its various aid programs. Nearly 40 percent of all enrolled students now receive some kind of aid, and for a large fraction of these, getting it is crucial to the decision to attend college. The greater part of the aid students receive returns to institutions as tuition, fees, room, and board. Since state appropriations for most public institutions depend chiefly on formulas geared to enrollment, federal aid that enables students to attend these institutions has a multiplier effect by attracting state funds.

3. Washington was also a munificent patron of science and scholarship. Federal support for basic research grew rapidly. A drive to encourage and assist "centers of excellence" through grants to institutions as well as student fellowships led to new or enlarged graduate programs in many fields. Many public institutions were able to become strong in areas previously dominated by the private universities. Federal money was generously distributed and fed rivalry. Grants and loan guarantees were available for construction of dormitories and later, academic buildings.

During this time, federal support of research became essential to the budgets of a relatively few institutions, but leading ones in every dimension. About a hundred universities, both public and private, were the great beneficiaries of the federal policy of funding academic science. By 1978, federal expenditures in its support were $4.5 billion and accounted for 75 percent of what higher education spent on scientific research.

Today, the federal government plays a major role as a patron of colleges and universities. In 1978, the dollar value of all kinds of federal support amounted to between an eighth and a sixth of their aggregate current fund revenues. Almost all of the federal dollars are made available through student aid or research support programs.

The New Situation: Fewer Students, Less Income, Higher Costs

The buoyant and optimistic atmosphere that characterized the growth period just described is increasingly replaced by a pessimistic one, as higher education comes to terms with its need to live not only with an end of growth but with actual retrenchment.

Three factors account for the declining prospects. First, demographic changes will bring lower enrollments; second, inflation raises costs; and third, a new purpose now guides federal funding.

1. Early in its work, the Commission concluded that because of demographic changes, enrollments will decline significantly in the next fifteen years. This is unwelcome news for all of higher education and, in particular, for the parts that had recently expanded so rapidly. Conflicting or opposing views of enrollment prospects are frequently heard. We believe that the interests of the segments of higher education most affected by the predicted changes will be better served by planning for orderly retrenchment than by denial that it must come. The facts are indisputable.

Since 1965, growth in college enrollments has been slowing down. It now seems to have ended. The number of eighteen-year-olds in the population has already reached its peak. Fifteen years from now, there will be only 75 percent as many as the baby boom generation produced. If we look at the larger age range that covers the greater part of traditional students—the numbers of eighteen to twenty-four-year-olds—we find that this group will also be in a long and deep decline, although it will begin to shrink two years later.

Two statistics further support the prediction that there is no significant reservoir for growth in the numbers of students of traditional college age. First, the fraction of eighteen-year-olds who graduate from high school is historically high. At present, it is 75 percent, about where it has been since 1966, after a period of rapid growth. The other is the fraction of high school graduates who go on to college. This is also higher than it has ever been. But it, too, has peaked: from 1950 to 1970, this proportion rose from 43 percent to 62 percent, and it has changed little since. Still another factor is that, with the large increase in college-going, the purely economic advantages of college education over immediate post-high school entry into the labor force seem to be declining. Taken together with the decline of eighteen-year-olds in the population, these are powerful reasons to predict that the growth of enrollments will not resume in the next fifteen to twenty years.

Demographic decline will not affect the country uniformly. The Northeast will probably suffer most, while parts of the Southwest may escape entirely and even continue to grow. Consequently, our recommendations and conclusions will be appropriate to most of the states but not to all of them.

Experience so far gives at least a broad indication of what kinds of institutions may be particularly affected by enrollment changes. Complete data are available only to 1978, the immediate past when total enrollments were just levelling off. In the private sector, which so far was only slightly more hard hit than the public, the small liberal arts colleges in small town locations serving nearby populations are the first to have been affected. Among public institutions the comprehensive colleges had significant declines, but the greatest student losses to date are in the two-year institutions—nearly 15 percent of the public and 20 percent of the private already have been affected significantly. This suggests what the future will bring, and also suggests the kinds of pressures on public policy that are likely to arise on behalf of institutions in trouble.

The falling-off of the cohorts of college age is paralleled by a rise in those at older ages. They will have fewer children and, soon, grandchildren, about whom to be concerned, and will be more interested in supporting increased services for themselves than in supporting colleges.

Some in higher education hope that non-traditional students who are outside the usual college-going ages will make up for the losses that demographic changes bring. It is true that this is a time of sweeping social change—alternative life styles embraced by young people now, the place of child-bearing and marriage in womens' lives, earlier retirement and increased vigor of the elderly—all of these forces point to new types of students, and they are indeed growing in numbers. However, most of them are part-timers who do not enter full-fledged degree programs because of typical economic and family constraints. For this reason, it is highly unlikely that their numbers will grow enough to begin to replace the declining number of full-time, full-program, traditionally aged students. We have confidence in our prediction, and our recommendations are based on it.

2. Inflation further worsens the economic situation, especially of private institutions that rely heavily on endowments and gifts. Static stock prices in the face of inflation, which has been gaining momentum since the late 1960s, erode substantially the real value of these two sources of funds for the private sector.

All this generates pressure to raise tuition. From 1966 to 1977, average tuition at all private four-year institutions rose more than 9 percent each year, compared to a 6 percent annual increase in the Consumer Price Index. Tuition increases have continued in the past two years, but at a lower rate.

For a few institutions—those with the widest reputations and the longest lists of applicants—increases in tuition can solve the financial problem, though not without consequences that are undesirable on other grounds, particularly a narrowing of the social composition of their student bodies, after a period of successful conscious effort to broaden it. But for the majority of private institutions, what may be an unavoidable measure in the immediate situation carries great financial risks in the longer run. Since public institutions have been much slower to raise tuitions and fees (until 1974, they had risen less than the cost of living) the "tuition gap"—difference between tuition and required fees at more or less comparable private and public institutions—has been widening. Even if the tuition and fees of public and private institutions increase at the same rate, the tuition gap gets larger in dollar terms. When private institutions raise tuitions, they face a substantial risk of losing enrollments even faster than they otherwise would, and an ever larger share of a declining total goes to the institutions that charge less.

The importance of gifts from individuals (usually alumni) and from business corporations to the financing of higher education is great. Grants from private foundations are another major non-governmental source of money. It is clear that any change in the tax laws or other governmental policies that led to a significant reduction in this income, would seriously worsen the financial position of many institutions. So would a sharp falling-off of support from private foundations.

Continuing inflation also has unfavorable effects on publicly supported institutions. Shifting demands of an older population on state budgets leave governors and legislatures less willing to provide large annual increases for higher education. The slowing of enrollment growth and the prospect of future decline add to this reluctance. The same pressures have already led to significant rises in tuition and to wider differentials between tuition rates for out-of-state students and those for residents.

3. The final feature of higher education's changed financial position comes from a change in public policy beginning in 1965: federal dollars are now used to support different purposes than they did during the boom period.

What has changed in the last fifteen years is that there has been a great shift in the relative dollar weights: the present two-to-one ratio in favor of student aid was then just the reverse in support of research. The central thrust of the new student aid program is egalitarian: to provide financial assistance to students from low-income families who might not otherwise be able to go to college. By contrast, programs of research support are basically meritocratic, even elitist, in orientation. The change did not result from one set of values replacing the other, but from legislative recognition of a new and additional public purpose that higher education can serve.

The two programs have quite different clienteles. Student aid programs involve almost every college and university in the nation, and nearly all have benefited from them. Most of the support of science goes to a relatively few institutions. The end of growth in research support does have a major impact on them, and they are major institutions. Because of their prestige and the quality of the programs they offer, they are consistently oversupplied with applicants at both undergraduate and professional school levels, and the fact that student aid has increased is almost irrelevant for them. Thus the change in federal programs has a largely negative effect on the most visible and audible part of higher education.

Chapter 3

Federal Regulation

It is the business of a university to provide that atmosphere which is most conducive to speculation, experiment and creation. It is an atmosphere in which there prevail "four freedoms" of a university— to determine for itself on academic grounds who may teach, what may be taught, how it shall be taught, and who may be admitted to study.

Justice Frankfurter caught the American academic tradition in these words not so long ago. There are times when they can be read by the faculty and administrators of our colleges and universities as a remembrance of things past. The distinguishing mark of American higher education has been its independence and autonomy. It was as true on the whole of the public institutions as of the private ones, and in contrast to the centralized direction and control by government ministries that characterizes Continental higher education.

Equal opportunity regulation is administered today in a way that is not in keeping with our tradition. The enforcement problems are the most difficult, most important, and most enduring ones that federal regulation presents for higher education. But not for it alone; these are very difficult questions for everyone, everywhere they are raised.

The goal of public policy is to change long-established patterns of behavior of individuals and institutions and, even more fundamentally, to change people's attitudes. This is an inherently difficult task; many believe an impossible one. Nonetheless, as a society, we are committed to it. The repeated ratification of this goal by Congress in new legislation, and its continued reinforcement in the courts testifies to the commitment. Further, equal opportunity in higher education is particularly important since it actually does reduce social inequality. As the attention given the *Bakke* case showed, discrimination in higher education has great symbolic as well as substantive significance.

However, this broad general commitment does not resolve continuing conflicts over the costs of achieving these goals at the expense of other values. These conflicts reflect a more basic American dilemma: the tension between the ideal of equality of opportunity and the reality of inequality of condition—the tension between traditional individualism and a new egalitarianism. In the specific context of higher education, this expresses itself in the tension between the accepted academic principle of selection on the basis of merit, and the egalitarian principle of proportional representation.

Each major branch of government played an important role in developing equal opportunity policies, from the initial Presidential Executive Order (11246) forbidding discrimination in hiring by federal contractors in 1940, to the Civil Rights Act of 1964, and the continuing series of court decisions that have since interpreted and applied the Act.

Congress, in passing the equal opportunity laws and providing for their enforcement, tried to emphasize voluntary cooperation, persuasion, and conciliation rather than litigation as the primary way to achieve compliance. However, events took a different course. The legislation gave the responsible agencies neither clear standards for compliance, nor adequate enforcement powers. The agencies in turn found it difficult to set standards by regulation, and did so only very slowly. They lacked resources for effective mediation and conciliation. Aggrieved individuals and groups, feeling that the agencies were not doing enough to protect their rights, turned to the courts. The judicial mode, rather than administrative processes, became the most important way to seek compliance. Accordingly, the courts—not the agencies—have played the dominant role as the forum for hearing complaints and shaping the substantive content of equal opportunity policy.

In the absence of effective administrative regulatory power, a strong judicial role is inevitable. The courtroom is certainly preferable to the barricades for deciding sensitive issues of discrimination. But too heavy reliance on litigation is costly. The decentralization of the courts, the several stages of appellate review, and the complexity of public-law litigation all add to the length of the proceedings. Even though formal procedures do alter as the courts' role in shaping public law expands, it is often difficult to be sure that all important interests are heard and their claims adequately evaluated. Specific court decisions may produce significant unintended consequences for parties not at the bar. Further, the adversarial cast of the trial process fosters tensions that may continue for years, tensions inimical to "that atmosphere which is most conducive to speculation, experiment and creation."

We reject two alternatives to the present system, though both have wide support. First, we believe that it is not the cure to abolish the whole apparatus of legal compulsion, beyond the broad constitutional provision for equal treatment under the laws. Many do and argue one, or both, of two propositions: (1) the goals are illusory, because the problems are inherent in human nature, and (2) the procedural problems are merely particular examples of the general problem inherent in any regulatory legislation of broad reach, and are certain to reappear in one form or another as long as there is any regulation.

Another view that we reject holds that nothing more needs to be done, that the present system, with all its blemishes, has effected real change in colleges and universities, and that regulated and regulators are learning to adapt to each other. Those sharing this view also believe that further adaptation will occur naturally without any efforts at large scale restructuring of the process. A further and even stronger form of this position says that restructuring will only lead to new problems, ones now unanticipated, with new kinds of adaptation needed on both sides before even the present level of workability is reached.

We believe that regulation is needed. We strongly support the country's newest demand on higher education—that it rid itself of every kind of discrimination. But we believe that a faster, surer, and less adversarial way to meet that demand must be found for the difficult years ahead. Significant improvements in the present regulatory apparatus should be made. The Commission believes they can be made.

THE NEED FOR EQUAL OPPORTUNITY REGULATION

Discrimination marked higher education over our history, just as it has every other sector of American life. Blacks, women, and Jews—at one time or another—have been denied access to the academic world. Women's opportunities for faculty positions at colleges and universities, for instance, were limited by recruitment based on the "old boy" network, by anti-nepotism rules that were unfair to capable wives living where no other suitable academic jobs were available, and by the heavy weight given in criteria for tenured appointments to the numbers of scholarly publications, with no allowance made for time devoted to raising children.

In 1970, one half of all Black undergraduates were still in predominantly Black colleges and universities. There were 500,000 Black students—7 percent of undergraduate enrollments—compared to their 10 percent share of the nation's recent high school graduates.

Only 2.2 percent of the 350,000 faculty members around the country were Black. Almost all were teaching in historically Black institutions.

Though 22 percent of the American faculty were women, less than one-third had teaching jobs in doctoral-granting or research universities. Few, indeed, were in tenured professorial ranks.

This was the situation sixteen years after *Brown* v. *Board of Education* and six years after the new Civil Rights Act. Title VI of that act had specifically addressed discrimination in all federally funded programs such as education. In that year, colleges and universities first began to feel the heavy hand of federal investigators on a large scale and regulations initially applied to other sectors were now extended by the government to the academic world. Since then, all of the newer regulations have included higher education from the first.

And the regulatory effort has made a difference, despite the turmoil it has led to on many campuses. From the perspective of every ethnic minority, the handicapped, the aged, and women—all those for whom the laws were designed—there have been outcomes that might not otherwise have been realized. The numbers of minority and women students and faculty who have come into the higher education system within the past decade reflect their increased opportunities. Black high school graduates now attend four-year colleges at a rate higher than their proportion in the population, and enrollments of women and all other groups earlier denied opportunity continue to increase.

But, granting that opportunity is greater and that discrimination is waning, intense competition for academic jobs that is already appearing, and that will worsen as enrollments fall, creates a buyers' market for faculty. Many institutions of all kinds might narrow their field of candidates for appointments out of a desire to use the particular excellences of research universities as a model, when in fact other qualities are more relevant to their needs. It will take real effort to assure that all institutions continue to include non-traditional candidates in tenured appointments, and that new "open-door" policies do not in practice become revolving doors.

All these considerations are the basis for the Commission's conviction that regulation continues to be needed. Having said this, we then had to consider the distinctive nature of higher education, and the specific problems it poses to equal opportunity regulation, even if the machinery were to work with optimal smoothness.

PARTICULAR PROBLEMS IN REGULATING HIGHER EDUCATION

No matter how much procedures are improved, some intractable problems are bound to remain to make it difficult to regulate equal opportunity in colleges and universities. The hardest problems center on faculty appointments and promotions. They come from the very nature of academic activity and the way that higher education has traditionally functioned. It is worth noting that it has traditionally functioned in a way that brought a high degree of excellence and some extraordinary accomplishments, both for itself and for the nation.

Tenure System

Tenure is at the heart of academic organization. The end of growth in enrollments will mean a more than corresponding decline in demand for new faculty. The high proportion of tenured faculty, its relative youth, and the newly legislated rise in the retirement age combine to intensify the appointment problems for at least the next fifteen years. More women are earning doctorates in all fields, and many of them will be looking for academic jobs. By 1977, a quarter of the Ph.D.'s awarded were to women, compared to fewer than 14 percent in 1970. Thus, there will be more women qualified to teach and few positions available. Every slot will be subject to fierce competition, and the competitive tensions will grow as the new faculty moves up the promotion ladder to tenure.

Minorities, especially Blacks, are in a somewhat different position. Here, qualified candidates for academic employment are still in high demand. Nonetheless, many women and Blacks will not be hired, promoted, or given tenure. Some among them will perceive themselves as victims of discrimination, sometimes rightly so, and some will complain.

Under present procedures, statistical comparisons play a central role in determining whether discrimination in employment exists. For instance, the regulatory goal in enforcing the Executive Order has been to achieve statistical parity between the workforce of the employer in question and the relevant labor pool. Standards for selecting the appropriate pool are therefore crucial, but the concepts in current use were developed in the context of blue-collar or entry-level management employment in business organizations. These standards may be inappropriate to faculty appointments and promotions.

In upper-echelon executive and professional employment, specialized training, prior experience, and subjective criteria are central to the hiring decision. These considerations are also particularly important in promotion and tenure decisions in higher education, where commitments made may span the entire professional life of those appointed. Labor pool concepts are elusive. Different academic institutions, and departments within them, draw from different recruitment pools. Catalogues of earned degrees or rosters of scientific or specialized personnel do not necessarily represent the number of people actually available or suitable for faculty appointments. These important issues have not been directly addressed by the administrative agencies concerned. Moreover, regulations relating to availability pools and workforce utilization analysis have not yet taken into consideration the problem of limited job opportunity caused by the combination of the high proportion of tenured faculty and declining demand for higher education.

Public Disclosure and Confidentiality
of Faculty Dossiers

A serious collateral problem is how to reconcile regulatory oversight, public disclosure laws, and the traditional confidentiality of faculty dossiers. A faculty dossier contains a mixture of public information (degrees received, honors, books published), semi-public information (scholastic transcripts, qualifying examination scores, national board scores), and confidential information (letters of recommendation, peer review evaluations of scholarship and teaching performance, along with invited outside evaluation of research and publications). Unlike student records that regularly mark the academic seasons with final grades, evaluations, and commentaries, the faculty dossier grows by fits and starts. Usually, vital documentation is added to the dossier during the appointment, reappointment, promotion, and tenure decision process.

The faculty dossier has traditionally had a high degree of confidentiality. Academic peer review, through promotion or tenure committees, generates confidential assessments, evaluations, and comments. Access to these files is restricted; they are not available for direct review even by the person under consideration.

Strict confidentiality has been considered necessary to protect the integrity of the peer review process, and an institution's desire to make offers and commitments only to the most qualified person available for any particular appointment. Peer review helps maintain standards of academic excellence. Confidentiality protects the process in two ways: it promotes open, honest, and (in theory) unbiased evaluations of the candidate's qualifications while protecting his or her reputation from injury.

Any other use of the faculty dossier creates a problem of proper balance between public rights and private rights, disclosure and confidentiality. Increased government regulation is paralleled by an increased government need to inspect, collect, and review private actions to assure compliance with regulatory standards. Regulations under the Executive Order and other equal opportunity programs provide that a contractor or a federal fund recipient must allow the government investigators complete access to all records. If the on-site compliance officer believes the situation warrants further review by regional or Washington staff, the agency may ask to remove or copy the academic personnel file under review. However, once the institution relinquishes the file, the public agency may not be able to keep the material confidential. The Freedom of Information Act (FOIA) gives the public the opportunity to inspect and review the record of the regulator and the response of the regulated. Individuals whose interests are directly involved have broad access to all the materials.

In this situation public and private rights clash. Publicity threatens the traditional peer review process. The various interests at stake — maintaining academic standards, public accountability, elimination of selection bias — raise important policy issues. However, these issues have been left to ad hoc, case-by-case determination, without either public discussion of the issues or development of regulatory standards to guide agencies and institutions.

Collegial Nature of Higher Education

Faculties of academic institutions are unlike most other groups who work together. While there is a hierarchical structure which reaches from the student, through the teaching instructor, on to the various levels before tenure is reached, to deans, to the president, to the governing board, and it would be fatuous to claim that deference to the next level is not present, it is also true that in a basic sense colleges and universities are run collegially. One of the major attractions of academic employment is the individual's sense of independence. Furthermore, the most important feature of collegiality, as it bears on regulating equal opportunity, is that judgment by peers is its highest value.

In the final analysis, faculty status is not won in the courtroom. Remedies that compel employment or tenure ignore the sociology of the collegial structure. Less drastic remedies, such as ordering back-pay, may recoup financial loss, but litigiousness is not an attribute that enhances standing with colleagues. An individual litigant may win the immediate battle at great emotional and economic cost, only to lose the academic war.

Members of the groups for whose benefit the equal opportunities laws were enacted do not themselves want to enter the academic ranks at the expense of academic quality. Although there are occasional exceptions, and some may question how quality has been defined, those appointed do not want to discard the concept of merit. Like the public, they would rather that the academic badge continue to be honorably awarded by the judgment of peers.

The collegial nature of higher education is not a matter of convenience or indulgence; rather it is the efficient adaptation of organizational form to purpose. In a hierarchical organization, commands generally are executed, even if the internal resistance is high. The same cannot be said of a collegial one. If procedures and sanctions for achieving equal opportunity in higher education are to be effective, they must be compatible with the way colleges and universities naturally govern themselves.

Interacting Choices of Students and Institutions

Another special feature of higher education is that it has traditionally been characterized by interacting choices of institutions and students, with the result that different colleges and universities have distinctive curricula and academic standards. Institutions, or state systems, set their own requirements for admission, retention, and graduation in order to offer coherent programs of instruction at a level their student bodies can meet. The other side of this, of course, is that students choose the institution they want. For many, the possibility of attending a particular kind of college is an important element in deciding to go beyond high school.

Since most students attend their nearest high school—and it must accept them—this is a point of sharp distinction between secondary and higher education. Yet secondary schooling is now a widely used model in setting compliance standards on issues involving equal opportunity for students in higher education.

This had led to some of the thorniest problems and to many of the well-publicized issues on admissions, grades, and curriculum in recent years. It must be remembered that, earlier, most state universities, while traditionally open to all high school graduates, always had high drop-out rates because many students admitted could not meet the academic standards.

A combination of vigorous enforcement and raised consciousness has undoubtedly prodded many academic institutions into broadening the social composition of their student bodies and giving up long-standing discriminatory practices. Nonetheless, difficult problems remain to be solved whenever a student challenges a college or university on its admissions policy or academic standards.

All of these problems complicate the regulation of equal opportunity: declining job opportunities in higher education, the tenure system as it relates to labor pool concepts and workforce utilization analysis, the need for confidentiality of dossiers, the collegial nature of higher education, and the interacting choices of students and institutions. The problems will persist in the years ahead with the best apparatus for enforcement.

THE PRESENT REGULATORY APPARATUS—
HOW IT FUNCTIONS

It is useful to discuss enforcement of the equal opportunity laws in colleges and universities today in terms of: (1) the substantive content of the laws forbidding discrimination and the standards for applying them; (2) the agencies presently responsible for enforcement; and, (3) how the procedures are operating to create problems.

Legal Basis

A case for discrimination rests on either of two claims: (1) if one of two people in a similar situation has been denied opportunity on the basis of some irrelevant condition, such as race, sex, national origin, religion, age or handicap; (2) if a practice, ostensibly neutral on its face has, in fact, a disparate impact on a person who is a member of a disadvantaged (protected) group.

Three different standards are now in use for determining unlawful discrimination: constitutional, statutory, and contractual. Complainants relying on Amendments V and XIV of the Constitution must offer evidence of an intent to discriminate. Statistical disparities in outcomes may be used as evidence of such an intent. Someone charged with a violation must, therefore, be able to rebut an assertion of intention to discriminate.

Legislation enacted by Congress presents a different situation; it usually does not set statutory standards for discrimination. These are more often set implicitly by the agency applying the statute. Increasingly, the courts are setting the standards. Generally, only the results are considered, rather than any evidence of intent to discriminate. For instance, a finding of unlawful discrimination can be made under Title VI or VII of the Civil Rights Act on statistical evidence that an ostensibly neutral hiring practice has a disparate impact on minorities or on women. An employer charged under Title VII has to show that he did not discriminate even inadvertently.

The contractual standard of discrimination is the most demanding. Executive Order 11246, enacted in 1940, as amended, set equal employment standards for contracts between the federal government and its contractors. It obliges the latter to undertake affirmative action to remedy under-representation of certain groups employed; it is not directed toward proving acts of past discrimination.

Agencies Involved

There are now seventeen constitutional provisions, executive orders, and federal laws affecting equal opportunity in higher education. Most have been enacted or issued since 1970.

At least eight different government agencies are directly responsible for enforcement of these laws, and several more have responsibilities because they grant federal funds to colleges and universities. In addition to the federal agencies' responsibilities, the federal courts have jurisdiction over private suits brought under these statutes. (State constitutions and non-discrimination laws also exist in plenty but the Commission's report is limited to the discussion of regulation by the states in Chapter 4.)

This bewildering array of regulations can be put into two main categories. One focuses on employment, and concerns the faculty—hiring, retention, and promotion to tenure. Responsibility for enforcement is divided among the Department of Labor, Office of Federal Contract Compliance Programs (OFCCP), the Department of Justice (DOJ), and the Equal Employment Opportunity Commission (EEOC).

The other set of equal opportunity regulations affecting higher education is directed toward policies on students—admission, promotion, graduation—and toward programs for them— such as curriculum and facilities. (Titles VI, IX, and Section 504 are all primarily student-oriented statutes, but in certain situations they also relate to employment discrimination.) Primary responsibility for the enforcement of these laws, known as "programmatic," is concentrated in a single agency—HEW's Office of Civil Rights (OCR). (In May 1980, HEW became HHS, the Department of Health and Human Services.) However, for public colleges and universities, the jurisdiction is shared with the Department of Justice.

Much of the friction that has developed between higher education and the government is a result of the sheer numbers of laws, agencies, and people involved in the daily task of investigating, evaluating, and deciding that an institution is not in compliance. Different agencies' styles conflict; decentralization brings uneven results in different parts of the country; inexperience in higher education of many of the investigators also accounts for some of the trouble; and, finally, the chief remedy available is a cut-off of all federal funding.

Procedures Used and Sanctions

The various agencies have developed differing procedural styles that affect enforcement and standards. For instance, the orientation of EEOC is on voluntary settlement of individual complaints. In large measure, the agency relies on private litigants to develop the substantive standards of Title VII. In contrast, enforcement of the Executive Order program is seldom triggered by individual complaints. Its enforcement agency

(OFCCP) focuses on elimination of "systemic" problems through contractual promises. It emphasizes "result-oriented" procedures and specific numerical standards in affirmative action plans and does not consider an employer's actual history of discrimination.

In addition to the problems created by the varying standards and procedures of the several enforcement agencies with shared purposes and overlapping jurisdictions, there is difficulty within agencies because of their decentralized structures. Decentralized control frustrates the development of uniform standards and procedures. When agency outcomes differ with regional offices, rather than resulting from real distinctions in institutions' practices, the process appears to be subjective and arbitrary. This can discourage initiatives toward voluntary compliance.

A gap between theory and practice, discernable even at headquarters in Washington, becomes even more pronounced when actions in the field are compared with the policies as defined in Washington. The problem is exacerbated by the lack of experience with higher education of the compliance coordinators, or equal opportunity specialists, who investigate equal opportunity questions on campus. In both OCR and the Department of Labor, they are employees in low or middle grade positions and not highly paid. A recent vacancy announcement for such positions in OCR listed experience as a condition of employment, but not a bachelor's degree or even college attendance. In some cases, education is accepted as a substitute for experience, but it is obvious from the job descriptions that experience is the crucial factor. What is looked for is experience in various "community programs designed to promote equality," "special experience" demonstrating "knowledge of the causes and effects of discriminatory practices against minorities and women," and experience "working with or promoting equal opportunity for handicapped persons." Experience with or particular knowledge of the regulated institutions is not sought. From the perspective of academic administrators and faculty, for whom competency and achievement are important, the inexperience with higher education of the federal on-site compliance agents is a serious irritant.

In contrast to the variety of procedures and forums available to bring complaints, there is relatively little flexibility in remedies available once a violation has been established. Nine laws provide that the only sanction for violation of statutory or regulatory standards is termination of both federal funds and federal contracts either to the particular non-complying institution, or to the entire system of higher education to which it belongs.

Like other forms of massive retaliation, this sanction is too powerful to be completely credible, and too broad and indiscriminate to be a useful instrument of influence. Since both research and student aid funds are subject to these sanctions, fund termination represents, for almost all academic administrators, the difference between institutional health and life-threatening illness. Though to date no institution has had its federal funds terminated under the equal opportunity laws, responsible administrators take the threats seriously. Even if the formal procedures leading to termination do not go forward, there are informal, and sufficiently alarming, ways of delaying expected federal funds. In contrast, since it has never been imposed, the prospect of a cut-off has an aura of unreality for faculty. Yet the achievement of the goals of non-discrimination and equal opportunity depends primarily on changes in attitudes and behavior at the faculty level.

The threat of fund termination operates to divide the academy, administrators against faculty and even faculty against itself. Traditional departmental autonomy is seen as threatened. Faculties in the sciences and humanities may have different perspectives on the nature of objective recruiting procedures, but it is contract money for science that is at stake if the humanities faculty fails to meet the regulatory standards. The essential point is that a fund cut-off makes sense as a sanction against hierarchical organizations, and is inappropriate and generally ineffective in collegial ones.

Sometimes the agency responds to complaints filed by an individual or group. Other times the agency is responding to a pending renewal of a government grant or contract to a college or university. It then becomes the duty of the equal opportunity agency to investigate the situation and make determinations about possible discriminatory behavior. In these cases the agency takes on a dual function; it is both advocate and judge.

To many in higher education, however, the government does not appear to act neutrally. Too often the agency's participatory role becomes confused; the line between investigation and decision is not clearly marked. In some instances funds have been delayed or deferred even before a hearing on the merits of the discrimination issue. These are sensitive and complex decisions and must be fair in substance; they must also appear to be made in an impartial and fair manner. Although that is the essence of due process, present agency procedures do not always recognize and respect the boundaries between advocacy and judgment.

THREE CASE HISTORIES

Matters of procedure will in the end have a great influence on how effectively and how speedily the goal of the government's equal opportunity enforcement efforts is reached in higher education. The broad substantive aim of the laws is now generally accepted in the academic community, or at least it accepts the need to comply with them. What is at issue is who should decide what constitutes discrimination, on the basis of what standards, what should be done about it, and who decides that. These procedural questions are inevitably complex, and systematic discussion of them tends to take on an abstract quality that makes for difficult reading. Yet it is in procedural questions that some of the knottiest problems of regulation lie, in other areas as well as in colleges and universities.

In order to illustrate how the complicated machinery described above actually operates in regulating equal opportunity and non-discrimination in higher education, we present three case histories. The first two are hypothetical, although drawn from actual cases. The last is a brief account of an actual case with a long history, the case now known as *Adams* v. *Califano*.

The Case of John Doe, Student

Chem 220 is one of the most famous courses offered at Oxbridge, a leading private research university. The course is famed for its rigor and for the fact that any student who gets a grade of "B" or above is practically assured admission to medical school. Only 250 students can be admitted and because of its reputation it is always oversubscribed. The class is given in the Holsworthy Lecture Room, the only one large enough for a class that size. Holsworthy is located on the top floor (third) of the Old Science Building, a magnificent late-Victorian building.

John Doe, a senior at Oxbridge, is a thirty-seven year-old Black veteran. He lost one of his legs in the Vietnam War and uses crutches to get around campus. John wants to go to medical school. Last year John was one of the few minority students enrolled in Chem 220. It was difficult for him to get to Holsworthy, and he generally arrived late. He received a "C" in the course, which was the highest grade received by any of the minority students in the course. This year John applied to the state medical school but was not admitted there, or to any other medical school. He ranked below the fiftieth percentile in the national Medical College Admission Test.

The hypothetical situation could lead to various charges of discrimination or unequal treatment. Of course, a claim does not mean the charge is proved. However, the period between an initial claim and a final decision can be long and the process costly for all concerned.

John Doe, a Black student in a private institution, may raise claims against Oxbridge under the following statutes requiring non-discrimination in education programs: Title VI (race), the Age Discrimination Act, and Section 504 of the Rehabilitation Act of 1973 (handicap). In addition to these programmatic claims, Doe may use the link between the course, Chem 220, and admission to medical school to assert that both Oxbridge and the state medical school violated several non-discrimination-in-employment statutes, specifically Section 503 of the Rehabilitation Act of 1973 (handicap), the Vietnam Era Veterans Readjustment Assitance Act of 1974, and the Age Discrimination in Employment Act of 1967. Although these employment-based claims are certainly more attenuated, two courts have said that the term "employment agency" in similar statutes should be liberally construed to include law and medical schools.

John Doe has a private right of action under these laws and therefore could immediately bring suit against Oxbridge. However, he might prefer to take his complaints to the agencies responsible for enforcing the relevant laws and ask them to investigate his charges. For the programmatic statutes the relevant agency would be the Office for Civil Rights (OCR). The relevant agencies for the employment-based claims would be the office of Federal Contract Compliance Programs (OFCCP) in the Department of Labor and the Equal Employment Opportunity Commission (EEOC).

On the basis of these facts the regulatory agencies might determine that Oxbridge has violated the law. The third-floor classroom presents an access problem for a handicapped student. Oxbridge may have to move the class, build ramps, or install an elevator to be in compliance with Section 504. In addition, the statistical evidence on the number of minority students admitted to Chem 220 and the lack of any minority students receiving a "good" grade may lead to a finding of discrimination based on disparate impact under Title VI. If any of the programmatic claims ultimately are resolved in John Doe's favor, Oxbridge may conceivably lose its federal funding of student financial aid and of several projects under government contracts as well.

John Doe is just one student; multiply him by the number of potential student claimants on the campus and it is easy to see why academic administrators are concerned about the impact of these laws.

The second example, involving two faculty members, will illustrate further aspects of these problems.

The Case of Associate Professors
Robert Roe and Mary Moe

Old State is the flagship institution in the public system of higher education in the state of Newconsin. It is a highly respected research university with several outstanding graduate degree programs. In the past, Old State's sociology department has not had a strong reputation; but in the last six or seven years the department has increased its full-time positions from eight to twenty-one, and it has increased its emphasis on research as well as teaching excellence. Throughout this period Old State was also actively seeking to increase the size of its Black faculty. Old State has several major contracts totaling more than $1 million with the federal government.

Robert Roe, a Black male, and Mary Moe, a white female, have teaching appointments in the sociology department. Professor Roe had taught for several years at another college and had completed all but his dissertation when he was recruited and hired as an associate professor by the department three years ago. He asked for and received a commitment to pay him $15,000 during the first year of his three-year contract if he received his Ph.D. (which he did) by the time he arrived on campus to begin teaching in the fall. This was $3,000 above the rate which the sociology department was paying for new Ph.D.'s.

In the spring of his second year, Professor Roe was evaluated by the department and the decision was made not to renew his contract. The reasons given for non-renewal were that his performance in teaching and scholarship were below the standard the department wished to maintain. During the two years he has been at Old State,

Roe had not produced any scholarly publication and the student enrollment in his "Black America" course fell dramatically. He is involved in community activities and is chairman of the local branch of the NAACP.

Mary Moe is an older woman who returned to graduate school to complete her graduate work after her youngest child entered high school. She received her doctorate from a prestigious institution. She was hired as an instructor (at a salary of $9,500) in the sociology department seven years earlier. Her contract was renewed, and she has received regular promotions. She is now an associate professor.

Mary Moe's research work concentrated on studies of the blue-collar workforce. In the past two years she has increasingly focused her research on the role of the working-class woman in American society. She has published extensively in this area and has several women graduate students who came to Old State to study with her specifically. She has been active in organizing a women's group on campus. This year, her final year on contract, she submitted her dossier for consideration by the faculty tenure committee. The committee acknowledged her teaching excellence but felt her recent publications were "insufficiently scholarly" in view of the objectives of the department and therefore denied her request for tenure. Old State has an "up or out" rule and, as a result, Professor Moe must seek a teaching position elsewhere.

This case also presents a multiple statute/multiple forum situation. On the basis of these facts Professors Roe and Moe may both be able to make claims under several statutes with the following agencies:

Professor Roe

XIV Amendment	Private Suit (individual or class action) in federal or state court.
Title VI (discrimination on the basis of race)	Complaint filed with OCR: in addition may file class or individual private suit under Title VI.
Title VII (non-discrimination in employment)	EEOC/DOJ: individual complaint investigation, may lead to a "right to sue" letter or after review EEOC may refer the matter to the Department of Justice for filing of a "pattern and practice" suit against a public institution.

Executive Order 11246; as amended by Executive Order 11375	OFCCP/DOL: individual complaints referred to EEOC; investigation of systemic discrimination and contract compliance enforcement by OFCCP/DOL. OFCCP or EEOC may refer the matter to DOJ for further action.

Professor Moe

XIV Amendment	Private suit (individual or class action) in federal or state court.
Title IX (discrimination on the basis of sex in educational programs)	Complaint filed with OCR; and Professor Moe has a private right of action under Title IX.
Title VII (non-discrimination in employment)	EEOC/DOJ: individual complaint investigation, may lead to a "right to sue" letter or after review EEOC may refer the matter to the Department of Justice for filing of a "pattern and practice" suit against a public institution.
Age Discrimination in Employment Act	EEOC/DOJ: Same as above.
Equal Pay Act	EEOC/DOJ: Same as above.
Executive Order 11246; as amended by Executive Order 11375	OFCCP/DOL: individual complaints referred to EEOC; investigation of systemic discrimination and contract compliance enforcement by OFCCP/DOL. OFCCP or EEOC may refer the matter to DOJ for further action.

Assuming that Robert Roe and Mary Moe ultimately prevail on any of these claims, Old State may have to reinstate him and grant her tenure. Old State also might be subject to an order requiring equalization of salaries between them, and an award for back-pay. And here too, the institution's contracts with the federal government might be delayed or terminated because of the contract compliance program under the Executive Order. Furthermore, the complainants may also allege violations of various state antidiscrimination or fair employment practice statutes.

These cases are hypothetical, but identical real situations have triggered multiple compliance reviews by several different agencies. Each agency has its own perspective, and its own perception of the facts. Therefore, identical facts may have different outcomes in the several agencies and perhaps among different branch offices of the same agency.

Adams v. Califano

An actual, rather than a hypothetical, example of the problems created by duplication and concurrent jurisdiction, rendered even more complex by the interaction of courts, administrative agencies, complainants, academic institutions, the state legislature, and the governor is provided by the course of the proceeding *Adams* v. *Califano*.

The Adams case has a long history of agency action, inaction, and reaction. More than ten years ago the Office for Civil Rights (OCR) of the Department of Health, Education and Welfare (HEW) as it then was, began to review several public education systems, including higher education, to determine whether they were in compliance with the prohibitions of Title VI against race discrimination. In 1970, dissatisfied with the pace of agency procedures, the NAACP Legal Defense Fund (LDF) initiated a class-action suit against the government, and requested an order from the federal district court in Washington, D.C. requiring the agency to enforce Title VI in ten systems of public higher education. All had a prior history of de jure segregation.

By 1975, of the ten states originally involved (none of which were parties to the suit against the government), two had refused to respond or negotiate with OCR, and their cases were transferred to the Department of Justice for prosecution. (To date, in one of these cases, no further action has been taken.) One other state was then negotiating a settlement; and one state countered by bringing suit against HEW. The six remaining states attempted to negotiate with OCR to develop state plans to promote racial integration in their formerly dual systems of higher education. Again dissatisfied with the agency's performance, the LDF returned to court in 1975. OCR approved the initial state plans in 1974, but later repudiated them. In early 1977 they were all found unacceptable by the court. Thereafter each of the six remaining states has worked to develop new plans acceptable to the agency. By 1979, five state plans had been granted provisional and then final approval by the agency.

The plan for higher education submitted by one state, North Carolina, was provisionally approved in May 1978 but denied final approval in March 1979. OCR announced that it was going to institute formal administrative proceedings in the case, possibly leading to cutting off all federal funds to the state's higher education system. Meanwhile all grants and contracts for the University of North Carolina involving federal funds were referred to OCR. The state brought suit against HEW and OCR requesting the federal court in North Carolina to enjoin further action by the agency against the state, or funding delays. The court granted a temporary injunction prohibiting immediate withholding of federal funds. Administrative hearings in this matter were to begin in January 1980.

During all this time, other complainants, dissatisfied by lagging federal enforcement efforts under other education-based antidiscrimination statutes (Title IX and Section 504, sex and handicap) initiated similar suits against the agency. In 1977, consent decrees in all these actions bound OCR and other governmental agencies to observe strict enforcement schedules for processing complaints and eliminating the backlog of cases. In July 1979 the Women's Equity Action League and other groups requested that officials of HEW be held in contempt for failure to observe the terms of the 1977 agreement with respect to enforcing Title IX.

This bare recital cannot convey the high emotional pitch of those involved—complainants, state officials, and federal regulators. To date, the case has involved six consecutive Secretaries of HEW, six General Counsels, and six Directors of OCR. In the past two years there has been a complete turnover of the agency senior administrative staff; each change of leadership within the agency has been accompanied by shifts in policy.

After years of federal enforcement and state response, the public institutions in many of the *Adams* states still bear the marks of their history and remain predominantly white or black. The academic administrators responsible for running these systems have faced years of agency uncertainty and ambiguity while managing the complex politics involved in assuring state legislative support for the increased academic budgets promised in their plans. The economic and emotional cost has been high. Yet at no point has the federal agency clearly defined its standard for measuring compliance.

For instance, notwithstanding HEW's long-term involvement with the application of Title VI to systems of higher education, no separate regulations about it have ever been issued. In 1977, the court ordered HEW to issue desegregation criteria to assist the six *Adams*-affected states. This approximates regulatory policy, but court-ordered criteria are not regulations. Under the Administrative Procedure Act agency rule-making procedures may vary in degree of formality but even informal procedures require a period for public review and comment on proposed regulations, giving all interests a chance to be heard before regulations are issued that may affect them. On the critical issue of applying Title VI to higher education then, the appearance of impartiality and expert evaluation which ought to accompany rule-making procedures was absent.

In the *Adams* case, both the plaintiffs and OCR have applied legal and regulatory standards developed in the context of elementary and secondary public school education with little examination of the appropriateness of these standards for higher education. These define equal educational opportunity in terms of an integrated unitary model of education. But, in some respects these standards are not relevant to the world of higher education, in which voluntary choice of institution by the student, and frequently of students by the institution, is so important. However, the agency has apparently taken no notice of these considerations. Furthermore, these standards may have an unintended harmful effect on the Black colleges in the *Adams* states. Almost all of these institutions have played an important role in providing educational opportunity to minority students, and many believe there is a continuing need for their services.

The absence of clear standards creates other problems. Varying standards applied in essentially similar situations, or standards that shift over time raise questions of fairness. Both factors caused friction in the *Adams*-affected states. Many administrators ask why their particular states were subjected to the Title VI enforcement proceedings, when other states with similar histories and dual systems escaped. Admittedly, agency power is discretionary, and in the face of limited enforcement capability, the agency must have priorities. Nonetheless, the use of this power appears discriminatory and arbitrary to those subject to agency action, and contributes to the belief that standards shift erratically as agency personnel change. In the *Adams* states, for example, OCR emphasized the entry of white students into Black institutions for several years. Now the *Adams* court-mandated criteria and a judicial admonition to take "into account the unique importance of Black colleges" has shifted the agency emphasis to the number of Black students entering traditionally white institutions. The policies and budget commitments made by the states in the earlier period may not be appropriate to these new goals. Shifting priorities and resources in systems of higher education is a long-time process not easily compatible with sudden shifts in regulatory directions.

RECOMMENDATIONS FOR PROCEDURAL REFORM

The real issue and the hard question the Commission posed about regulation of equal opportunity in higher education remains: is the social cost in terms of time, money and effort presently expended by all parties—regulatory, regulated, and client group—worth the result that has been achieved?

The Commission is convinced that the duplication of effort created by administrative agency overlap, the enervatingly repetitive responses from the institutions that result, the variations in standards for compliance, and the early and frequent resort to the courts that puts an adversarial cast on the relations of government and higher education are all strong arguments for reform.

Council for Equal Opportunity in Higher Education

Recommendation 1

The creation of a unified and consolidated administrative system for promoting and implementing the equal opportunity laws in higher education: The Council for Equal Opportunity in Higher Education. A key feature is the use of institutional equal opportunity assessments reports as the basis for Council action.

Organization. Our recommendation calls for a new Council to replace present mechanisms and to unify and consolidate the responsibilities for higher education presently shared by all agencies. The Council would be an independent agency within the Department of Education, reporting to the Secretary. It would be responsible both for implementation and enforcement and deal with all questions relating to college and university students as well as faculty and administrative employment. It would also be responsible for developing equal opportunity policy for higher education, balancing the public interest in efficient and effective enforcement of the laws, the needs of particular groups who have been burdened by discrimination, and the interests and needs of colleges and universities.*

> The Council and staff would have at least five members appointed by the President with the approval of the Senate, to serve staggered terms. It would not have regional offices, and would be divided into three sections all in Washington: the Council itself, a General Counsel's office, and a Hearings office.
>
> The responsibilities of the Council would include: receipt and review of institutions' self-evaluation reports; development of policy and issuance of rules and regulations; enforcement through selective compliance reviews and remedial orders; investigation and resolution of individual complaints; and provision of policy guidance on issues bearing on the problems of compliance (for instance, tenure, privacy, confidentiality, and peer review). The Council would have formal power of decision for all claims arising under the equal opportunity laws as well as the power to impose sanctions and issue cease and desist or other remedial orders for violations. Final decisions of the Council would be subject to judicial review in the federal courts of appeal.
>
> The General Counsel would be responsible for supervising enforcement including initiating complaints, or receiving and investigating or prosecuting complaints filed by individuals or groups. On request, the General Counsel could also issue advisory opinions. This office would be responsible for developing and training a corps of assistants who would be specialists in equal opportunity for higher education. Informal dispute resolution services, such as mediation and conciliation and other non-adversarial third-party intervention techniques, would also be available to assist in settling complaints.
>
> The Hearings Office would consider matters not resolved through mediation. After hearing cases, the Hearing Officers would prepare written reports and recommendations.

Institutional Assessment Reports.   Institutional equal opportunity assessment reports are a key feature of our recommendation and central to the development of mechanisms for effective reform. Every institution would be required to make,

*Peter Clark, Thomas S. Gates, and A. Leon Higginbotham, Jr., dissent from this recommendation. See comments page 89–93.

publish, and file with the Council an evaluation of its promises and performance over the entire range of equal opportunity goals on a regular basis. This assessment report would incorporate the present affirmative action plans and replace the federal equal opportunity information reports now required.

Several important purposes would be served by this procedure. It meets the need for institutional and public accountability in a way consistent with the collegial and generally decentralized structure of colleges and universities. It develops information to increase awareness of discriminatory patterns and to promote institutional initiatives. It encourages more effective agency rule-making, responsive to the realities of the academic marketplace. Publication of the report exposes institutions to the critical review of their peers, provides relevant information to potential buyers and sellers of academic services (whether students, faculty, or contractors), and thus deters continuing patterns of discrimination. Finally, a good-faith assessment process emphasizes the real objectives of these laws—to provide genuine equality of opportunity, rather than to focus on numerical goals as ends in themselves. Thus academic departments that are not obliged to set numerical hiring goals—either because there are too few qualified candidates in the relevant labor pool to state a meaningful number, or because the department's faculty is statistically balanced or in excess would still be subject to this assessment process.

This Commission cannot, nor should it, set the standards for a good-faith assessment. The substantive standards must evolve from collective experience yet remain responsive to institutional diversity. It is important that the process reflect the organizational structure specific to each institution. It should begin with the faculty and administration of each institution together mapping the locus of responsibility for various types of personnel decisions. Thus, if the departments in a given institution are responsible for all new hire decisions, the departments would be responsible for analysis of their employment performance and for determining their future objectives, and would be held responsible for their efforts. Where there is overlapping or dual responsibility, for example, between the budget committee of an academic senate and a promotion and tenure committee, both groups should participate. The purpose of these jurisdictional analyses is to pin-point responsibility and make the process more responsive to the decision-making structure of each institution. Some colleges and universities now review their equal opportunity efforts in this manner. Most do not. Typically, present agency practice tends to force institutions to respond in an administrative and bureaucratic mode, rather than in their familiar collegial style.

Effective equal opportunity policy must have strong support at the top. The assessment process will reinforce this leadership. Similar analysis should be made of the adequacy of campus-based equal opportunity grievance and complaint procedures. All of these analyses and departmental reports would be incorporated into a final document, subject to a period of review and comment by the academic community of each institution.

Every institution would be required to report regularly (every two or three years). If the Council had no objection within ninety days of receipt, the report would then constitute *prima facie* evidence that the reporting institution was in compliance with the requirements of Executive Order 11246, as amended.

If the Council filed specific objections, the reporting institution would have sixty days to respond with an amended report. The Council would investigate and assist the institution in developing adequate procedures, taking into account the quality of the effort shown in the initial report. If the Council still had objections, or believed the institution not to be in compliance with the equal opportunity laws, it would start hearing procedures within thirty days.

This procedure would supplant the current Executive Order pre-award compliance review process and replace or incorporate current equal opportunity reporting requirements. Some institutions are now reporting in this way. In the proposed system all institutions, not only those with government contracts, would have to report in this fashion. What might be different for many institutions, however, could be the way in which the information was developed and used. It would not be a routine bureaucratic function. A narrative report would help emphasize that equal opportunity is a continuing process, not a set of target numbers.

The process does not eliminate governmental regulation. It places greater emphasis on institutional initiative and responsibility rather than relying, as the present system does, almost exclusively on regulatory police power. It is appropriate to move in this direction because there are now enough directly concerned people in faculty positions to participate actively in the assessment process. By involving the faculty directly, our proposal gives responsibility, credit, and incentive to those who in fact hold the key to reform.

Procedures for Enforcement. All complaints by students, faculty, academic administrators, or others under the equal opportunity laws would be filed with the General Counsel's office. If

indicated, the General Counsel would promptly refer each matter to the Federal Mediation and Conciliation Service or some
other independent and neutral mediation office. All claims
initiated by the Council (such as "pattern and practice" complaints or non-compliance claims) arising out of its legal enforcement responsibilities would also be referred to mediation.
The goal would be a satisfactory resolution of the dispute
through informal and confidential third-party intervention procedures, before the hardening of attitudes that results from a
formal adversary process sets in. If, in the mediator's judgment,
no satisfactory settlement can be achieved within a reasonable
time, the matter would be referred back to the Council where
the complaint would then be referred to a Hearing Officer, for
preparation of a written report with a recommended disposition
or order. If exceptions were filed, or if the case were of special
importance, such as one involving a pattern or practice of discrimination, or an individual case of major precedental value,
the Council itself would review the report or order. Any party
dissatisfied with a final administrative order could then seek
judicial review in the federal circuit court of appeals.

For a reasonable period, complainants would be limited to
administrative remedies. This would not deny individuals or
groups their right to go to court, but would provide a more coherent and impartial system for administrative resolution of the
problems. To meet standards of fairness, the Council must act
promptly.

> In cases of complaints filed by individuals, if not resolved through
> mediation within ninety days of the initial complaint, or if no final
> decision had been issued by the Council 180 days thereafter, com-
> plainants would have the option to bring suit. It is more difficult to
> set an appropriate time table for class complaints or public actions
> brought by the Council. These could involve multiple claims, and
> many different parties with varying interests. In these cases, it seems
> appropriate to extend the mediation period to one year. Thereafter
> class complainants could initiate suit if no final decision or order had
> been issued by the Council within eighteen months.

Wider use of mediation and other informal non-adversarial
dispute resolution techniques is an important element of our
proposals. Mediation is most effective when it is perceived to be
genuinely neutral and independent. These services could be

provided by the Federal Mediation and Conciliation Service (FMCS), an experienced agency already in existence.

> FMCS has eight regional offices, seventy-one field offices and a large staff of full-time mediators which could be augmented if its responsibilities were broadened to include equal opportunity cases in higher education. Alternatively, a special office for mediation in higher education could be established as a division of FMCS. Such an office would be able to provide the necessary degree of specialized skill, training and understanding for effective mediation. In some instances, private mediation organizations, including those of higher education associations, also might be able to provide these services.

Varied Remedies. The Council must command more flexible and responsive remedial powers than the only administrative sanction now provided: termination of all federal funds and loss of eligibility for receipt of funds in the future. If the new Council is to replace courts as final decision-maker for most cases, it must have the power to order a range of sanctions and remedies now available only to the courts, including the issuance of cease and desist orders, provision of back-pay, salary equalization, or ordering "targeted" fund-terminations limited to a particular program or offending department or school, as well as the ultimate power to order termination of all funds to the whole institution or higher education system.

This recommendation for varied sanctions is closely linked to the creation of a coherent and uniform administrative process. Several agencies with overlapping jurisdictions applying differing sanctions would create more confusion, not less. Only if the Council is seen as providing fair hearing procedures, and ordering sanctions appropriate to the situations, will it achieve the authority to give its decisions the degree of finality they should have.

Phase-in and Review. In putting these proposals into practice, two further questions must be considered: the provision of a period to phase-in the new regulatory system, and a method for monitoring and evaluating its effectiveness.

Many of the present enforcement agencies were initially unprepared to deal with the equal opportunity laws and regulations and were overwhelmed by their responsibilities. To prevent such overload, a new regulatory system must have time for organization and staffing before assuming full responsibility.

> We recommend that the new system of structured self-regulation be phased in over a two-year period. During the first year, the institutions would plan and initiate their self-evaluation processes, and the Council would begin to build an organization and hire staff. In the second year, the institutions would file their first self-evaluation reports, and the Council receive and review them. By the beginning of the third year, the Council should be fully staffed and prepared to assume all its responsibilities. During the phase-in period, the agencies now responsible would continue enforcing the laws and investigating complaints in higher education.

Once the new system had operated for a substantial period, a review and evaluation of its effectiveness should be undertaken. Some monitoring would occur in the normal course of the governmental process. The Council would submit annual budget requests, which it would have to justify both within the executive branch and in appropriation hearings before Congressional committees. Since the system is concerned with protecting civil rights, it would be subject to review by the U.S. Commission on Civil Rights. Additionally, the courts would review the Council's performance in the course of appeals from its orders, or its failures to meet the timetable for action. In such cases, the whole record of the Council's actions would be before the courts.

What is also needed is an evaluation of the system as a whole to judge how well it has succeeded in advancing the policy objectives and reducing present adversarial tensions. In the past, regulatory systems established in the name of reform have failed to achieve their goals, yet they continue to exist. An appropriate review taking these factors into consideration at the end of, say, eight years, could be provided by a "sunset" provision in the initial legislation that required Congressional re-authorization of the agency after the review. If not re-authorized, the new agency would be phased out.

This review should be undertaken by an ad hoc public commission, whose members were drawn from outside the executive branch. The review could also be used to determine the desirability of an extension of the agency's scope to other institutions.

Political Feasibility.   Our proposal for administrative reorganization raises serious questions of political feasibility, since it requires legislative action by the Congress. While the recommended change in the responsibility for enforcement of the programmatic statutes could be made by Executive Order, new legislation is needed to transfer the jurisdiction of employment cases in higher education from EEOC to the proposed new Council, to give it the broad array of remedial powers suggested, and to require that these are used before appeals to the courts can be made. Further, the proposed Council would be more likely to have the status it needs, especially vis-à-vis the courts, if it is created by law rather than Presidential fiat.

> A less sweeping reorganization plan might be more easily achieved politically; one that respects the present division between student-oriented and employment-oriented regulation. Two bureaus could be developed to take over the responsibilities for higher education shared by the present agencies. One, responsible for student-oriented programs, would be part of the Secretary's office in the Department of Education. The second, responsible for equal employment regulations for faculty and administrative employees, would be part of the Secretary's office in the Department of Labor. Each bureau would develop policy and enforce the laws and regulations in its domain. A higher education advisory board would be created to coordinate the work of the two bureaus, reviewing proposed regulations and issuing advisory opinions. But the power to issue final orders or regulations would remain with the Secretaries of the two departments.
>
> The Commission considered this alternative, but rejected it as much less likely to result in the substantial improvement of the regulatory process that is needed. The more diffuse structure would make procedural reform more difficult, leaving the problems and burdens of duplication and overlapping jurisdictions that plague the present system. The line between policy relating to student programs and policy relating to employment is often difficult to draw, and a coordinating board with only advisory powers might well be ineffective in trying to maintain the boundary. Even more important, it would be harder for two overlapping, and sometimes competing, agencies to achieve the change in regulatory style and attitude toward those it regulates, than it would be for a single new agency. These changes lie at the heart of our proposals.

FINANCIAL INCENTIVES

The new Council we recommend focuses on the procedural reform needed before equal opportunity can be realized in a way that is consistent with the traditions of the academic world. Much current discussion of regulatory reform in other areas emphasizes the contrast between incentive and command, prescribing more of the former and less of the latter. Earlier we suggested an important non-monetary incentive for voluntary compliance with equal opportunity laws and regulations: regular publicly reported and publicly reviewed institutional self-assessment would be *prima facie* evidence of compliance with the Executive Order. Thus institutions seeking federal contracts would be eligible to receive them.

For the most part, financial incentives are inappropriate in the area of equal opportunity. However, the Commission has two recommendations based on the useful role such incentives can play.

Matching Funds for Expenditures on Plant to Aid Handicapped

Recommendation 2

Federal matching funds should be available to colleges and universities for expenditures on facilities to help the handicapped. A minimum qualifying expenditure by the institution, and a maximum grant for each institution per year should be set.

There are troubling questions about the recent regulations governing access for the handicapped. The financial impact of the requirements on the institution is interrelated with internal academic decisions on whom to admit and how to teach. But, in any case, substantial additional current expenditures in the annual budget or even from capital are often needed to alter buildings and make other changes to meet the actual needs of the handicapped and to comply with the laws. Our recommendation has the aim of providing an incentive for institutional effort that might not be produced by commands alone.

Matching Funds to Enlarge Supply of Minority Candidates for Faculty Appointments

Recommendation 3

The existing federal fellowship program for Black and other minority Ph.D. candidates should be strengthened by providing for federal matching of university contributions. Restrictions on fields of study in the present program should be removed.

We observed earlier that the number of Blacks qualified for academic employment, as measured by their share in the annual flow of new doctorates, is still small and barely increasing. The federal government now offers special fellowship programs for Black and other minority Ph.D. candidates. This support lowers the substantial financial barrier that most minority students face in undertaking doctoral study leading to academic careers and enlarges the pool of qualified minority Ph.D.'s for faculties to draw on to meet affirmative action goals. Roughly a thousand minority doctoral students and about the same number of professional students will receive fellowship support in 1980, if the program is fully funded, as it should be.

The present program could be improved in two ways. First, if the universities were required to make a matching contribution from their own resources, it would probably increase the willingness of Congress to fund the government half of the program fully. Second, the fellowships awarded to an institution in any given year cannot now be spread among more than five fields of study within the arts and sciences, and each of these disciplines is required to be a "national priority." These restrictions should be removed. With these changes the program would add to the total resources available and make a more effective contribution to expanding academic opportunities for minorities.

OTHER FEDERAL REGULATION AFFECTING HIGHER EDUCATION

The increasing amount of government regulation affecting higher education reflects an increasing amount everywhere in society. In one area after another—housing, safety of products, and of working conditions, the environment—administrative agencies are being asked to do for everyone what the courts did in the past for individuals.

1. One type of regulation relates to financial accountability for grants specific to academic institutions, chiefly student aid and research support. The rules describe the purposes and terms of federal grants, loans and contracts, designate who is to receive them, and set reporting and auditing requirements.

In the last fifteen years new student aid programs, with their rules on eligibility, application procedures, and reporting, brought new administrative paperwork to colleges and universities. While the volume and scope of rules governing research grants changed relatively little during this time, requirements for procedural formality and record-keeping for audit purposes became more elaborate and stringent, with a corresponding increase in both their administrative and psychological costs. The substantive impact of the rules concerning financial accountability is important, and is discussed in Chapter 6 below. The purely administrative costs of financial accountability are small, and for all but a few institutions have been far outweighed by the benefits of the programs that entail them.

2. Another broad range of laws and regulations concern general health and welfare, pay, and the environment. Some have been in place a generation or more, most are relatively new. Many were applied initially to business enterprises and only recently extended to colleges, universities, and other non-profit organizations. One sub-group of laws includes social security, workmen's compensation, fair labor standards (wages and hours), occupational health and safety (OSHA), and retirement income (ERISA). Laws aimed at protecting the environment form another sub-group.

The general health and welfare, pay, and environmental regulations are of concern to higher education primarily because of their costs, a concern that is magnified by higher education's current economic difficulties. It is hard to estimate these costs with precision: for the representative institution they might account for 5 percent of the annual operating budget, including Social Security taxes, the largest single item. This estimate is, of course, a broad average; the actual figure varies widely from institution to institution. Small institutions have been forced to change their accounting and record-keeping procedures and add new kinds of administrative staff. On the other hand, large institutions may already have such procedures and staff, but they are much more visible to the regulators, and may be scrutinized more regularly and thoroughly.

We believe these general health and welfare measures are here to stay for all society, in substance if not detail. It is neither realistic, nor free, nor fair, for academic institutions to expect to be exempted from them. It is not free; if they were exempted, they would be less able to recruit high-quality staff, especially non-academic staff, in competition with other employers. It is not fair because it would require the lowest paid employees of the sector to absorb the costs by foregoing the benefits of these regulations, rather than passing them on to be shared among faculty, senior administrators, students and their parents, and the taxpayers of the fifty states.

While the Commission does not mean to minimize any problems which regulation creates, we believe we accurately reflect the assessment of the academic world that those created by health and welfare rules and the administrative requirements of financial accountability are not the most serious ones confronting it.

CONCLUSION

As we have seen, the equal opportunity and non-discrimination laws pose far more serious problems than those described above. They do more than add to operating costs—they can affect the way colleges and universities perform their characteristic tasks. The problems are likely to increase as competition for academic jobs grows. Issues of discrimination in hiring and promotion will be a continuing focus of strain. Issues on the fairness of academic standards applied to students, including questions of retention and graduation will also persist, aggravated by increased competition among institutions for students.

The Commission's recommendation for a new Council to unify and consolidate application of equal opportunity laws to higher education embodies an administrative system, rational in form and substance, coherent, and fair. We believe the Council would:

—Encourage colleges and universities to take the initiative.

—Provide an effective range of sanctions that could be applied fairly.

—Reduce bureaucratic duplication and establish uniform standards, with self-regulation as the chief instrument of reform.

—Encourage the development of a corps of administrative advisors with the requisite training and experience, both in higher education and equal opportunity enforcement.

—Use mediation to prevent polarization of attitudes on both sides.

—Provide an efficient, fair, and impartial way to resolve conflicts, if mediation fails.

Proposals for new legislation to achieve these objectives face serious obstacles. First, the process of legislation itself would threaten the present equilibrium among the protected groups, their bureaucratic advocates, and the institutions now the objects of complaint and the targets of enforcement. In particular, women, Blacks and other ethnic minorities, the handicapped, and those who look for governmental protection against age discrimination might view these proposals as weakening their position. From their perspective, the gains they have won to date are the result of their own determined efforts to get the courts to enforce the laws. The question is whether they could be convinced, as we are, that the gains in institutional responsiveness and speed of decision offered by the new procedures would outweigh this change.

Second, the proposed administrative machinery would appear to some, especially those not directly concerned, to be the creation of another special-interest bureaucracy, with its attendant increase in regulatory intrusion and litigation. The off-set for higher education—that it wipes out a much more complex administrative structure with little power of real decision and highly productive of litigation—is less visible.

This leads to the final and most difficult problem: if the reorganization of agencies and procedures for enforcing the equal opportunity laws and regulations proposed for higher education is a good idea, why is it not applicable to their enforcement in general? Perhaps it is, but it is outside this Commission's scope to propose changes for other sectors. We believe that higher education suffers particularly from procedures developed in other contexts, especially from those appropriate to compulsory public schooling, and to blue-collar, clerical, and entry-level jobs in business or public service. Though our proposal is indeed a sweeping change, it is more suitable for try-out in the reasonably well-defined area of higher education than for extension to the whole range of equal opportunity law enforcement at one step. If adopted and successful, it could then well serve as a model for other sectors.

The various national associations of colleges and universities, the organized academic interest groups, have a role to play in a reformed system. The history of regulation in the United States in almost all fields shows strong governmental reliance on industry groups to inform the regulatory process. So far, the academic interest groups have not provided strong leadership on this range of issues. The diversity of institutional interests represented by the higher education associations has been an obstacle to much unified action, but the problems of regulation are ones in which this diversity is less important. There are two specific tasks they are well able to perform. One is to develop standards for self-evaluation for different kinds of institutions, and to offer assistance to the institutions in using them. The second is to develop facilities for assisting in non-adversarial methods of dispute resolution—mediation, conciliation, and other third-party techniques—and to offer these to individuals as well as to institutions as a step short of government entrance into the disputes. More broadly, the associations could serve as clearinghouses for information on the new system, disseminating the successful (and unsuccessful) procedures rapidly and broadly.

In the end, the colleges and universities must accomplish what no administrative reform can do alone. Educational opportunity is fundamental to the principle of equality. Twenty-five years ago the Supreme Court in *Brown* v. *Board of Education* underscored this point in the context of elementary and secondary education:

> It [education] is required in the performance of our most basic public responsibilities. . . . It is the very foundation of good citizenship. Today it is a principle instrument in awakening the child to cultural values, in preparing him for later professional training, and in helping

him to adjust normally to his environment. In these days, it is doubtful that any child may reasonably be expected to succeed in life if he is denied the opportunity of an education. Such an opportunity . . . is a right which must be made available to all on equal terms.

These words teach an equally important lesson for higher education. While not everyone goes to college, the possibility must be open to all who can use it. Colleges and universities must provide a model of equal opportunity in action.

COMMENTS AND DISSENTS

Dissent by Peter Clark

The Commission's critique of the "inexperienced," excessively "adversarial," "litigious" administration of the equal opportunity statutes in the field of higher education would apply with similar force to all other sectors of the society subject to equal opportunity legislation. The Commission has not proven the case that higher education should be exempted from the burdens borne by everyone else. To the contrary, since higher education serves as a self-conscious source of moral criticism and social change for the society, it may prove useful that higher education be subjected to the same governmental procedures as is everyone else.

Dissent by A. Leon Higginbotham, Jr.

While I have been impressed generally with the excellence of the Commission's Report and its findings, I must dissent from its analysis and recommendations on federal regulation of higher education as stated in Chapter 3. I fear that the majority seems far more comfortable with what it calls the past "American academic tradition" than it is with the challenges of the seventies which have been marked by frustrations inherent in the efforts to assure greater access to higher education to those who had been traditionally excluded or at least discouraged. By

Recommendation One the Commission seems to identify more closely with the problems of present college administrators and present tenured faculty than it empathizes with the victims of discrimination.

Perhaps the sensitivity of the Commission is most dramatically demonstrated by the very first paragraph of Chapter 3. Quoting Mr. Justice Frankfurter, it endorsed his view of the " 'four freedoms' of the university—to determine *for itself* on academic grounds *who* may teach, what may be taught, how it shall be taught, and *who may be admitted to study*." (emphasis added) They say that this statement captures the "American academic tradition," and then they lament that "equal opportunity is being administered today in a way that is not in keeping with our tradition." Bluntly, I am not enthralled with the "academic tradition" of Justice Frankfurter's time, when he was professor at Harvard Law School or when he was on the United States Supreme Court.

When Justice Frankfurter taught at Harvard Law School women were precluded. None were admitted to Harvard Law School until the 1950s. In addition, during that time it was rare if there were more than four or five black students in the entire Harvard Law School. Today at Harvard Law School there are 453 women and 148 blacks out of a total enrollment of 1,624. What has caused the change from the old American academic tradition? Did the change take place because of what the majority calls the "sociology of collegial structure" or is the change in the composition at Harvard Law School and at most universities partially attributable to the pressures of present civil rights statutes? How much change would have taken place if we had relied on what the majority calls "institutional opportunity assessment reports" as "a key feature . . . to the development of mechanisms for effective reform?"

Similar questions arise when analyzing blacks and women in medical schools during the last decade. In 1968–69 there were 793 blacks and 3,136 women out of a total of 35,833. In 1979 there were 3,627 blacks and 16,140 women out of a total of 63,800 medical students. The self-evident truth is that even though administrators may have felt hassled by the multiple civil rights acts and related administrative agencies, it has been a decade of more options for blacks and women. I believe that the proposals of the majority run the serious risk of turning the clock back to the status quo of the "American academic tradition" of the early sixties.

The civil rights laws were not designed to give college faculties any special immunity from the challenges of equal opportunity which confront our society generally. I can think of no rational reason for, as the majority phrases it, a "reform" which supports the Commission's first recommendation. With the multitude of professions in this country why should we carve out a special niche or council just for the higher education community?

If higher education is entitled to the special prerogatives of its independent Council for Equal Opportunity in Higher Education—reporting directly to the Secretary of Education, why shouldn't bankers be entitled to their Council for Equal Opportunity in Banking—reporting directly to the Treasury Department? Why shouldn't labor unions also have their special Council for Equal Opportunity in Employment—reporting directly to the Department of Labor? Why shouldn't physicians have their special Council of Equal Opportunity in Health Services—reporting directly to the Department of Health? In fact, why shouldn't any group have its own council reporting solely to its favorite department? Tragically the bottom line and inherent logic of the majority's report is: Why shouldn't the EEOC and all other civil rights agencies be abolished so that each "unique" interest will have its special council to give it the extra sensitivity it believes its discipline deserves?

Each of these professions requires certain subtleties in judgment which are not dissimilar to the problems one finds in higher education. The majority asserts:

> "In the final analysis, *faculty* status is not won in the courtroom. Remedies which compel employment or tenure ignore the sociology of the collegial structure. Remedies short of compelling employment, such as back pay, may recoup financial loss, but litigiousness is not an attribute which enhances standing with colleagues. An individual litigant may win the immediate battle at great emotional and economic cost, only to lose the academic war." (emphasis added)

If one deleted the word "faculty" and substituted one of several other professions in its place, the same argument could be made. I submit that it is better for victims to endure the emotional and economic cost of litigation than to win neither the "immediate battle" nor the academic war.

Even if one could accept the Commission's general recommendation for the creation of a council for equal opportunity in higher education, the mechanisms which have been suggested are unworkable and anti-democratic. When it comes to dealing with colleges and faculty, the majority stresses "the collegial and generally decentralized structure of colleges and universities." Yet what does it ask of its new administrative agency? It stresses that it "would not have regional offices, and would be divided into three sections, *all in Washington*: the Council itself, a General Counsel's office, and a Hearings office." (emphasis added) Why is it that after having emphasized the importance of decentralization at colleges and the fact that at colleges one of the major attractions is the individual's sense of independence, the Commission comes down with the most centralized organization possible for the government regulator? A centralized organization confined solely in Washington would preclude effective investigation, effective follow-up, effective enforcement of the laws, and even effective conciliation.

Of course, the present regulatory system can be improved and I have the impression that some progress is being made. However, in my view, what the majority proposes is not a reform for equal opportunity in higher education, but is instead a deformity which would slacken the pace and delay the day in this nation when racial, religious and gender discrimination can become merely a tragic relic of our past.

I know that the substantial gap between me and the majority results solely from disagreement as to methods and not as to ultimate goals. I have been privileged to serve on several national commissions, both public and private, over the last 20 years, but I have never had colleagues who are more amiable. All the majority have records of strong statements in support of equal opportunity. But the fair measure of our societal success in eliminating the barriers of bigotry and discrimination cannot be, and has never been, reflected in egalitarian pronouncements; rather, the true test must be in the ultimate results of the market place, whether it is in commerce or in academia. In my view if the nation takes seriously the majority's proposal to dismantle and restructure the present civil rights federal regulatory process, I fear that the progress of the future will be miniscule, if there is any at all. Enacting the majority's proposals could result in keeping further from the mainstream those who for so many years have been traditionally excluded or discouraged and who at long last are securing partial access to the system. The ultimate irony will be that such a demise was precipitated by brilliant scholars and administrators who have spoken so boldly for social and racial justice, while proposing a regulatory process which precludes their attainment.*

Comment by Thomas S. Gates

I share the concern of the majority about the need for making better progress in achieving the goals of non-discrimination and equal opportunity. However, I join in Judge Higginbotham's view that maintaining the present mechanism and trying to improve its procedures is preferable to creating a new agency.

---

*There is a counter-report to the views of the majority which is expressed with eloquence in the National Urban League's recent report "The State of Black America in 1980." There Vernon Jordan emphasizes that "blacks and their special problems have gone out of fashion in government, politics and civil concern." It is my hope that the special problems of blacks, women and other minorities will not go out of fashion with prestigious foundation commissions.

Chapter 4

Role of the States

W hat our colleges and universities look like a generation from now will be determined more by actions taken in individual states than by any other single factor. It is not a new role— the dramatic transformation that took place in the generation just ended was also due to state initiative, imagination, and responsiveness to changes in society.

But entirely different conditions characterize the two periods. What the states did from 1950 to 1975 was in response to forces that are now disappearing. There simply were not enough places in existing institutions for all the eighteen-year-old high school graduates who wanted to go to college.

The need to expand was a challenge to which the states were equal. They had rising revenues from economic growth to pay for it, they had broad public support for the policy, they found the human resources to staff the new institutions that they created. It was not an easy job but it was an agreeable one. Governors and legislatures could respond to the forces of growth without intimate participation in colleges and universities, or detailed appreciation of their complexities.

By contrast, the decisions the states have to make in the next generation will have a profound impact on the quality, rather than the quantity, of higher education. The big job ahead is retrenchment, and the greatest problem is how to adjust capacity to demand without sacrificing essentials. Which state-supported programs to consolidate, which to strengthen, which to eliminate, which institutions to give extra support are all hard questions to answer. The forces supporting particular colleges and universities are always vigorous and especially difficult for elected officials to resist.

Another vital consideration is the place of private institutions. In many parts of the country, the private colleges and universities lend a variety and have qualities that are essential to the character and strength of the whole state system. Further, the larger the share of a given student body in public institutions, the greater is the cost to the state's taxpayers. Unless a conscious effort is made by state officials, private institutions will suffer disproportionately during retrenchment because of market forces. So the job ahead is neither pleasant nor easy.

Our recommendations for the states are made in this context. They are broad because we are not able to prescribe for each state, and there are even some in which the population changes will run counter to the national trend. We focus on procedures for insuring quality and variety in the face of retrenchment. We also focus on the importance of the composition of the various state boards that will have to face the hard decisions.

Our recommendations can be divided into three groups:

—The composition of state higher education boards.
—Dealing with retrenchment.
—Collective bargaining.

We close with some observations on regulation at the state level.

THE COMPOSITION OF HIGHER EDUCATION BOARDS

Recommendation 1

Members of state higher education boards should be widely respected individuals who bring to the boards experience and demonstrated abilities, and who will consider the health of the entire higher education community within the state. No more than one-third of the members should be representatives of higher education, public or private.

Higher education boards vary widely in their degrees of influence, not only because their powers under enabling statutes vary, but because of the political interplay that makes it possible for the boards' recommendations to be ignored by governors or legislatures. Considering the great impact that their decisions can have in the next generation, the Commission believes that it is of first importance for these boards to be strengthened. Their standing, in fact, must be so great that it should be impossible for political figures to ignore their recommendations without drawing considerable public criticism.

We believe that the chief way to strengthen these boards is by strengthening their composition, not their powers. They can only function effectively if their membership is distinguished enough to command public and political respect. Meeting the challenges created by excess capacity will require extraordinarily able and qualified people. They must be respected by both the legislative and executive branches and by higher education, in both its public and private sectors.

If the boards are to be regarded as balanced, objective, and highly competent bodies, they should be composed primarily of lay members. Boards should also have substantial representation from both public and private institutions if they are to be seen as knowledgeable about both sectors, but biased toward neither. Nine states have already included the voice of private higher education in such state-wide boards. Further, in order to maintain their independence from other state agencies and their credibility with legislatures, the number of ex-officio members from the executive branch should be held to a minimum.

The boards must view their charge as representation of the public interest. Defending either the public or private sector, or serving any narrowly defined special interest, is inconsistent with the obligation taken on by a member. The terms served should be long to keep the perspective as long as possible, and to give members a degree of insulation from political pressures. Finally, the boards must be provided with adequate staffs which they themselves hire.

Very few existing boards have the strength we recommend. There are presently three main types among the states. The strongest are the consolidated governing boards, responsible for approving programs and submitting budgets for all public four-year institutions and, in some cases, two-year community colleges as well as all post-secondary vocational educational schools in the state. A few states are unusual in that their consolidated boards include private institutions in the planning and coordination for the whole system. Even though this type of board has a similar structure wherever it exists, some are not able to act with the authority of others. The Board of Governors of the University of North Carolina and the Board of Regents of the University of Wisconsin exercise strong authority, for example, while similarly structured governing boards in Florida, Mississippi, and North Dakota are less able to do so.

The second type is the regulatory coordinating board, which, unlike consolidated ones described above, does not actually govern institutions but acts as an intermediary between the separate boards of particular institutions and the political authorities. The final type—the advisory coordinating board, limited to making recommendations to the state government— has the least formal authority. The effectiveness of both the regulatory and advisory boards depends heavily on their place in the political process—on their relationships to the governors, the legislatures, and the institutions themselves. Where these relationships are good, as in the state of Washington, the board's recommendations carry considerable authority and have been described as having the "weight of governance." Other states with such boards scarcely heed their recommendations.

Our recommendation was influenced by these actual differences, leading us to the conclusion that the composition, rather than the powers, of the boards is what is most in need of improvement.

DEALING WITH RETRENCHMENT

It is imperative that each state deal directly and intelligently with the underlying situation of declining demand, since the problems created by excess capacity could well be intensified by unwise decisions. Strategies are necessary to reduce the temptation for public institutions to compete for students in undesirable ways. Moreover, ill-considered competition between the public and private sectors, as well as among the public institutions, can lead only to an erosion of both academic standards and financial strength everywhere in the system. The decisions to be made are complicated enough to require board members who are exceptionally well qualified to make them, even without the other considerations of maintaining independence and public confidence discussed in the previous section.

The Commission sees five ways to deal with the problem. Taken together, they would protect the variety of institutions a state must have to fill all its needs, and also protect the quality which all higher education should have. They are interdependent and the higher education boards must not lose sight of this.

1. Each state should examine the structure of its entire system so that the mission of each institution and its place and weight in the system is clear.
2. Each state should make periodic quality reviews of all public individual colleges and universities.
3. The allocation of state appropriations should reflect these reviews. The formulas on which they are presently based need revision.
4. The traditional state policy of supporting the flagship research universities is wise and should not change.
5. All institutions in a state, public and private, should be licensed in order to prevent fraudulent or deceptive practices.

Defining the Missions of All Public Colleges and Universities

A necessary first step for the states to take in protecting the quality and diversity of the higher education it offers is to look at the system as a whole. It is already quite typical that two institutions, serving the same or overlapping geographical regions and offering similar programs, are each unable to attract enough students to use fully the resources available. Each, in this atmosphere of competition for students, will find it difficult to prevent a slow deterioration in the quality of its academic programs. Both the financial resources and the incentives to maintain quality are undermined. How can a state board decide on the best course?

We believe that an examination must be made of the purpose served by every college or university in the system as a whole, and of its strengths and weaknesses, in order to place the importance of each in the state structure. In most states the definition of institutional missions is the joint responsibility of the state board and the institution or central system office in question.

The degree of detail of this definition varies from state to state. At one extreme, the Nebraska legislature has set forth the "role and mission" of each public institution in precise and extensive detail. For the University of Nebraska at Lincoln, undergraduate instruction is the first priority, graduate and professional instruction and research is second, and public service is third. The role of the state colleges is limited to providing undergraduate instruction in general academic, occupational, and professional degree programs. The bill defining missions for public higher education in Nebraska, for example, states that:

> Kearney State College may maintain its existing baccalaureate general academic, baccalaureate occupational, and baccalaureate professional degree programs and shall limit new baccalaureate degree programs to the needs of its unique service area generally defined as the state's central region. Kearney State College shall not independently award the master's degree in business administration after September 1, 1980.

More frequently, however, states rely on vague statements of mission. These should become more specific: they should identify the programs to be offered at each public institution and set forth in broad terms the public purposes, and the student population, that the programs will serve. Only if the statements of mission provide this detail will they be a useful tool in bringing order to the decisions that must be made.

State legislatures on occasion intervene to modify statements of scope and function that have been agreed upon. For example, the legislature and Governor of Ohio mandated eight medical programs in spite of the objections of the Board of Regents and several of the institutions involved.

Statements of mission not only define the role of individual institutions, but also how one segment of public higher education relates to another. Each segment should reassess, and if necessary, redefine its mission as the public sector contracts.

The great state research universities have a mission important enough and face problems serious enough for separate discussion below.

State colleges and non-research universities face especially troubling problems, and may require changes in their missions. These institutions will probably be heavily affected by the decline in enrollments, and therefore by decreases in appropriations. Their more advanced programs will probably suffer the most, and they may have to eliminate some of their master's and professionally oriented programs, concentrating instead on undergraduate programs, with particular emphasis on the occupational and vocational ones. In some cases, public colleges may be forced to merge, or to become branch campuses of larger institutions.

The two-year community colleges were the fastest growing component of public higher education during the boom. Their mission is clear. Through a combination of low tuition, which currently averages less than $400, and open admissions—the entrance requirement is at most high school graduation—they provide a unique degree of open-access to higher education that no other set of institutions matches. They have successfully attracted students of all ages, and now account for close to one-half all enrollments in public colleges and universities. While the importance of the community colleges' mission will not change in the 1980s, the early figures on the effects of the demographic changes suggest that the demand for this kind of institution will also fall. State boards should keep a sharp eye on the competition that will probably develop between state colleges and community college systems. The mission of the former may evolve and come to resemble that of the latter more closely. It is also true that a few states—Massachusetts is an example—overbuilt their community college systems, particularly in suburban areas, because they expected higher day-time enrollments than actually developed. These states are already troubled by excess capacity in this sector. All states should formalize arrangements for transfers from two-year to four-year colleges.

In summary, to put it simply, a state board cannot decide whether an institution with flagging enrollments and declining quality should be closed or its mission changed until it knows what other institutions serve similar functions, and how strong they are. If higher education boards are to use peer group evaluations of quality, which we discuss in the next section, rationally and consistently, they must first determine the mission of each public institution in the state.

Periodic Quality Reviews

Recommendation 2

Each state higher education board should arrange for periodic reviews of the quality of educational programs at every public college and university within the state. The reviews should be conducted by academic peer groups. Their reports, along with the institutions' responses, should be published after a one-year delay. To the greatest extent possible, each state should make use of regional and other accrediting associations in organizing the reviews.

Intense competition to attract students can be antithetical to efforts to maintain quality. Any institution that maintains high admission standards, decides what courses to offer on the basis of academic excellence rather than popularity, and maintains strict grading systems will tend to lose students to less stringent competitors. As this happens, its appropriations drop, and it loses some financial resources that are needed to maintain quality. Although an institution may want to keep up traditional standards of excellence, that becomes hard to do. And it becomes even harder as more institutions begin to feel the pressures. The number of institutions unable to resist lowering standards is sure to grow unless the states have a better way of planning for reduction in capacity than they now have.

These considerations convinced most members of our Commission that some evaluation by the state of the quality of programs provided by public colleges and institutions within it is essential. In making this recommendation, we are well aware of the disquiet, if not outright opposition, it arouses in many. Anxieties about threats to institutional autonomy are understandable.

Nevertheless, we believe that the process is necessary for two important reasons. First, quality reviews can be of special value to a particular institution. Candid evaluations made by competent and disinterested examiners can warn that certain programs are slipping; they can guide administrators in allocating resources within the institution; and they can help institutions as a group to resist the sacrifice of academic standards to competition for students.

Second, decisions to redefine an institution's mission and change its role in the system are difficult for a legislature to make. But elected officials may find it easier to vote for changes in an institution's role in the system, or in the programs offered, or even to close an institution if they can present convincing evidence supplied by independent observers.

These evaluations of quality must be made by highly credible and independent reviewers. While the authority to order reviews of academic programs should be vested in the higher education boards, the review process itself should be carried out by visiting teams of recognized scholars, drawn largely from the academic world. In almost all cases, the higher education boards would draw upon the resources of regional and other accrediting associations to organize and conduct the reviews. We expect that these reviews would become integrated with the regular work of the accrediting associations. Normally the function of the board would be limited to ordering the review, publishing the report of the peer group, and in the case of a clearly unfavorable report, recommending appropriate action.

Public disclosure of the results of program reviews, if made known widely to prospective students and their families, could well contribute to the further decline of a college that is found to be functioning at very low standards. In this respect, the process can only work to the advantage of the more competent institutions. However, an adverse finding could endanger a program or institution that might be marginal but not meretricious. In order to avoid putting any institution at undeserved risk, there should be a year's grace period before publication of the results of academic program reviews. At that time, the institution's response to the report could be appended to it. Alternatively, institutions could have the right of appeal of an unfavorable report or board recommendation and request a second review.

In any case, publication is an essential part of the process. Only broad dissemination of the results of the reviews is likely to create a climate of opinion that will support change. Without publication, all involved in the process would find it too easy to suppress or ignore unfavorable reports.

The thorny question of whether private colleges and universities should be included in the review process remains to be answered. On the one hand, higher education boards are unlikely to make forceful recommendations, and legislatures are unlikely to accept closure of public institutions, if the private sector escapes scrutiny. The pressure to include it will be particularly strong in states with substantial student aid programs for residents who enroll in private colleges and universities within the state.

On the other hand, the private colleges and universities are likely to view the process as an undesirable intrusion into their autonomy. They see a potential for conflict of interest since the process is controlled by the higher education board, whose chief loyalties may be viewed as lying with the public sector. This is a powerful additional reason for the private sector to have substantial representation on the board.

The Commission believes on balance that participation of both sets of institutions is desirable, and that the state should invite the participation of private colleges and universities in the academic program review process but not require it. If private institutions accept, state boards will gain direct knowledge of their quality, useful to the boards as they weigh policy questions and set expenditure levels for the public sector. Boards of trustees of the private institutions will also gain from the reviews as they plan their own futures. All would benefit—the states, the institutions themselves and the students. While participation of private institutions in the review process should be voluntary, we believe it would work in their own interest.

Ideally, the necessary adjustments to declining enrollments would be most effectively made by the institutions themselves, both public and private, rather than imposed by state governments. Yet we feel that the incentives built into the system, the limitations of the market as an instrument of discipline for publicly funded institutions, and the consequent one-sidedness of the public/private competition, all demand some more self-conscious, more systematic, and more widely applied process of quality control than now exists. What is at stake is the integrity and financial strength of higher education in a state.*

Financing Formulas for Public Higher Education

In addressing the problems of maintaining quality in public higher education, budget-makers and legislators must consider the effects on colleges and universities of the way appropriations are determined. Budget recommendations and appropriations for each public institution are now typically based on the number of students currently enrolled, usually expressed in terms of full-time equivalents. In effect, each institution receives a certain number of dollars per student, so that the institution's budget rises and falls proportionately with its enrollments.

Appropriations formulas vary considerably from state to state and are quite complex. Different formulas are used for different types of institutions, and for different programs, activities, and levels of instruction within the same institution. In Ohio, the budget for each public college or university is derived from sixteen different formulas, each highly detailed, while in Louisiana the formulas are much simpler, with little distinction among institutions.

Major colleges and universities do undertake some functions and activities that are not enrollment related. The extension services of colleges of agriculture at major land-grant universities, their externally funded research programs, and the hospitals affiliated with their medical schools are the primary examples of such activities. For the majority of colleges and universities, however, the scale of most of their activities is dependent upon the number of students served.

Enrollment-driven appropriations formulas were particularly well-adapted to respond to increasing demand for higher educa-

---

*William Friday and James Killian dissent from this recommendation. See pages 119–121.

tion. They created a strong incentive for public institutions to admit more students, and thus played an important role in accommodating the rapid influx of students during the enrollment boom.

Unfortunately, the same process does not work in reverse. In the event of a decline in enrollments, public colleges and universities that receive enrollment-driven appropriations will experience a decline in their appropriations that is proportional to the decline in their enrollments. However, many of the costs of operating a college remain unchanged as enrollments decline. Tenured faculty must be paid, buildings must be maintained even though they are no longer full, and the library must continue to operate. Total operating costs will decline less rapidly. State appropriations will consequently be insufficient to operate the institution at the new, lower enrollment, at least as it was previously operated, and some cutbacks on expenditures will be forced that can seriously affect the quality of instruction offered.

This is precisely the prospect that public higher education faces in the next few years. The appropriations formulas now in use allow a mismatch between costs and revenues to develop as enrollment drops. They put immediate financial pressure on all public colleges and universities that experience enrollment declines—those that will continue to function as they are, as well as those that will have to modify their programs.

Although enrollment-driven appropriations formulas can inflict hardships on particular institutions, they fail to highlight directly for state legislatures the need to reduce capacity. By providing a fixed number of dollars per student, the formulas obscure the fact that operating many institutions well below capacity must ultimately increase the cost to the state of providing public higher education.

Finally, enrollment-driven formulas powerfully reinforce the incentives for public institutions to compete for students in undesirable ways, by providing a sizable premium for each additional student that they enroll.

A few states have already instituted changes in the budget process. In some, legislatures have mandated a fixed percentage decrease in the budgets of all public colleges and universities, leaving to the higher education boards, or the institutions themselves, how to cope with these reduced budgets. In a sense, this approach is equitable, since it distributes the burden of contraction equally among institutions, but evenly shared debilitation is not a solution to the problem of maintaining quality. Similarly, efforts to devise appropriations formulas that make increasingly fine distinctions among programs and services offered by the institutions may spread the burden more equitably, but they will do little more.

A number of states have made regulations designed to increase faculty productivity by increasing student/faculty ratios or the number of student contact hours expected of each faculty member. However, only minimal savings are possible without compromising academic standards, or running up against the constraint of faculty tenure.

One possible remedy that could be applied more widely is a substantial reduction in the enrollment-driven portion of appropriations. States could adopt appropriations formulas which combine a flat basic grant that covers a portion of each institution's overall budget at current enrollment levels, with a per-student allowance that provides the remainder of the appropriation. The per-student allowance would differ for upper and lower division undergraduates and graduate students, as it does now. Similarly, both the allowance and the base grant would vary among different types of institutions. But in all cases, the base grant would be a substantial fraction of the total appropriation. Under this formula, institutional budgets would still decrease as enrollments decline, but much less steeply than they now do.

In the short run, each public institution would find it easier to maintain an adequate financial base from which to develop new missions, or plan an orderly contraction. Since the proposed formula would make public institutions less dependent on enrollments, it would reduce, though not eliminate, the intensity of the competition for students that can lower academic standards.

In effect, the revised formula would shift the financial pressure caused by declining enrollments from colleges that will be short of operating funds to state legislatures that will find they have to spend more to keep a particular institution open than they would under current appropriations formulas. We recognize that constituency pressures or "log-rolling" may still inhibit legislators from voting to merge or close academic programs. Since the proposed formula relieves some of the financial pressure on the institutions, and makes it easier for them to endure declines in enrollments, its use could conceivably aggravate the problem of excess capacity. But by putting a clear price—the amount of the flat base grant—on keeping an institution open, a formula of this type should focus legislators' attention on the costs of failing to reduce capacity and force them to deal with the underlying problems of declining demand.

The major purposes of proposing a quality control mechanism and a change in the formulas for financing public higher education are interdependent. Each of these proposals is offered in an effort to reduce the temptation to compete for students among public institutions as well as between the private and public sectors. We hope to dull the incentive to compete by quality degradation, and to encourage excellence.

The Importance of Public Research Universities

Two-thirds of the finest research universities in the country are in the public sector. Thirty years ago there were relatively few. Today, virtually every state has at least one, and many of them have several. Because of their excellence, they attract students and faculty not only from around the country, but from all over the world. They now face an uncertain future, along with the private research universities, because federal support which is so central to their operation, and which in some cases even brought them to their present states of excellence, can no longer be counted on to the degree it was during the expansion period. But, in addition, they have another threat spared the private institutions. Retrenchment within a state can mean that their share of the total higher education appropriations is reduced, due to pressures from other types of institutions on the legislature. Some of these universities may find themselves no longer able to maintain their quality.

In addition to these "flagships," most states have smaller universities with graduate and professional schools. The number of these has grown and they are regionally distributed, often serving metropolitan areas. Admission policies in these universities are more selective in some states than in others. Tuition is usually low, sometimes only slightly higher than at community colleges. While some of these newer state universities have accomplished a great deal in a short time, the academic caliber for the majority is not to be compared to that of the nationally known flagships.

Yet, the emphasis of these flagships is not one that appeals to most governors or legislators who often believe that they sacrifice teaching to research. Political pressure is also developing that favors increased appropriations to doctoral granting institutions in metropolitan areas, rather than to the traditional flagships. Several states favor distributing support for graduate education and research evenly among all their universities, rather than concentrating on keeping up the quality of the leading ones.

The Commission believes that the traditional policy of support for flagship institutions is the wisest one for the states to pursue. These universities represent a unique and valuable asset to the states and to the country as a whole through their contributions to research, professional training, and public service. They now have 65 percent of all enrollments in research universities. Their wide development in the public sector, and consequent wide access for students, is one of the most important transformations of the last three decades.

Minimum Standards of Academic Conduct

Recommendation 3

In order to prevent clearly deceptive or fraudulent practices, each state higher education board should establish and enforce minimum standards of academic conduct that all institutions must meet in order to be licensed to operate within the state.

As competition for students intensifies, institutions are tempted to use deceptive recruiting practices and lower their standards to prevent a steady erosion of their financial base. In ideal circumstances, well-intentioned institutions would not enroll unqualified students. But these are not ideal circumstances, and fierce salesmanship can compromise an institution's integrity.

A few colleges and universities have gone beyond aggressive recruiting techniques and have begun to use highly questionable practices. These are expected to become more widespread, and include:

—encouraging enrollments in programs of study for which job opportunities are limited;

—offering programs without adequate facilities or faculty;

—awarding credit for life experience, for non-collegiate preparatory work, or credit by examination, that is unwarranted in relation to actual accomplishments;

—reducing standards of performance in order to retain tuition-paying students (grade inflation);

—failing to provide adequate information on admission, grading, credit, and retention standards;

—admitting students who are unprepared for college without providing adequate counseling or remedial programs, and

—using the accreditation and licensing authority of a home campus to franchise academically deficient branch campus operations.

The clearest example of this kind of misconduct so far is the proliferation of out-of-state branch campuses, operating at locations that are hundreds of miles from the home campus. In some cases, library and other facilities are grossly deficient or non-existent, faculty are recruited off the streets, and academic quality, by any standards, is abominably low. Yet the branch campuses enjoy the prestige of the home campus whose name they share, and the institution can reap a quick profit, often by tapping a captive market such as a military base. In Maryland, fifteen out of thirty branches of out-of-state institutions closed their operations rather than submit to review by the state higher education board.

Some institutions may engage in questionable practices without being aware of their exploitative nature. Though aggressive recruiting techniques, improper granting of credits, or grade inflation, even when they overstep the bounds of acceptable conduct, do not justify the license revocation of an otherwise reputable institution, at some extreme these practices degrade the quality of education to the point that the offender no longer should be considered an institution of higher education. We expect such instances to be rare, but some mechanism must be set in place to establish minimum standards of academic conduct, and when necessary, to revoke the license of an institution that consistently fails to meet them. In most cases simply bringing unacceptable practices to the attention of an institution should be sufficient.

We emphasize that what is at issue here is not whether the quality of educational offerings of reputable institutions of higher education justifies the cost of keeping them open. Rather, we are proposing minimum standards of conduct designed to provide a degree of consumer protection from clearly deceptive or fraudulent practices. Since any accredited institution is eligible to receive federal student aid, its practices and programs have an implicit stamp of approval. However, the traditional accrediting associations cannot effectively control, nor do they want the responsibility for controlling, abuses like these.

No institution of higher education should be exempt from this licensing review process. The model legislation developed by the Task Force on Model State Legislation for Approval of Postsecondary Educational Institutions and Authorization to Grant Degrees of the Education Commission of the States is a useful guideline. This vests state higher education boards with the authority to prohibit the kind of abuses discussed above. Where additional statutory authority is needed, it should be promptly sought.

At present, exemptions are sometimes granted to institutions which (1) are accredited, (2) existed prior to a certain date, (3) are regulated by a state professional board, or (4) are incorporated as non-profit institutions. With adoption of the model legislation, such exemptions should be dropped.

And finally, each state higher education board that does not already have it, should be granted authority to revoke the license of any institution, public or private, that consistently fails to meet minimum standards of academic conduct. We believe that this authority will rarely need to be exercised.*

---

*Peter Clark comments on this recommendation, see page 121.

FACULTY COLLECTIVE BARGAINING

Recommendation 4

The states should reinforce the role of individual institutions in the collective bargaining process. Specifically:

(a) The states should designate the individual governing boards of public colleges and universities (where such exist) as the bargaining representatives of management on academic issues affecting the institution.

(b) The states should insist on institutional autonomy over personnel, academic, and planning decision.

Faculty unions are a relatively new development in higher education, and most of them are in public colleges and universities. The movement began with the passage of public employee bargaining legislation, which twenty-five states and the District of Columbia now have, and the first faculty unions were organized in 1969 at Central Michigan University, City University of New York, and Southeastern Massachusetts University. Today, 25 percent of all college and university campuses (600) and 30 percent of all higher education faculty are unionized. It is predicted that this will go to over 250,000 faculty on more than 1,000 campuses by 1990, although the rate has slowed considerably in recent years.

The greatest concentrations of faculty unions are in the two-year colleges and in the comprehensive four-year colleges. The faculties in these new types of institutions have traditionally played only minor roles in formal governance procedures. They object to the intrusion of executive agencies and legislatures and try to protect their prerogatives through unionization.

Fears had been widespread that faculty unionization collective bargaining would distort governance procedures, would change the professional roles of the faculty by inhibiting scholarly production, would lower education standards, would reduce innovation and experimentation, and perhaps most importantly, would weaken the criteria used to evaluate peers.

Experience so far has been that these fears are overdrawn. Even in institutions with a traditionally strong role for the faculty in decision-making, union contracts frequently have been useful in formalizing and assigning faculty responsibilities. New grievance procedures have resulted in due process for all personnel decisions and have also created, on the whole, more systematic and consistent evaluation criteria. The process by which conflicts are resolved has changed, but the standards of academic quality and peer review for major appointments usually have not.

However, collective bargaining has brought about a more subtle and troubling change in the way conflicts between faculty and administration are resolved. Many decisions formerly made on campus are now raised to higher political levels. Typically, the "employer" who bargains with a unionized faculty is not the individual institution, but a state-wide authority. In ten states, the higher education boards represent management by law. In most other states, a state employee bargaining office responsible to the governor conducts the negotiations. This office usually consults with central system management, but rarely with campus administrators. Thus, the presidents of public institutions, who are the immediately responsible administrators, are little involved in bargaining. In many instances, faculty unions lobby state legislatures and governors, a trend that administrations try to counter by adopting a policy of full disclosure of institutional budgets to union leaders.

The general rate of pay for the faculty of public colleges and universities is essentially a political matter. It is unavoidable for bargaining over salaries to take place at a state-wide level, and for governors, the state legislatures, and state higher education agencies to influence the negotiations. Academic issues, however, should be negotiated at the institutional level, where academic rather than political considerations are involved, and where bargaining is likely to be more collegial.

In order to bring about an appropriate division of collective bargaining responsibilities, a number of writers have suggested that the bargaining process be split. The general level of faculty salaries would be negotiated at the state level, while such other academic issues as teaching loads, criteria for promotion, and the pay scale used at a particular college would be negotiated at the institutional level. Bi-level bargaining can permit the needs of the particular institution and its faculty to enter the bargaining process, and preserves the negotiations from interference by political or state education authority. Because the constraints of state laws, which are designed for traditional public employees, do not take the peculiar nature of faculties and of higher education into account, imaginative administration is required to bring off bi-level bargaining. When relations between administration and faculty are good, informal coalitions can achieve these ends as well. In New Jersey, public colleges use local letters of agreement that accommodate the needs of both parties and thus achieve the objectives of bi-level bargaining.

It has also been suggested that the operating budgets of public institutions be split, so that the base for faculty salaries can be appropriated with some ease, while negotiated salary increases, which must be ratified in the legislature where they may meet political opposition and delays, can be appropriated at another time. Splitting budget appropriations in this fashion can avoid holding up an institution's entire appropriation because of failure to reach agreement on salary increases, and should make the bargaining process work more smoothly.

Even with these improvements, faculty unionization poses a problem for institutional harmony. Unionization contributes to the proliferation of state regulation by encouraging an adversarial relationship between state government and the faculties of public colleges and universities.

Collective bargaining will become more difficult as enrollments decline. Procedures to be followed during retrenchment are appearing more frequently in contracts, and some faculties that feel the need for job security are demanding contracts that specify the reverse order of seniority as the basis for cut-backs in salary. It is probably unwise to include specific retrenchment procedures in faculty contracts. Instead, contracts should include provisions for faculty participation in developing retrenchment policies. We also note that retrenchment increases the need for long-range fiscal and academic planning. Contract disputes should not be permitted to blind agencies and institutions to this fact.

In the end, governance on campuses that have faculty unions becomes more political and less cooperative, even under the best circumstances.

REGULATION: STATE OVERSIGHT AND ADMINISTRATIVE AUTONOMY

Colleges and universities in the public sector have much more government regulation to cope with than private ones. Since they are actually governed by the state, the state institutions need to deal not only with a large and growing cadre of federal investigators, but also with an equally burgeoning corps of state agents. The past thirty years have been marked by steady increases in state efforts to insure accountability for the use of state funds, as institutions grew in size, numbers, and sophistication.

Paradoxically, in the coming period of declining enrollments and retrenchment, the states are likely to increase further their regulation of the public sector of higher education, and also to make inroads into the regulation of the private sector. Financial stringency creates more pressure, rather than less, to ensure that state dollars are properly spent and state-mandated administrative procedures are adhered to.

Our Commission explored the magnitude of the regulatory burden through ten studies prepared for us on current practices in the states of California, Florida, Louisiana, Massachusetts, Nebraska, New York, Ohio, Texas, Wisconsin, and Washington. From them we concluded that regulation is already placing a heavy burden on public institutions in terms of dollar cost, paperwork, and faculty and staff time usually without improving either their accountability or quality enough to justify the burden.

These studies show that state regulation of higher education has its origins in a number of different sources. Some regulation is mandated directly by legislation. Additional regulation is required by higher education boards. A third, and increasing, source of state regulation comes from the growing complexity of state systems and the consequent increase in problems of governing them.

The California study reported that "literally hundreds of regulations are issued each year from the central office of the California State University and College System; most require detailed reports and they constitute a far greater burden on campus managers than the reports required by an equally regulatory national government establishment." During 1976, the

University of Wisconsin system had to deal with thirty-nine separate audits; eight ordered by the state legislative audit bureau, eight by HHS, one by the Navy, and twenty-two ordered by the Regents of the University itself. In the state of Washington, a community college that was required to submit fifteen reports on personnel transactions in 1973–75, expected to have to provide 300 by 1977–79. And there was no significant change in the number of such transactions over the period!

Although the dollar cost of state regulation is, of course, troubling, public higher education leaders are made even more anxious by their perception that it is eroding institutional autonomy. Academic freedom is fairly well protected. It has become an accepted principle in both public and private higher education. In the past, legislatures and governors have tried, sometimes successfully, to invade the traditional academic authority to decide who should teach and what is taught. Such attempts are now exceedingly rare. Administrative autonomy is less well protected by statute or tradition. Most institutions, except those sheltered by constitutional status (and in some cases even these), are not free to choose the procedural or administrative practices used to manage them.

The Washington study suggests that academic independence has been reduced by state handling of negotiations over faculty unionization and by legislation specifying requirements for student contact hours. The report cites twenty-six legislative resolutions calling for study of Washington's higher education system and audits of faculty utilization recently ordered at two senior institutions.

The California study also noted that while legislated regulations have not invaded the traditional preserves of academic freedom, they have "substantially intruded into areas such as curriculum, degree requirements, and personnel decisions which had previously been left to governing boards, academic administrators, and faculty." The study cited legislative mandates to award credit for remedial writing, to lay off faculty by reverse order of seniority rather than by program need or qualifications, and to disclose faculty evaluations to persons being reviewed for promotion or tenure. The study concluded that:

> The budget and audit process, letters of intent (accompanying budgets) and committee instructions, informal advice and agreed formu-

las have become major devices for regulating higher education. . . .
Higher education has not been singled out for expanded regulations, however; they have become more common in all state agencies
as the Governor, Legislature, and their control agencies have become
heavily involved in the management and administration of public
services.

The basic question of state regulation was posed by a senior
vice president of the University of Wisconsin:

> When do we reach the point of diminishing returns when the human
> and fiscal costs of increasingly rigorous and formal processes of mon-
> itoring and evaluation exceed the value of any changes or corrections
> resulting from such processes? I have an ever increasing feeling that
> we have reached and perhaps gone past this point of diminishing
> returns and that we need to give greater emphasis to the concept of
> delegation. . . .

The states must retain broad powers of oversight relating to
program content if they are to manage the redirection of institutional missions and the orderly contraction of the public
sector. However, most state regulations deal with procedural
rather than academic matters, such as central purchasing and
personnel administration, regulations restricting out-of-state
travel, central control over the disposition of overhead funds
and revolving funds, and increasing numbers of fiscal and management audits. In effect, state agencies, and more recently
state legislatures, are assuming an increasing role in the day-to-
day management of public institutions.

Not all public institutions can demonstrate the ability to
manage their tax dollars competently and efficiently. In a few
institutions, relatively routine managerial data are not available,
either to the administrators of the institutions or to the state
executive agencies and legislature. Some institutions still regard
as esoteric the financial and management controls that any
other economic enterprise would consider routine. Finally, public institutions must demonstrate to their external constituencies that they are capable of adapting to conditions of declining
demand by making a persistent and effective effort at restrain-
ing costs.

Most public institutions are competently administered. Nevertheless, state regulation imposes an increasing financial burden

on them, and is gradually moving the locus of administration away from individual institutions where the resources and capabilities for supervising routine administrative matters are greatest, to centralized executive agencies and state legislatures. Since the source of these regulations is also the source of the funds that support the public sector, the administrators and faculty of public colleges and universities are in a poor position to resist state regulation and oversight, even when it is not appropriate or cost-effective.

In a time of financial constraint, state regulation of public higher education, relating to administrative and financial policies as well as program content, is inevitable. As the California study of state governance reported,

> It is almost inconceivable that any other public agency would request that elected officials provide a budget and a program mandate and then would assert that state government should neither prescribe rules for the conduct of the program nor rigorously hold the program to an agreed set of objectives and methods for assessing the agency's accomplishment of those objectives. In the long run . . . higher education cannot successfully adopt such a strategy.

But if state oversight of public higher education is not to paralyze the institutional management process that it seeks to improve, it must delegate routine management authority, rather than attempting to manage each public institution from the state capitol. In the vivid words of the California study:

> A strong case can be made that intensive state regulation of universities is counterproductive: it costs money, stifles creativity and diversity, defeats effective administration, and at its extremes intrudes upon academic freedom. But the other elements necessary to substitute a policy of delegation for one of ever-advancing regulation are only now being developed. Mission statements and evaluation techniques must be devised and adopted that will create sufficient official and public confidence to sustain pleas for a special relationship between universities and state governments, turning on delegated authority and program accountability.

The vice president for business and finance of a moderate-sized private liberal arts college puts the issue more sharply.

He says:

> If the academy is as astute in analyzing its own future as it professes to be when it addresses itself to its customary disciplines, the realization may dawn upon it that in a world of diminishing resources it would by example teach others how not to grow, how not to render its services at inflationary costs, and how to become less gigantic as gracefully as possible.

COMMENTS AND DISSENTS

Dissent by William Friday

There are still another complicating set of circumstances facing higher education in its relations with state governments in the years ahead. Private colleges and universities have become in the last decade major claimants for state funds. In state after state, programs of public aid to private higher education have been established and funded. Here again, the aid formulas are generally tied to enrollment levels. Moreover, the preponderance of federal appropriations for the support of higher education is now for programs of student financial aid. The Basic Educational Opportunity Grant program is a powerful driving force in maintaining enrollment levels in both state colleges and universities and in private colleges and universities. For many private colleges and universities which have little or no endowment income and are thus dependent for their survival on student tuition payments, stability or even survival depends on enrollment levels. This is the case because their enrollments largely determine amounts of state aid, and because of the federal dollars that are funneled to them through student financial aid programs. This dependency on public funds is a novel situation for American private higher education, and it raises a series of difficult policy questions of fundamental importance.

Should the private colleges and universities be included in this quality control process? This question points to the single most important dilemma facing private institutions. The private institutions have a unique and vital role in American higher education, and they are an essential part of the diversity of the system.

This quality of diversity is the consequence of the fact that they are private or independent institutions. As many of them become more dependent on state funds, and indeed as they assert a state obligation to provide for them some form of aid, can they continue to be private and independent in the historical meaning of the words? This is one of the most important questions to be faced by the private colleges and universities themselves, and by all of higher education. Simple assertions of the virtues of diversity do not suffice to answer the question, and more and more the relationship of the two sectors of higher education may become antagonistic as they compete for state appropriations.

Earlier in this report we said, "Accountability for public money is inescapable." As public funding to the private sector increases, this accountability almost certainly will soon require that private colleges and universities participate fully in the quality assurance process which should be conducted by academic peer groups through the established state governance or coordinating structures for higher education. If they are to receive public assistance from the state and participate in federal aid programs, then they ought to share in the responsibility for assuring that academic standards and quality are protected. Otherwise, public policy requirements regarding the use of public funds and avoidance of costly duplication and wastefulness would be applied to one segment of higher education and not to the other while both are being funded from state and federal sources. A voluntary program in all likelihood could not meet public policy requirements for academic accountability.

Dissent by James R. Killian

I do not concur in the recommendation "that each state arrange for a periodic review of the quality of educational programs at every public college and university within the state" and with the statement that "inclusion of the private as well as public sector is probably desirable." Long experience leads me to fear the intrusion of the government in reviews of program quality. I fear that the assumption by the states—or the federal government—of accreditation will inevitably lead to dangerous governmental control even though the original arrangements seek to avoid harmful governmental influence on academic decisions. While the report suggests that state should "invite but not require private colleges and universities to participate in the academic program review process," I fear that the public institutions would feel that the non-participation of private institutions would be discriminatory, that pressures would inevitably increase for the mandatory inclusion of private institutions, and that indeed the adoption of the recommendation in this report would be but a "first step on the slippery slope to public control." I recognize the dangers inherent in the possibility that weak public institutions will be kept alive by state funds and that private institutions will take the brunt of declining enrollments. Nevertheless, I much prefer to leave the review process to the non-government, regional, and other accrediting agencies with every effort being made to strengthen these accrediting agencies.

Comment by Peter Clark

Under "Reviews of Program Quality," (p. 104) the Commission says, ". . . we believe states should invite, but not require, private colleges and universities to participate in the academic program review process." On p. 109, it goes on to say, "Each state should empower its higher education agency to license all institutions for operation within the state, and should establish and enforce minimum standards of academic conduct as a condition of licensing, in order to prevent fraudulent and deceptive practices. No institution of higher education should be exempt from this licensing process."

One cannot object to protection from "fraudulent and deceptive practices." It is not difficult to imagine, however, the use of this licensing power by some state bureaucracies to advance the interests of public institutions, adversely to private colleges and universities, during the period of intense competition for students and for funds that we all believe will come. Every effort should be made to protect *private* colleges and universities from state government control over their very survival.

Chapter 5

Financial Aid

About nine billion dollars are spent each year by the federal government on aid to students, making this by far its largest contribution to higher education. In addition to helping millions to go to college, this is a most important source of revenue for almost every college and university in the country. As we looked at the problems and complexities of federal financial aid to students, we asked these questions:

—Should broadening student access—that is, basing grants on need measured by family income—remain the guiding principle?

—If it should, does it?

—Is "choice"—that is, enabling students to choose more expensive institutions—still a valid purpose for federal programs?

—If it is, do the programs work?

—What is the effect of financial aid on who actually pays for a student's education—the parents, the student, or the taxpayers?

—Are students and families with higher incomes receiving help from financial aid programs that is inappropriate, considering their stated purpose?

SHOULD WIDENING ACCESS REMAIN THE CENTRAL PRINCIPLE?

Who goes to college today? What kind of college is it? The answers to both these questions are startlingly changed since 1950, and contain the most radical transformation of higher education in our history. It is the result of government initiative. The state governments made the most important contribution by creating and financing new kinds of colleges. The federal government, through its grant programs, helped large numbers of students to go beyond high school who might otherwise not have been able to. It is fair to say that many millions of Americans are now college graduates who would not even have enrolled a generation earlier.

The present massive federal financial aid program came in the wake of the legislation resulting from the civil rights movement and the war on poverty. There was public recognition that profound inequity in educational opportunities still existed in the United States, that college graduates and professionals were disproportionately from middle- or higher-income families, and that education beyond high school can help to open the door for all to the benefits of upward mobility in income and quality of life. Yet it was only in 1972 that increasing access to higher education became the explicit goal and dominant theme of the major grant program, the Basic Educational Opportunity Grant (BEOG).

It is not obvious that the present federal policy of basing aid to students on financial need is the wisest one, or that all reasonable people support it. Since there are strong alternative views, the Commission examined them with care.

Many Americans think that the aim of making it possible for everyone to go to college is unrealistic, that there will always be some who are unsuited, and that only those who can truly benefit should be given financial assistance at public expense. This view points out that the present policy is wasteful at times, that some students who do not belong in college nevertheless enroll, that they themselves fail to benefit, and that some generally promising students are held back when the level of instruction is lowered to meet the needs of those without adequate preparation or ability. The conclusion of this view is that any subsidy for higher education should be a privilege, not a right.

If this view is accepted, some criterion for aid is required in addition to simple financial need. We discussed several possible alternatives. One would be to measure academic achievement through a national test. Such a standard would in effect eliminate broadening access to higher education as a national goal since family income and academic achievement are strongly correlated. The winners in such an unconstrained contest would come overwhelmingly from the upper regions of the income distribution where participation is already high.

A second possibility also would use an academic standard but one that places the student in a local context more appropriate for judging accomplishment. The student would be required to graduate from high school in the top half or even two-thirds of the class, making it possible for students from poor families to get financial aid, but excluding those who were especially limited academically.

Another possibility would be to condition a federal grant on some kind of national service performed either before or after college. If the service followed graduation, a further incentive could be to use it as a basis for cancellation of all or part of a loan repayment obligation.

A fourth possible criterion would be to require all students who do receive federal grants to help themselves while in college, either through working or borrowing. The logic is that society should be willing to invest only in students who are themselves willing to invest energy and money because they recognize their self-interest in going to college. Government and students should be in a partnership.

A final alternative might be for the federal government to have only one role—to guarantee the availability of credit, giving up grants entirely and making students face whatever net costs of education in tuitions and other prices emerged from the policies of the institutions and the states. For those unable to meet the price, the federal government would encourage private lenders to make loans available by underwriting the risks of non-payment. This approach would remove the government entirely as an agent in redressing inequalities of income, leaving whatever help is available to students from poor families entirely up to the accident of residence, and to the political process in their states.

From society's point of view, this would effectively prevent overinvestment in higher education. However, it could lead to substantial underinvestment. Many people are not sophisticated enough to realize the benefits of a college degree; many resist putting themselves in any kind of debt; and many do not realize that beyond their personal gains from higher education, some part of the benefits to the whole society returns to them.

After considering these alternatives, the Commission concluded that the goal of federal financial aid should continue to be to help poor students who want to go beyond high school. But we also want to emphasize that self-help is important—no student should be fully supported through grants, that parents should contribute as much as possible, and that some part of the program should reward academic achievement in an inexpensive but symbolically important way.

This is a middle course between the shortcomings of the present program which allows some waste to both students and government, and those of one substituting prior academic achievement for need, since those most in need would be handicapped in any competition.

WHO SHOULD PAY FOR HIGHER EDUCATION?

In answering the questions we posed, the Commission found itself repeatedly confronted with perplexing problems because financial aid policies also have a large influence on who pays for college. What should be the balance among parents, students, the taxpayers of the fifty states and of the nation as a whole? The following discussion is not meant to answer these questions fully, but should throw some light on what financial aid can do and should do.

One fact often overlooked is that the colleges and universities themselves pay a significant part of each student's costs. Almost all of higher education is subsidized in this sense because tuition usually does not cover the institution's full cost of educating a student. In the case of public institutions, this subsidy is great—two-thirds or more of the costs are met by state appropriations. In the case of private institutions, which subsidize all students out of their endowment income, gifts, and other resources, the subsidy is much smaller, but it is not negligible.

The Role of Parents

Since the present system of aid to students is based on need as measured by family income, its central assumption is that parents' contribution should be as large as possible. The view that the parents should not be assessed as heavily as current rules demand has been gaining attention and support. This trend shows itself in an expansion of the number of students defined as independent, a growing reluctance of parents to contribute as much as they are now expected to, and various proposals to make it easier for students to borrow at low cost. In short, the basic assumption of the federal program is now being widely questioned by the public, and these questions are influencing Congressional decisions. The newest laws governing financial aid no longer rest squarely on the original premise of maximum contribution from the student's family.

The case for reduced parental contribution has been advanced primarily by the middle-class, reeling under two burdens that are particularly hard for it to bear. First, rising costs of keeping a student in college are worsened by what inflation does to the family's income. Second, there have been deep changes in the traditional ways in which parents and children view each other, brought about principally by the sexual revolution and by the youthful questioning of our country's basic premises which began in the 1960s. Both of these factors undermine the solidity of middle-class parents' conviction that it is in their own best interest to put aside enough money in the family budget for their children's education beyond high school.

But the United States has more than a middle-class, and the Commission had to ask how changing financial aid policy in its interest will affect parents in other income groups. We concluded it is more fully in the public interest to maintain the original premise that families should make the largest possible contribution to their children's college education. This should remain the foundation of the system—keeping down the level of federal spending, preventing serious inequities among income classes from developing, and bolstering family ties at a time when many are fragile.

The determination of whether students are genuinely independent of parents' support is important to the amount of financial aid they receive. In 1976–77, roughly 25 percent of all students receiving federal grants claimed to be, and it is true that many young people are achieving independence at a relatively early age. Simultaneously, however, a number of families have discovered how to fulfill the letter of the definition of independence while avoiding its spirit. As a result, there are many inequities in the system. Two students may come from similar backgrounds, but one may be largely supported by parental sacrifice while the other—having learned to play the system—may enjoy a substantial federal grant. Nothing illegal may be happening, but some families put their children into a somewhat contrived state of financial independence before the college bills begin to accumulate. A consistent and credible resolution of this question must be found before it impairs the effectiveness of the entire federal financial aid program, and undermines its public support.

It is a clear and serious distortion of the purpose of publicly financed grants when they go to children from the upper ranges of the income distribution. Since the resources are scarce and the problem to which they are being directed is large, it is simply not the federal government's responsibility to subsidize upper-income families in this way. There already is a public subsidy available—and it is a large one indeed—in the still relatively low tuition of public colleges and universities. And students from these families should be given reasonable opportunities to work and to borrow. But to define them as financially independent—and therefore eligible for grants—is unacceptable.

Married students are now classified as financially independent, and in many cases the kind of inequity discussed above is involved. When these students receive grants, two families have shifted to all taxpayers what they would themselves otherwise have paid.

Present federal programs make no provision for lending to parents. This omission is strange, because such a feature could connect the principle that parents should pay as much as possible with the reality that middle-income families are feeling hard-pressed to pay college bills out of current income. Some parents do borrow now on a commercial basis from banks. There is no systematic information about the character and scale of borrowing, but what can be learned from interviews with bankers suggests that the range of experience is wide and that it varies greatly in different parts of the country.

It is clear that some parents who would like to borrow to pay for their children's education are more successful than others in getting loans. In order to give concrete form to the principle of maximum parental contribution, we believe the federal lending program should be extended to parents.

The Role of Students

Some element of self-help should be expected of every student who gets financial aid. The Commission believes that even in the case of a poor student attending an inexpensive institution, and however modest the contribution, this principle must be maintained.

Two practical reasons support our conviction. A dollars and cents stake encourages students to choose programs with care and to give them serious attention. The other important consideration is that the chance to go to college must be viewed for what it is—a chance to grow personally and to improve prospects in every way. Federal grants must be protected from being viewed solely as a welfare program and, to some extent, it has been.

At present, the basic federal grants do not cover the full cost of education, and there is a requirement that they can not be renewed unless the student can show satisfactory academic progress. These are features we support. However, the first—the so-called half-cost rule of the BEOG—has the very serious limitation that it operates to reduce the award of the poorest students at the colleges with lowest tuitions. The second requirement, while excellent, is not strictly enforced.

A short description of financial aid packages as now calculated will help to put some light on students' present obligations. The underlying principles of need-based financial aid are simple to describe but complicated to apply. The measure of need is the difference between what education costs the student and how much the immediate family can contribute. Calculating the out-of-pocket costs is fairly straightforward, especially for a residential student. Although foregone earnings can be a major element of the cost for a poor student, they are not explicitly calculated. Ideally, a financial aid package constructed for the student has three elements in varying proportions— grants, loans, and money earned through a work-study job. In practice, institutions simply do not have the resources to meet all students' needs as calculated, and sometimes, but not typically, a student is forced to drop out or to switch to part-time status.

Though the self-help principle already exists as an element in the way the financial aid package is calculated, in practice it is very difficult to apply to a dependent commuter student who is living at home, and whose expenses are so small relative to the grant that frequently the student does not need more money. The situation is quite different for students in a residential setting who receive federal grants. Almost without exception, they have to work or borrow to pay some part of their costs above the grant.

The Commission recommends that all financial aid packages contain an element of self-help: work, borrowing, national service, or parental contribution. We also recommend more opportunities for off-campus work in schools and hospitals.

Borrowing is one aspect of self-help. We believe that loans should be readily available to form part of each financial aid package. While there has been a great deal of attention given to student defaulters, there is something to be said for many—not all—of them. To a certain extent, the blame which many have eagerly assigned to former students should more fairly be shared with others. The system has given students unclear signals about whether the purchasing power advanced was "really" a loan or, if it was a loan, how binding their obligation was to repay.

No student should expect the government to foot the entire bill. In many cases, they will need to work. In other cases they will need to borrow. Many will need to do both.

The Role of the Government

If the family is too poor to help a student pay for higher education, and if the student has no other source of money, he or she can be described as financially needy. Such a student should legitimately have as much help from the government as possible, and federal grants are presently based on this principle as we have seen. This means, of course, that the taxpayer provides the money.

It is money well spent. Most of the students who have been helped by the Basic Grants and state governments' wide-access institutions have chosen programs that emphasize specific occupational training. Typically, those who enroll in the more expensive and selective colleges have looked more to graduate study for professional training. The whole country has the benefit of a more highly trained labor force and a better educated citizenry. The students themselves have a greatly increased chance for better lives.

However, the problem is still with us—while much has been accomplished in increasing access to higher education, more needs to be done. Opportunities for Black high school graduates, for example, have substantially improved, but for all children of poor families the results are less impressive. The top-quarter of students of proved academic ability manage to get to college whatever their family income. But for the remaining three-quarters, the family's place on the income scale is still a highly significant determinant of whether a student is able to go on beyond high school.

To keep its focus sharp, we recommend several important modifications of the Basic Grant program.

A renewed commitment to the goal of wide-access requires making young people aware of the opportunities that exist for help in going to college in time, and in a form, to reinforce their personal faith in their own goals. Today, technically correct information is often made available so late that, for practical purposes, it is useless. Students should learn about the nation's commitment to access before they are tracked early in high school to a program that does not prepare them for college.

Moreover, whatever information is distributed must convey more than the message: "There is a lot of public money available to help you pay for college; here is how to get some." It is a waste of taxpayer money to encourage young people whose chief motivation to go to college is that they do not know what else to do and that they can be paid, so to speak, to enroll. They must realize that higher education confers advantage only on those who are willing to work at it, and the federal literature on basic grants must stress this point, rather than mislead. The need for this caveat is especially great in the near future when institutions will be doing all that they can with seductive claims to attract high school seniors in order to increase enrollments.

Taxpayers in the states have an equal interest in making sure that students without the necessary motivation do not enroll. In contrast to the federal money which focuses on students from poor families, most of whom attend public institutions, over half of the states' money is used by students to attend private ones.

But to look at the obligations of the taxpayers in the states in a positive way, they have already supported the most important effort to increase access to higher education in our nation's history. Community colleges and many of the new four-year institutions are a great success because of their wide distribution that makes it possible for many poor students to live at home, and because the tuitions are so low. In the coming period, taxpayers and legislators should recognize that this remains the country's most important way to help poor students to go on beyond high school. It is in the public interest to keep tuitions low in the first two years of all open-access public institutions.

SHOULD CHOICE REMAIN A GOAL OF FEDERAL FINANCIAL AID?

The other side of both federal and state financial aid programs is that they help to determine which colleges students choose. This is an appropriate federal role in our opinion but it should be separated from the fundamental purpose of insuring access.

Ever since the first large federal program to help students pay for their higher education (the G.I. bills of 1944), financial aid has had the effect of also helping them to choose more expensive colleges and universities than they could otherwise afford. There are substantial grant and loan programs operating today, other than the Basic Educational Opportunity Grant program, that serve students of all income classes. They exist side by side with the access thrust of the major program and in some cases overlap and intrude on each other's purpose.

Unless there were to be a drastic scrapping of all these other programs, a prospect neither politically feasible nor necessarily desirable, federal financial aid will continue to serve the choice function—that is, it will have a large influence on enrollments in particular institutions. The struggle for enrollments will become an issue of survival for many colleges, especially the private ones, and the pressures on Congress to shape financial aid rules so that they benefit the institutions will be great.

The Commission believes that it is appropriate for the federal government to help students and their parents to choose private institutions about which they feel that "it costs more but the extra cost is worth it," and are willing to go in debt to pay for it. However, we believe that the way to accomplish this is through helping students and their families to get loans for higher education, and not by helping the institutions directly. Thus, the Commission endorses one of the basic premises of the 1972 legislation—that aid must go primarily to the student.

The difference between tuitions at public and private institutions of similar type and quality, known as the "tuition gap," is a serious problem for private institutions. Two substantial student grant programs now address it, and we recommend that they continue. It is likely that the gap will be somewhat reduced as the states raise tuitions in public colleges and universities under the pressures of rising costs and competing demands from the public. In the previous chapter we emphasized both the self-interest and obligation of the states to shape their policies so that the burdens of retrenchment are shared by the public sector. However, even with the best state policy, wisely administered, the private institutions will be hard pressed. But, the dangers of federal policy directed toward helping a particular institution, or class of institutions, are great for both higher education and society. Letting institutions benefit from what students choose to do with their aid money is a far wiser course in the light of American convictions about economic competition and academic freedom.

We believe that strengthening the loan program is the best and fairest way for the federal government to help both student choice and higher education, particularly in its private sector, in the years ahead. One of the major recommendations of this Commission is the creation of a National Educational Loan Bank to make loans readily available to students and their parents.

Grants give students from poor families a "choice"—but it is the choice between going to college, or not going. It is appropriate for all students, from the lowest to the highest income groups, to have federal help if they want to choose to spend more on their higher education, but that help should come from loans, not grants.

RECOMMENDATIONS

The federal financial aid programs constitute a system, but not by design. It is a complicated one resulting from different national purposes at different times in our history since 1944. All of the programs are important to those who receive money from them, but some work better than others, and some require modification to fit our principles.

Since we present a coherent overall program which takes into account the interrelationships among the different parts that now exist, our recommendations cover all parts of the system, although not all need revision.

The first group of recommendations—from one through ten—aim to increase access to higher education. The major recommendations are:

—Keeping tuitions low in the first two years of all open-access institutions. (Recommendation 2)

—Modifications to the Basic Educational Opportunity Grant (BEOG), substituting self-help for the half-cost limitation, raising the 1980 maximum award, adjusting the award for inflation, and prompt action by Congress on appropriations, both initial and supplementary. (Recommendations 3, 4, 5, and 7)

—Increasing College Work-Study appropriations. (Recommendation 6)

—A single schedule of Expected Parental Contribution. (Recommendation 8)

—Elimination of Social Security benefits for college students. (Recommendation 9)

—Access and Retention Awards as a modification of the present Title III program, "Aid to Developing Institutions." (Recommendation 10)

The second group of recommendations addresses the problem of the best way to help students to choose more expensive institutions through the financial aid program. This group has three sections:

—The creation of the National Educational Loan Bank to replace all existing federal loan programs for students. (Recommendation 14)

—The contribution of the Supplemental Educational Opportunity Grant (SEOG) and State Student Incentive Grant (SSIG) programs. (Recommendation 15)

—A discussion of the contribution of state student aid programs.

Recommendations 12 and 13 add a small program with a purpose new to federal grant aid: Merit Scholarships.

The final Recommendation (16) assesses the future of federal spending for financial aid.

The further discussions are intended for those readers interested in background on our proposals and their detailed workings.

Keeping Tuitions Low in First Two Years of Open Access Institutions

Recommendation 1

The central purpose of federal financial aid programs should continue to be lowering the financial barriers to access to education beyond secondary school.

Recommendation 2

Tuition should remain relatively low in community colleges and in the first two years in other open-access institutions.

These recommendations are central to the Commission's purpose of broadening access. If the federal basic grant program is improved in the important ways we propose, it still will not be able to provide enough help to the students most in need if tuitions are raised at the institutions most of them attend. These are the colleges in which the only qualification for entrance is high school graduation.

It must be recognized that the first two years of college for such students is an important personal testing time. They try it out, discover they can profit and go on, or decide they do not like it and drop out. The Commission believes it is therefore important to keep tuitions low in the first two years of all open-access institutions, both in the community colleges and those offering four-year programs.

Once the sorting has been accomplished, those who stay enrolled can reasonably expect tangible reward, and this is the case for charging juniors and seniors a larger proportion of the costs of their education. The aim of our recommendation is to establish priorities for the states in responding to the emerging pressures to raise tuitions in public colleges and universities. In our judgment, it is fairer to impose higher costs on needy juniors and seniors than it is for the states to change their policies of providing wide opportunity in low-cost, open-access public colleges.

> **Further Discussion.**   Long before the federal government engaged in its systematic effort to increase access, states had their own programs that made higher education widely available. The first state colleges were founded in the nineteenth century. The main features were to provide sufficient capacity to permit broad admission policies, and to keep tuition low. This older system allowed students to try out college, and frequently they never advanced beyond freshman year. It avoided two of the less attractive features of the current system of financial aid: means tests and debt.
>
> The response to the booming demand for higher education by the states (described in Chapter 4) was the most important effort to expand access ever made. But it poses problems for the states that the older system did not, because then less than one-quarter of eighteen-year-olds wanted to go to college. Now that participation rates are twice as high, the costs of the earlier method throughout public higher education are great, and the taxpayers are not willing to provide as large a general subsidy. A different and new model is growing in popularity, combining higher tuition and fees with relatively large amounts of financial aid.
>
> The Commission's recommendation is directed towards public understanding that it is essential for the states not to apply the new model to the open-access institutions they created.

The Basic Educational Opportunity Grant
(BEOG) Program and Self-Help

Recommendation 3

Public grants should not fully cover the cost of education
for any student.

Recommendation 4

Appropriations for the BEOG program should be large
enough to provide each eligible student the full amount
of the award which the legislation allows. If a supplemental appropriation is required to achieve this end, it should
be forthcoming.

Corollary:

The Department of Education should publish and make
widely available a booklet containing the appropriate
forms, tables, and instructions so that an individual can
calculate his or her own BEOG.

Recommendation 5

The half-cost rule should be rescinded, and a self-help
requirement should be applied.

Recommendation 6

To support renewed emphasis on self-help, spending on
the College Work-Study program should be increased by
$100 million.

Recommendation 7

The maximum BEOG award should be adjusted once every
two years (i.e., once every Congress) to reflect changes in
the consumer price index. (A maximum of $2,400 in 1980
would roughly compensate for inflation experienced since
1972 when the program was created.)

The Basic Educational Opportunity Grant is the centerpiece
of the federal financial aid program. In its short history since
1972 it has accomplished more than any previous federal effort

in widening access. The award rules are complicated. Commuter students from poor families attending low tuition (i.e., $400 or less a year) institutions full-time are the chief recipients. If they enroll in higher tuition colleges, these students can receive larger grants. In addition, several other small federal programs are open to these students, and most states have some money for student aid. But the BEOG is the most important source of funds for students from low-income families.

The Commission recommends action by Congress on four features of the program:

1. It is funded through annual Congressional appropriation. Often, Congress has not acted soon enough, or the appropriation has not been large enough for each student actually to receive the full amount of the award the regulations would allow. This is a serious handicap for poor students, and particularly for entering freshmen. Congress must act in time, and must vote whatever supplementary appropriation is needed.*

2. The present half-cost rule limits the grant to $750 a year for a student from a poor family who attends a tuition-free institution. The Commission believes that this is not enough to remove financial barriers to access for these students. Although it is money not available to the student or family when he or she was a high school senior, it offers little compared to the nine months' wages possibly foregone. We believe that the half-cost rule should be rescinded and a self-help requirement substituted for it. In the case of the poorest student this self-help sum should be $500.

3. The College Work-Study program should be increased by $100 million in order to support the renewed emphasis on self-help. This represents almost a 20 percent increase in the current program of $550 million per year.

4. It is important for the maximum award to be adjusted regularly so that it reflects higher prices. We recommend that the maximum should be set at $2,400 for 1980 and that each Congress should review the level.

*Peter Clark dissents from this recommendation. See page 162.

Further Discussion. The BEOG program was originally intended to provide aid not only to poor students but also to some regarded as coming from middle-income families. The Middle Income Student Assistance Act of 1978 (MISAA) has extended eligibility for a BEOG even higher within the region of middle-incomes; the highest family income (for a standard-size family) that qualifies for some assistance increased from $15,000 to $25,000. As a result, perhaps an additional 1.5 million students are now eligible, and there is reason to believe that most institutions will have roughly twice as many BEOG recipients in 1979−80—the first year when MISAA will have an impact on the number of recipients—as in 1978−79. MISAA was Congress' response to the feeling of middle-income families in recent years that they have been especially hard-pressed to pay the costs of college. In extending the range of incomes of families eligible for federal grant aid, Congress also extended its purpose. Under MISAA, the BEOGs subsidize "choice," to some degree, in addition to their original goal of subsidizing "access."

One of the program's major shortcomings is its failure to inform eligible students in a timely way how large an award to expect. The problem stems from the inconsistency that, on the one hand, the law refers to the program as an "entitlement," but on the other, it is funded through annual appropriations in such a way that the funds may not be available to give each recipient as large a grant as has been authorized. What is needed is for Congress to make the language of the law and its own practice in appropriating funds consistent. Ideally, the size of the grant available to a particular student attending a particular institution should not be subject to the ups and downs of the annual appropriation process.

If Congress accepts the need to protect the size of individual grants by making supplemental appropriations when necessary, a sensible further step would be to make it easy for the applicants to estimate their own awards. The main requirement is to make widely available a compact package with forms, relevant tables, and clear instructions. It would be similar to the tax package distributed by the Internal Revenue Service, but it could be much simpler. The underlying arithmetic is straightforward, and in most cases, the computations would be roughly comparable to those for a federal income tax return for a family with only earned income and some deductions.

With these changes, protecting the BEOG program from being seen, in any sense, as a welfare program, rather than as a means of enhancing educational opportunity will be especially important. Although MISAA helped provide that protection by extending the range of the income distribution eligible for BEOGs, most of the money will still go to students from poor families. Preventing public grants from covering the full cost of education provides part of what is needed. Strict enforcement of the requirement that a recipient make satisfactory progress in his or her educational program as a condition for renewal of a basic grant will also help.

The most unsatisfactory feature of the present BEOG program is the half-cost limitation. Its aim—to leave a gap between the cost of education and the grant—is one the Commission supports. The gap is to be financed by the efforts of the student and the family. However, the half-cost limitation operates to reduce the awards of the poorest students attending the least expensive institutions. We propose an alternate procedure for calculating BEOG awards for all recipients in order to incorporate the principle of self-help, thus preventing the grant from fully covering the cost of education.

The amount of the award would be the lesser of (a) the maximum allowable award minus the expected contribution from the student's family or (b) the cost of education minus the sum of the expected contribution from the student's family and $500. Five hundred dollars thus becomes the minimum self-help contribution of the student and his family.

With the maximum BEOG award of $2,400 that we recommend, this procedure builds into the BEOG program a self-help gap of exactly $500 for a BEOG recipient whose cost of education is below $2,900, and one of at least $500 for all other BEOG recipients. This means that the grant to students with maximum need attending tuition-free institutions as commuters would be $1,000.

BEOG recipients with higher costs of education typically receive a package of financial aid, made up by the financial aid officer, that contains elements in addition to the BEOG. For such students, we recommend that self-help average $750, with a range of $500 to $1,000. These numbers are broadly consistent with the self-help expectations built into the computations performed by the major need analysis services.

It is important to underline that the self-help principle is much easier to apply in a residential setting than for a commuter student. Despite this difficulty, the spirit of the proposal is to encourage the student to make a financial contribution.

The half-cost limitation originated in a compromise between public and private institutions, and its repeal would raise an important political problem. Those institutions in the private sector that are heavily dependent on tuition income from students in their local markets and compete for them with local public institutions support half-cost tenaciously.

One Schedule for Expected
Parental Contribution

Recommendation 8

**Only one schedule of Expected Parental Contributions
(EPCs) should be authorized for distributing federal funds
to parentally supported students. The guiding principle
should be for parents to contribute as much as possible.
The definition of the independent student should reinforce
that principle.**

Another shortcoming of the present financial aid system is
that it fails to insure that parents contribute as much as possible
to their children's education. The methods for determining how
much a family is expected to contribute were recently changed
by the passage of the Middle Income Student Assistance Act,
and the results have drawn close scrutiny. There is growing
unease about the present arrangement because it allows two
conflicting systems of need analysis to operate side by side, and
routinely to provide quite different answers to the question of
how much a particular family should contribute. The methods
used are less objective and more value-laden than was assumed—
at least tacitly—to be the case. It is now possible for the college
financial aid officer to suggest that a middle income family use
the schedule which gives it a lower obligation. This is a serious
inequity.

Further, the current arrangement confuses both the parents
and students whom the system is supposed to serve. Although it
is easy for the specialist in financial aid to explain the discrep-
ancy between the two systems of need analysis, the typical parent or student cannot, and is led to wonder why, if each process
is designed to generate an "objective" measure of ability to pay,
the results can differ so dramatically. Moreover, the fact that
both systems have government approval does not help clarify
matters. The Commission believes that there should be only one
schedule of Expected Parental Contribution.

We also believe that an appropriate boundary must be drawn
between financially dependent and independent undergraduates, since serious inequities result when students are classified
as independent inappropriately. If the boundary is drawn too

restrictively, some who should have a large grant will not receive it, if too loosely, some families will succeed in shifting to society at large a financial burden which they should properly be carrying.

Our concern with the importance of this modification is that we believe that parents should make the maximum possible contribution to their children's education and to the extent that contribution declines, it must be replaced by public funds.

Further Discussion. The two major conflicting systems for determining the EPC are first, the Uniform Methodology (UM) of the American College Testing Program (ACT) and the College Scholarship Service (CSS) and second, the BEOG methodology of the Department of Education.

For as long as the two systems have existed, they have differed, but the exact nature of their difference changed dramatically with the passage of MISAA. Previously, the BEOG schedule was more demanding than the UM over those ranges of income for which both were defined. For example, in 1977−78 a typical family with income of $14,000 should have contributed about $700 according to the UM and about $1,900 according to the BEOG methodology. The effect of MISAA was to alter the BEOG schedule in such a way that it remains above the UM schedule for low incomes but falls below it for high incomes. The two schedules cross at about $18,000 of income. Some incomes for which the BEOG schedule is defined are so high that they do not actually give rise to a BEOG award, but the existence of the two schedules creates confusion, especially with respect to middle-income families. While parents in those families may welcome the incentive the new BEOG schedule creates for financial aid officers to request the lower of the two EPCs, the new juxtaposition of the two schedules has introduced a substantial element of instability into higher education's pricing system.

If there is to be only one schedule of EPCs authorized for allocating federal financial aid, who should establish it? The obvious candidates are CSS−ACT, on the one hand, and Congress, on the other. The systems of ACT and CSS were unregulated for a long time. All that changed a few years ago, and now, in order to qualify as a mechanism for distributing federal money, the UM must conform closely to specific guidelines established by the Department of Education. Interestingly, the BEOG methodology for determining the EPC is exempted from the force of those guidelines. The BEOG methodology has always been governed by Congress in some sense. Before MISAA, the Department of Education would simply propose a schedule that Congress would typically approve, though it always has had the power to veto it. With MISAA, Congress has taken a more active role by writing directly into the legislation the schedule for translating a family's available income into its EPC.

The case for having Congress set the schedule is that the funds at issue are public, the schedule to be derived is closely analogous to a tax schedule, and the derivation of the EPC should be carried on in a "politically legitimate" environment.

The major reservation about giving Congress the assignment is that the legislature may be better suited to working out political compromises than to doing objective need analysis. The recent history of MISAA at least partially illustrates the problems. When forced to choose between the conflicting views of constituents, on the one hand, and some academic analyses, on the other, over the intensity of the middle-income squeeze, Congress, predictably, lined up with the constituents. All of this may be another way of saying that spending on financial aid will be greater if Congress is, in effect, measuring the aggregate need in the system than if an alternative agency were performing that function. Such a result would please parents, students, and institutions, and worry those who monitor the aggregate level of federal spending.

Closely related to the task of constructing the schedule of EPCs is the matter of drawing an appropriate boundary between financially dependent and financially independent undergraduates. Inevitably there will be difficult cases. It seems best to be strict in formulating the general definition of the single independent student and, simultaneously, to create some mechanism for granting exceptions. Ideally, the procedure would strike a balance between intruding on the institution's autonomy and being so unobtrusive as to encourage inequities resulting from which college a student happened to attend. Marriage also raises questions about independent status. Perhaps the same mechanism for granting exceptions could take marriage into account as one factor among others.

Consolidation of All Student Aid Programs in Department of Education

Recommendation 9

Social Security benefits for college students should be eliminated.

Future educational benefits for military service should be integrated with the Department of Education programs of financial aid.

When the Social Security program of benefits to students was enacted, the Basic Grant program did not exist. Since the purpose that justified it is now served by BEOG and other programs, there is no longer any reason for students to have Social Security benefits. Moreover, its criteria for award, in general, give recipients more money than they would receive under the basic grants; this is inconsistent with the basic criterion of need. The Commission recommends, therefore, that Social Security benefits for students should be eliminated. This would have the further advantage of saving $1,300 million annually. Applying these savings to improving Basic Grants and other Department of Education programs, as we recommend, would help to widen access since these programs serve that purpose directly.

Further Discussion. In 1965 education benefits were extended by the Social Security Administration to eighteen- through twenty-one-year-old full-time unmarried students who had a working parent leave the work force because of death, disability, or retirement. Not all the beneficiaries are in college; in 1972–73, one-fifth were in high school. This program is a full-fledged entitlement, and between fiscal years 1978 and 1982 benefits paid under it are expected to rise from $1.8 to $2.5 billion annually. However, this simple dollar total is misleading. The award rule is complicated, and if a student recipient were to drop out of school the government would make a full net saving of the student's allowance in some instances, while in others there would be only a partial saving because allowances to other members of the family would increase. Thus the cost of education benefits under Social Security is hard to estimate precisely.

Our recommendation for educational benefits for military service is essentially parallel. Education benefits as a form of deferred compensation for veterans have a long and honorable history. The landmark legislation was the Servicemen's Readjustment Act of 1944, and subsequently there have been three other G.I. Bills. Through November of 1976, 5.4 million Vietnam era veterans received training under the Vietnam Era Bill, 64 percent of them in college. The peak came in fiscal year 1976, when the government spent $5 billion on veterans' training and when 1.9 million veterans were enrolled in institutions of higher learning. Subsequently, both the spending and the enrollments have declined.

The terms of benefits for past service are already fixed and we make no recommendations on them. If, as seems likely, educational benefits will be used more in the future as an incentive in connection with military service, it would be desirable to tie them into the existing Department of Education programs. For example, a young man or woman who completed the ordinary two-year term of military service could be entitled to receive BEOG grants at one-and-one-half times the rate that he or she could otherwise claim. In that situation, it would also be appropriate to treat these veterans as independent students. The same argument would apply if other forms of national service also use educational benefits as an incentive to attract volunteers. In every case, such service would qualify as self-help.

Title III: The Secretary of Education's Access and Retention Awards

Recommendation 10

Four-year institutions making an outstanding contribution to the nation's goal of improving educational opportunities for young people from poor families should receive special awards. The Secretary of Education would designate the recipients, basing the decision upon an institution's proportion of students from exceptionally poor families, its rate of retention for students who enter as freshmen, and the record of its graduates in obtaining post-baccalaureate education. The award would be an unrestricted grant matching the aggregate BEOG awards received by the institution's students during the academic year in which it is made. This would enhance the present Title III program Aid to Developing Institutions.

"Wide-access" can become an empty rallying cry. It has another side that should receive more attention: whether students actually stay on, once admitted to college, and graduate. The recent introduction of new kinds of institutions now makes it possible for all students to find the kind of college appropriate to their academic needs. The trouble is that all too many colleges take the students in and turn them over frequently. The dropout rate is high.

The Commission believes that success in keeping students who are both particularly underprepared and particularly disadvantaged is an important aspect of broadening access that is not appropriately acknowledged in the present financial aid programs. One group of institutions notably successful in this way represents a national treasure worth maintaining. These are the historically Black colleges. And there are other institutions with similarly outstanding records, such as some in Appalachia that do as well for their ill-prepared white students.

Therefore, we are recommending new criteria for awards to such institutions—"The Secretary of Education's Access and Retention Awards"—to help them meet the costs and give them an incentive to keep up the good work.

We offer this recommendation as a modification of the present Title III program, "Aid to Developing Institutions." Title III was originally conceived to help colleges "out of the mainstream," especially Black colleges providing access for a pool of students uniquely disadvantaged, both economically and educationally. For this reason the program was continued even after federal policy changed in 1972 to focus on the needs of students rather than of institutions.

Congress has now mandated that a substantial part of Title III funds, 24 percent, should be earmarked for community colleges and private junior colleges. Small, predominantly white, financially weak colleges serving a middle-class student body are increasingly included. Without new criteria, this trend will probably continue since it is not easy to define a developing institution. Community colleges have made excellent contributions toward broadening access that we neither minimize nor ignore. However, we believe that public money at state and local levels is available to them. It is more appropriate for federal policy to focus on four-year institutions.

The program is not strictly a part of financial aid, but when it was enacted in 1965 the intention was to use it as a tool to improve access, and to give institutional aid accordingly. The Commission believes that its recommendation will guard the original purpose. It will be important to reexamine the program from time to time as race relations change and as new colleges develop which focus on the special needs of Hispanic-Americans and American Indians and prove to be successful in the same way.

We make no recommendation about how many institutions should receive awards, believing that this should be left to the Secretary of Education and the Congress. Our sense of the order of magnitude is that about 150 to 200 institutions would qualify, and it is on this basis that we have estimated the program's cost at $150 million per year.

Funding Special Remedial Programs at Authorized Level

Recommendation 11

Further to serve the purposes of the Secretary's Awards, the TRIO programs should be funded at the authorized level of $200 million per annum.

Bringing students from poor families with inadequate educational backgrounds successfully through college requires efforts begun while the students are still in high school and continuing in the first years of college. Special programs are needed to find such students who are capable of college work, to inform them about the opportunities, and to help them make the best of these opportunities by remedying deficiencies in preparation. The TRIO programs, directed to this end, have been effective, but could well use more money. The current appropriations have been about $140 million per year. We believe that it is important for the appropriation to reach the authorized level of $200 million. The money would be well spent.

Like the Secretary's Awards, these programs are complementary to the Basic Grants. They deal with the special problems and difficulties of access for educationally disadvantaged groups that the broader program does not reach.

The original programs referred to as "TRIO" are Talent Search, Upward Bound, and Special Services for Disadvantaged Students. More recently two more programs have been started—Educational Opportunity Centers and Educational Information Centers—and it is these five programs to which the title "TRIO" is generally applied.

Merit Scholarships

Recommendation 12

The federal government should establish a Federal Undergraduate Merit Scholarship program, providing 3,000 awards annually. Of these, 1,500 would be awarded on a nationwide basis, and 1,500 would be allocated to the states, each state's share to be proportional to its share of the nation's eighteen-year-old population. The scholarship would pay up to the full cost of education for four years at the institution of the student's choice. The actual amount of the award would be determined on the basis of need, with the exception of $1,000, which each scholar would receive. The whole of the award would be grant aid.

Recommendation 13

The federal government should establish a companion program of scholarships for seniors in American colleges planning to obtain professional or graduate training. Awards should be made on the basis of qualities of leadership, enterprise, and character that promise professional achievement, as well as on academic record. There should be 3,000 scholarships, to be allocated among the states for competitions to be run in each state. Each state should get a number of scholarships proportional to its number of senators and representatives in Congress. Every baccalaureate institution should be entitled to nominate at least five, and at most ten, candidates for the competition. Each scholarship would cover the full cost of education at the institution of the student's choice for the duration of his or her study.

The present financial aid programs lack any acknowledgment that academic achievement and personal qualities of character, energy, and leadership are important both to the individual and to the country. While the Commission affirms that grants must be based on financial need, we believe the time has come to make a modest move to honor these traditional values, ignored recently because of our intense efforts to make up for previous inequities. We are recommending two scholarship programs, one for undergraduates, and the other for college seniors who plan graduate or professional training. Both would reward academic achievement, and for the seniors, personal qualities would also be taken into account.

Many of the talented students who are likely to win the awards would no doubt have succeeded in going to college and beyond without them. But the symbolic value of the awards would be considerable. They are a way for the nation to make a statement about what has enduring value and what is worth admiring and nurturing. To reinforce the symbolism, we recommend that the competition should be conducted by a panel of distinguished citizens, appointed by the President, with Congressional consent.

The scholarships for professional and graduate training emphasize the additional function of higher education as a channel of social mobility. Students in professional and graduate schools are still drawn disproportionately from middle and upper-middle class families, and had parents who were themselves college-educated. By giving the graduates of each four-year college a chance to compete, the proposed program would counterbalance, to some degree, the cumulative advantages of those who begin the competition at an advantage.

Our recommendation is certain to evoke opposition: that definition of merit would perpetuate the status quo; that the students so honored can obviously fend for themselves; that this program uses scarce resources better devoted to expanding opportunity; that weaknesses in the system of need-based aid are already being exploited, and that this program would mount one more attack on the need-based system which, despite its fragility, is worth trying to keep.

Anticipating the arguments against the proposals was a way for the Commission to reinforce its conviction of their worth. We believe that widespread questioning of our national purpose among young people makes it important to convey a sense of opportunity that influences aspirations. The programs are modest in size and cost, but both could have a symbolic effect beyond these.

In 1979 prices we estimate that the two programs would cost no more than $80 million annually in full operation.

In making this recommendation, we are mindful of the admirable work of the National Merit Scholarship Corporation

(NMSC). The awards we propose would be broadly similar in conception to the 1,000 awards of $1,000 each which the Corporation now makes annually. A plan to permit the federal government to provide matching funds to NMSC to expand its program along the line suggested would be a further development of this recommendation in keeping with its spirit.

A Unified Loan Program, the National Educational Loan Bank

Recommendation 14

Congress should establish a National Educational Loan Bank (NELB) to make essentially unsubsidized, long-term loans to undergraduates and to students in graduate and professional schools. NELB should be authorized to borrow through the Federal Financing Bank, its obligations should be guaranteed by the Secretary of Health, Education, and Welfare, and it should borrow and lend without statutory limitation.

NELB should also make it possible for parents to borrow in a way that makes credit widely available to them on more uniform terms.

This is one of the Commission's major recommendations. It is essential for the federal government to offer a rational program of widely available loans on terms more equitable than those existing. Our convictions about the importance of helping parents and students—particularly those from middle- and upper-income families—to borrow to pay for higher education are set forth at length on pages 127—129. Separation of grants from loans and the principle of maximum parental contribution must be built into the entire federal financial aid program for it to have integrity. The two existing federal loans programs have many inequities and malfunctions. We recommend the creation of entirely new machinery to deal with the need to make a wider choice of institutions financially possible for students and their families.

The following sketch of the essential features of the NELB should be combined with the further discussion below for an understanding of how it would work.

—NELB is intended to make loans readily available to all students.

—Even if not eligible for financial aid, students will be eligible for loans.

—Except in rare cases to be decided by financial aid officers in the college itself, loans will not be offered to freshmen.

—Twenty-five percent of the cost of education will be the upper limit for loans to undergraduates, while 50 percent will be available to students in graduate and professional schools.

—Parents of all students will also be eligible for loans. The Commission leaves open whether they would borrow directly from the NELB or from commercial banks to which it provides capital for the purpose.

—Fifty percent for undergraduates, and 75 percent for graduate and professional students will be the limit on combined borrowing of students and their parents. Thus, a loan directly to a student will diminish, dollar-for-dollar, the amount that parents can borrow.

—Interest on loans made to students will accumulate from the start, and the cost to the student borrower will be the cost of capital to the government.

—Students begin repayment shortly after graduation, with some options, and have twenty years to repay. Parents will enter repayment immediately and have ten years to repay.

—The federal government will provide capital to NELB through the Federal Financing Bank, and guarantee loans.

—The NELB will have direct responsibility for collection of loans to students. The Internal Revenue Service can help, primarily in locating highly mobile recent graduates. We want to emphasize that it is *not* our intention to treat students' debts as tax obligations, but merely to provide NELB information on where borrowers can be found.

In addition to its central purpose of making a wider choice of institutions financially possible for students, the NELB would rationalize a lending system whose working has become haphazard, and whose costs are high in relation to its purposes. Interest rates now charged differ dramatically depending on the program under which a student borrows. The record of the current system in making capital available is spotty on a geographic basis. In some places capital is readily available; elsewhere it is not.

Further Discussion. There are now two federal loan programs: the National Direct Student Loan program (NDSL) and the Guaranteed/Federally Insured Student Loan program (GSL/FISL).

The government supplies most of the capital for NDSL. The student pays no interest while in school; subsequently, he or she pays 3 percent. The upper level on borrowing is $10,000, and the repayment period is ten years.

In GSL/FISL, the primary capital comes from the lenders themselves—mostly banks, or colleges and universities—rather than the government. The lenders' incentive to participate comes from government guarantees of the loans. In one of the two variants of this program (FISL) the federal government insures loans directly. In the other (GSL), it supplies reinsurance for state guarantee agencies who are the primary guarantors.

Interest rates for those in repayment are far below any realistic measure of the current cost of capital, making the programs extremely expensive. In the NDSL, the major sources of capital to finance new lending are what Congress appropriates and what former borrowers repay. Therefore the lower the interest rate for those in repayment, the larger the appropriations must be to maintain a specified level of lending. In GSL/FISL there is a spread between the 7 percent charged to those in repayment and the 12 to 13 percent that the originators of loans—principally commercial banks—were receiving in mid-1979. The government pays that spread on every dollar in repayment. The cost for that one item—the special allowance—is expected to be nearly $400 million in fiscal year 1979.

We propose that the NELB raise the cost of interest to the student borrower so that it equals the average cost to the bank of providing capital: the interest rate on federal government obligations of similar term. Specifically, its lending rate each year would be the average of the relevant government borrowing rates over the preceeding five years. The cost of capital would not be subsidized in the direct way it is in the GSL program, but the government's provision of capital through the Federal Financing Bank and absorption of overhead and default costs would permit a rate that is much less than what a commercial lender would have to charge students with nothing to offer as security but their future earning power. In addition to the value of the government guarantee, we do propose two elements of direct subsidy: the costs of administration, and the costs of failure to repay, through default or death, would be absorbed by the federal government.

NELB loans would be available to form part of each financial aid package, and also to provide assistance to students who do not receive financial aid. Any undergraduate could borrow up to 25 percent of the cost of education, with one exception: freshmen would not ordinarily be offered loans. Any graduate or professional student would be allowed to borrow up to 50 percent of the cost of education.

Students would begin repayment shortly after graduation. They would have the option of deferring the payment of interest and allowing it to accumulate until they enter repayment, and they would have a graduated repayment option. The time available for repayment would be twenty years. The college financial aid office would serve as the loan window for all students, as it does now for students receiving NDSL loans as an element of financial aid.

One appealing opportunity for a parent to share the cost of the student's borrowing would arise because of the accumulation of interest while the student is enrolled. Under GSL and NDSL the student incurs no obligation for interest until repayment begins. Under NELB, however, interest would begin to accumulate from the start. A parent could undertake to pay the interest while the student is enrolled, so that the amount borrowed, not that amount plus accumulated interest, would be the student's obligation on graduation. The general goal is to allow each family to make such arrangements in the way most suitable to its circumstances and thus encourage intergenerational transfers within the family to the greatest possible extent, rather than resorting to taxation and transfers through the Treasury.

The greatest difficulty with the current loan programs has been in collection. This is not surprising—neither the Department of Education nor colleges and universities should be expected to be effective debt collectors.

Loan collection from former student borrowers should be the direct responsibility of the NELB. In meeting it, the Bank would draw on two sources of help: the Internal Revenue Service and the existing state guarantee agencies. The IRS can be especially helpful in collecting from student borrowers. They tend to be much more mobile than the population in general, and the IRS is better able to keep track of them than any other organization. The Revenue Code already entitles the Commissioner of Education to request information on the location of borrowers from the IRS. It could provide much more assistance. Under suitable legislative instruction, the IRS could ask every taxpayer to report on his or her tax return the existence of an outstanding obligation to the NELB; to be the recipient of his or her repayments; and to provide NELB a list of respondents to compare with the Bank's list of borrowers.

The effect of reporting through IRS, as well as the use of its information on taxpayers' locations, would in our judgment greatly reduce defaults and improve collections. We do not believe it is desirable to go further and treat students' debts as tax obligations, however, allowing the IRS to apply the array of extraordinary powers given to it for tax collection.

The NELB must also be prepared to handle late repayments and defaults. Since the essential characteristic of student loans is the absence of collateral, the lender cannot take the conventional recourse of selling the collateral. The long repayment periods and the option for a graduated repayment schedule, starting small and growing as the borrower's income grows, do help minimize the borrower's cash flow problems (to be sure, at the expense of larger aggregate interest costs).

One possible additional mechanism would be to allow a borrower to defer payments further whenever his or her income fell below some critical level. If at the end of the schedule repayment period, some deferred obligations still remained, they could be forgiven. This, however, would weaken the concept of the loan as an obligation, and perhaps invite a wider evasion of repayments. It seems, on balance, desirable to provide only the usual path of escape from the obligation: bankruptcy. It is, however, important not to permit recent graduates an early resort to bankruptcy—this could undermine the whole program. The Commission, therefore, strongly endorses the provision of the Education Amendments of 1976 that permits no escape from obligations by bankruptcy until five years after repayment begins.

The NELB would replace all current programs of lending to students. Thus it would change the present roles of institutions now involved in educational lending: the commercial banks, the Student Loan Marketing Association (Sallie Mae), and the state guarantee agencies. Though some banks might be glad to abandon their current roles as lenders to students under GSL, and many do not now participate in the program, others would be reluctant to lose the business. After all, $600 million is now flowing annually to GSL lenders, much of it to banks. However, as we explain below, while we recommend that the banks get out of the business of lending to students, we see an important role for them in lending to parents.

Sallie Mae was created in 1972 as a Congressionally chartered private profit-making corporation to develop a secondary market in student loans. Under NELB it would become superfluous in its current form. One possibility could be to use Sallie Mae as the base from which to develop NELB, but it would have to be transformed to nonprofit status.

The state guarantee agencies now function as intermediaries between the lenders, banks and institutions, and the federal government, by guaranteeing the loans of the former under the protection of federal reinsurance. NELB would eliminate this function, but could use the existing state organizations, in effect though not in form, as branches to perform certain important functions.

Another important issue of transition would be the fate of outstanding NDSL collectibles, the stream of repayments from past lending. Currently, these repayments go to the institution originating the loan and are deposited in its loan fund to finance new loans; they can be used for no other purpose. The record is clear regarding the ownership of the stream of repayments. The legislation provides that in the case of the program's termination, repayments would be divided in the same proportion as past contributions of capital, which means that roughly 90 percent would belong to the federal government. The stream would certainly be a good asset for the NELB.

There is no experience to provide a direct basis for estimating the operating cost of NELB's program of lending to students: administration, collection, and default. These costs will vary over the life of the bank, with experience, and with the volume of loans. The indirect evidence suggests the following as reasonable figures for annual costs of the bank at maturity, in 1979 prices:

General administration	$ 50 million
Collection	$ 100 million
Default rate	5% of repayment stream

For a mature bank in a steady state, in which annual repayments and new loans are equal, the cost of defaults for the current (1978–79) volume of lending would be about $100 million per year. Thus on this estimate, the total cost of the NELB for the same volume of lending as the present programs would be $250 million per year. This, of course, makes no provision for the cost of capital, on the ground that this cost is met by the borrowers. That is the basic, important sense in which the loans are "unsubsidized.'

Parents of eligible students could be brought into the lending program in one of two ways. The first would be to allow parents direct access to the Bank as borrowers, in the same way as students. The second is to have the NELB provide capital to commercial banks on sufficiently favorable terms so that they would be willing to lend widely to parents at commercial rates.

Under either alternative, we propose that parents of students (including freshmen, and graduate and professional students) could borrow up to 50 percent of the cost of education. However, the combined borrowing of a student and his or her parents could not exceed 50 percent of the cost of education for undergraduates and 75 percent for graduate and professional students. Thus a loan directly to a student would diminish, dollar-for-dollar, the amount that his parents could borrow. Parents would enter repayment immediately and have ten years to repay.

On the first alternative, direct lending by the Bank, we propose that parents pay an interest rate slightly higher than the rate students pay; this would diminish the element of subsidy to parents. College and university financial aid officers could not effectively serve as the loan windows for parents; we propose that this service be provided by commercial banks, and paid for by the NELB on a fee basis. Loans to parents involve an evaluation of their capacity to repay, in terms of annual earnings, assets, and the like. The college financial aid office is not the appropriate institution for making this evaluation. The NELB would set general credit guidelines, and the banks would apply them to individual borrowers. Parents' eligibility for loans would thus be limited by banks' judgment of their capacity to repay. Since parents of college-age students are characteristically much less mobile than their children, the state guarantee agencies could serve as effective collection agents for the Bank on loans to parents. They could also help do the necessary job of coordinating parent and student loans to a family, and seeing that they fall within the overall limits for families. On the second alternative, the parents would borrow from commercial banks at market interest rates, and the banks themselves would be responsible for collections and bear the risks of default in the usual way. The NELB would provide capital to the banks for re-lending, at a cost that would provide sufficient margin to make the business attractive to the banks. Without direct experience, it is difficult to say what this spread would have to be. If it were less than the spread between government and commercial rates, this method would involve no extra capital costs to NELB. If not, the program would require a government subsidy to the banks, similar to that now involved in the GSL program.

The Commission has not resolved which of these alternatives is preferable. The case for relying on the commercial banks is that they can conduct the operation with greater efficiency than a government bank, and that the subsidy to parents is unnecessary. The other alternative has the virtue of providing a single unified lending program that is more certain to make credit widely available to parents as well as students. Further, the basic justification for a government lending program as a way of increasing students' choice justifies use of the government's credit for parents as well as for students.

One potential disadvantage of reliance on commercial banks for loans to parents is that they might be too conservative in assessing credit risks, and many parents might be unable to borrow. In part, of course, the degree of conservatism will depend on the spread between the banks' lending rate, and the rate NELB charges them for the money it provides for re-lending.

This sketch of how NELB would work to provide loans to students and parents obviously does not do justice to the numerous details of a complex system that would have to be provided for in practice. It does, however, show how the Bank would play three desirable roles in the overall federal program. First, it would substantially disentangle loans from grants, as the present system of highly subsidized loans does not. Second, it would offer a resource to all students—not only those qualifying for financial aid in terms of need—that would help lighten the current burdens of paying for college, making possible a wider choice of institutions, and helping both students and institutions. Finally, it would make credit widely available to parents, helping to increase their contribution to the cost of their children's education.

Funding for Other Programs

Recommendation 15

The federal government should maintain real spending on Supplemental Educational Opportunity Grant (SEOG) and State Student Incentive Grant (SSIG) programs in the years to come.

Both of these current federal programs are particularly helpful to poor students attending high cost institutions. They have been effectively used by the states and the colleges in this way, and private institutions benefit most from them. The Commission believes that it is appropriate for the federal government to help sustain choice by continuing the programs. We recommend that spending on them should be maintained in constant dollars.

Further Discussion. The Supplemental Educational Opportunity Grant program was formally initiated in 1972 but has its roots in the Higher Education Act of 1965 which established the first federal scholarship program for undergraduates. When the BEOG program was authorized in 1972, the earlier program became "supplemental," with the acronym SEOG. These grants are intended for undergraduates of "exceptional financial need." In practice, the program's special mission is to help relatively poor students attend relatively expensive institutions. The SEOG provides funds to the institutions and the financial aid officer uses them to supplement the BEOGs of students from poor families. In fiscal year 1979, $340 million was appropriated for the program. Somewhat more than half the money goes to the public sector, but on a per capita basis, it goes predominantly to private institutions.

The State Student Incentive Grant program began in 1972. It provides the states with resources for their own student aid programs. It is a matching program. Increases in state spending for need-based financial aid above base year spending are matched dollar-for-dollar, up to a formula-determined limit for each state, by a federal contribution. It may be viewed as a federal program of revenue-sharing with the states. It is the smallest federal program—$77 million was appropriated for fiscal year 1979. Its impact is greatest in states without substantial other student aid programs and in these states it has played a major role in calling forth new programs.

State Student Aid Programs

Each state has a student aid program, many of them small and a few quite large, although the federal programs are much larger than all of the state programs combined. Nevertheless, in any consideration of help given to students to choose more expensive institutions, these programs must be mentioned, because over one-half of the money granted is used by students to attend private institutions.

Five states have the most substantial spending on student aid programs, roughly two-thirds of all in the country. New York alone accounts for 30 percent of the total. Although the combined total of state grants is substantial it is, however, less than one-quarter of the federal program. Spending by the fifty states was about $700 million during the academic year 1977–78, compared to $4.7 billion by the federal government in fiscal year 1979.

A few state programs began early in the twentieth century, but most are quite new. In 1969, only nineteen states had programs of need-based aid. By the fall of 1977, only Alaska was without one, although it does provide some aid to students that is not need-based.

While we make no recommendations about these programs because of their great variety and different problems, they should be mentioned as a further aid to private institutions and an additional way in which students are helped by public money to choose more expensive education.

Spending in the Future

Recommendation 16

Apart from decreases associated with the changes recommended in this chapter, spending in the Department of Education programs should not decline in real terms in the period to come. That portion of the program of educational benefits under the Social Security Administration that benefits students in college should be phased out with the understanding that the Department of Education will have a high claim to the saving generated in this way.

There is obviously no precisely correct answer to how the scale of the Department of Education programs should change as we anticipate the future. Table 1 estimates the cost if the major recommendations were implemented in 1979. But what about the course of spending in the future? If the size of the typical college-age cohort were the only issue, there would be reason for total spending to shrink, because that cohort is expected to decline by about a quarter between 1980 and 1995. But there are other issues. The main current purpose of federal financial aid is to encourage new participants—typically from the lower portions of the income distribution—to obtain postsecondary education, and this effort has not yet gone so far that it can be judged fully successful. Taking the work yet to be done into consideration, a reasonable approach is to say that, in the period to come, the overall effort should not decline in real terms after the changes called for in this chapter have been implemented. Those changes, as shown in Table 1, imply, in fiscal year 1979, a reduction in cost of just over $800 million.

Table 1. Comparison of Actual Costs (Rounded) and Those Estimated Under Major Recommendations, Department of Education Programs, and Selected Other Existing and Proposed Programs.

	Actual Fiscal Year 1979 (in millions of dollars)	Estimated under Proposed Changes, Fiscal Year 1979 (in millions of dollars)	Change
Basic Grants (BEOG)	2,600	3,800	+1,200
Supplemental Grants (SEOG)	340	340	0
Federal Matching Grants to States (SSIG)	80	80	0
College Work-Study (CWS)	550	650	+ 100
National Educational Loan Bank (NELB)*	0	250	+ 250
Federal Direct Lending (NDSL)	310	0	− 310
Insured Lending (GSL)	970	0	− 970
Title III, Strengthening Developing Institutions	120	150	+ 30
Special Remedial Programs (TRIO)	140	200	+ 60
Federal Merit Scholarship Programs	0	80	+ 80
Sub-total (D. of Ed. Programs)	5,110	5,550	+ 440
Social Security Education Benefits for Students in College	1,300	0	− 1,300
Veteran's Education Benefits	2,400	2,400	0
Sub-total (other Programs)	3,700	2,400	− 1,300
TOTAL	8,810	7,950	− 860

*As the discussion on page 156 shows, there are two variant proposals on how the Bank would deal with loans to parents. The figures here refer to the one in which the commercial banks would lend to parents and the Bank would provide them with capital for these purposes. The assumption is that the spread between the commercial rate and the Bank's lending rate would be sufficient to induce commercial banks to provide these loans widely, and, accordingly, no cost is assigned to this part of the operation. The more expensive variant, in which the Bank lends directly to parents, might add an additional $100 million to these costs.

Costs of the Proposed Compared
to Existing Programs

The separate programs of financial aid interrelate; from the point of view of students and institutions, they form a single whole. We believe our recommendations give a coherence to the whole that is presently lacking. They are directed towards achieving major improvements in equity without increasing total federal expenditures.

What do our proposals cost? Table 1 compares actual costs from the 1979 fiscal year budget with estimates of what those costs would be if the major proposed changes were in place, under the conditions of 1979 for enrollments, price levels, income distributions, and so forth.

The table indicates that no change is intended for three items. Veterans' Benefits are simply outside the purview of this study. As for SEOG and SSIG, no change in funding is recommended. The Commission's view is that these programs are running well and that a continuation of the status quo in terms of broad direction as well as real levels of funding is desirable.

The Federal Merit Scholarship programs and the National Educational Loan Bank are innovations, but neither is expensive. The merit programs are inexpensive because they are small. The NELB will do a large volume of lending, but since it will make unsubsidized loans, its costs will include only administration, collection, and default. The net cost of providing capital, over time, will be nearly zero. For the purposes of making the comparisons shown in Table 1, we have estimated the costs of the NELB under the assumption that the volume of borrowing is what it was in 1978−79.

The changes in the BEOG program that we recommend will result in a substantial increase in its costs, as follows:

Altering BEOG award rule for commuting students*	− $ 60 million
Eliminating half-cost*	+ $ 300 million
Increasing the maximum award to $2,400*	+ $ 900 million
	+ $ 1,140 million

*Each calculation is made on the assumption that all three of the proposed changes are made. Since they interact, the cost of each single change, taken itself, would be different from the figures in the table.

In addition, the elimination of Social Security benefits for students would make more students eligible for BEOGs, at an estimated cost of $60 million, bringing the total increase in costs of the changed BEOG program to $1.2 billion.

In the aggregate, the actual cost of present Department of Education financial aid as well as of Veterans' Benefits, Social Security Education Benefits for students in college, and Title III (the Strengthening Developing Institutions program) is $8.8 billion in fiscal year 1979. The total cost of these programs, as altered and replaced by our proposals, including a $1.3 billion saving from elimination of Social Security benefits for college students, is estimated at just under $8 billion, a reduction of over $800 million.

DISSENT

Dissent by Peter Clark

This implies that, by establishing the program, Congress has created for itself some special obligation to fund it fully. The Commission's report does not justify any such special obligation. General higher education (as distinguished from specialized education and scientific research and training) has no special claim to assured federal support. Along with many other federally-funded public benefit programs, it should compete for support in the ongoing political process.

Chapter 6

Federal Support for
Academic Research

When Washington turned to the academic world for the nation's immediate needs early in the Second World War, the response of the scientists and scholars was extraordinary in every way—in rapidity, in commitment, and in brilliance. It proved to be a most productive partnership for both sides, one that is in large part responsible for our present world leadership in science and technology. Over a long generation beginning in 1940, federal support of academic basic research was provided more than unquestioningly, it was generously offered. Thanks to federal dollars, some of our universities are now centers of scientific discovery operating on a scale and at a level of excellence unimagined forty years ago. The reciprocal dependence of the government and scientists attached to American universities makes enormous contributions to the nation's health, prosperity, and security.

Enthusiasm for science and technology as well as for scientists continued to be widespread in the country until the late sixties. Public respect and trust sparked Congressional liberality.

More than any other factor, this explains the dramatic growth in federal support of basic research at colleges and universities and the development of a system that relied heavily on the scientific and academic community itself to award and administer the funds.

Over the last ten years, the partnership has become increasingly strained as public attitudes toward science, scientists, and universities grew increasingly critical and skeptical. Recent conflicts are due in no small part to this weakened public support. Uneasiness has developed on the university side that it must defend its choice of direction in research, must defend the well-established peer review system for making awards to individual investigators, must lobby for adequate appropriations, and must account for the use of funds in what it views as excessive detail.

The Commission examined the current situation with great care because, as we pointed out earlier, those most affected by the changed relationship with Washington are the most visible and the most audible intellectual and scientific leaders in this country: they are the foremost teaching institutions, producing graduates who in turn fan out as teachers to the rest of higher education; they produce the scientists and technologists who keep American industry strong and who make possible most of our technical, economic, and health advances.

Although the fears of the academic scientific community appear to be overdrawn in some respects, the Commission concluded that there is real cause for anxiety. If unchecked, the growing pressure on the individuals and institutions involved could indeed weaken the ability of basic researchers at universities to do what they can for the nation and for science and scholarship everywhere.

THE CURRENT SITUATION

The federal government now spends about $3.3 billion annually on academic research: roughly $3 billion for the natural sciences and engineering. $200 million for the social sciences, and $20 million for the humanities. Another $600 million is spent on a wide variety of campus activities, such as improving science teaching, disseminating scientific information, laboratory construction, traineeships, and fellowships. Also there are twenty-one Federally Funded Research and Development Centers (FFRDC) administered by universities for which an additional $1.7 billion in federal funds are budgeted annually. Only a small part of this money is used for applied research to meet specific federal and public needs. Most of it supports basic research, advancing scientific knowledge itself.

Of the 3,000-odd colleges and universities in the United States, roughly 600 receive federal research grants. About 100 of these are major research universities, each counting on $10 to $100 million annually in federal funds. This dependence is a most important aspect of each one's relationship with Washington.

Since research talent is heavily concentrated, about thirty universities receive as much money as all the others combined. This results from the way the government distributes grants chiefly through the peer review process, designed to single out the best research for support. Individual researchers submit unsolicited proposals to federal agencies which then call on qualified active scientists in each field to evaluate the scientific promise of the work proposed and the competence of the investigator to carry it out.

When Vannevar Bush proposed the creation of a National Research Foundation in July of 1945, he envisaged a single federal agency to be the exclusive source of government funds supporting basic research at academic institutions. The pattern of funding that has in fact developed relies heavily on "mission" agencies as additional sources, with the National Science Foundation (NSF) funding a broad spectrum of basic research at levels that complement the activities of the mission agencies. Like the Department of Defense during the 1940s and 1950s, the National Institutes of Health (NIH) now occupy a special position among the mission agencies, funding more than half of all federally sponsored academic research and sharing with NSF a particularly strong emphasis on basic research.

For the past ten years, federal funds have been scarce, at least by the standard of rapid growth that prevailed during the preceding thirty years. Only $6 million in 1938, federal funds for academic research reached $90 million annually at the peak of war-related funding in 1944. Then, fueled by the Sputnik crisis, the pressures of the Cold War, and public enthusiasm, it grew to more than $1.5 billion in 1969—a 250-fold increase in thirty years. The annual compound rate of growth during this period, measured in constant (inflation-corrected) dollars, averaged 15 percent.

Rapid growth faltered in the late 1960s and then came to a full halt in 1969. Since then, federal support, corrected for inflation, has remained roughly constant. Although growing at a fairly steady rate of 3 percent in each year since 1974, real expenditures on academic research in 1979 were only slightly greater than they were eleven years earlier when the period of rapid growth ended. Pressure to hold down the federal budget is almost certain to result in minimal real growth, and perhaps modest real declines in federal research expenditures at least through fiscal 1981.

Although science still enjoys broad public approval, a number of debates focus on scientific and technological developments that can plausibly be argued to have done more harm than good. Concerns about nuclear power and arms proliferation lead segments of the public to oppose vigorously some applications of basic research, and their arguments raise doubts in the minds of many more Americans about the social benefits of every advance in scientific understanding.

Today's skepticism results in no small part from scientists' own willingness to air their differences publicly on technical matters, such as the safety of nuclear power plants or the potential dangers of recombinant DNA research. Growing public reluctance to accept their judgment without question affects the manner in which research support is administered as well as its amount. Twenty-five years ago, the nearly unanimous opinion of scientists on which lines of research should be pursued, how scientists should manage and account for public funds, and the extent to which some research presents risks to the public health, safety, and the environment would have gone unchallenged.

STRAINS IN THE PARTNERSHIP

The changing public attitude toward science and scientists—as reflected in Congressional actions and funding agency response—has certainly not had any crippling effect on the quality of academic basic research in this country as yet. On the other hand, it has had some undesirable results. We call attention to them in a general way before turning to our specific recommendations.

The Commission believes that four current trends run counter to the best interests both of the country and of fundamental scholarly and scientific research: increasing pressure to even out the distribution of federal dollars; increasing desire to use those dollars for applied research to meet specific social needs; increasing and excessive financial oversight; and increasing Congressional unwillingness to make appropriations at a level that permits modest real growth, to fund projects fully, and to fund them steadily.

Peer Review System

The United States has always had a strong tradition of distributing the resources of society widely, rather than conferring them on a select group. The peer review system conflicts sharply with this tradition, and there are those who consider the system, and the concentration of support that it produces, to be unjustified. They feel that if the federal government is to support higher education, it should support all institutions, and that it should in large measure support them equally. This view has a number of adherents in Congress, where geographical concentration of support might be expected to gain few supporters and many opponents. Congress has been the source of considerable pressure to "democratize" the merit system of awards, or to replace peer review with formula grants that distribute federal support more evenly.

The Commission believes, along with most scientists, and historians and sociologists of science, that research by its very nature is a selective activity: the number of individuals capable of coming up with important new ideas is relatively small. The interplay among researchers is often as important an ingredient in the generation of new ideas and the conduct of productive experiments as the insight of any single investigator. Successful research is more often a cooperative than a solitary process, and the best researchers in any given discipline tend to assemble in a fairly small number of departments in order to work together.

The set of institutions with a concentration of talent varies from one discipline to the next, but not as much as might be expected. Cooperation and discussion among researchers often extend across disciplinary boundaries, so that a given university is likely to be particularly strong in several related fields. There is a kind of "halo effect," whereby distinguished departments lend prestige to a university as a whole, and indirectly to other, perhaps distantly related departments, increasing their ability to attract first-rate researchers.

In short, the current institutional and geographical distribution of funds is not arbitrary. It reflects the distribution of scientific talent and is in turn a consequence of how successful research is naturally conducted. The supporters of the system argue that if the federal government wishes to fund first-rate scientific research, it has no choice but to concentrate support on the best institutions.

In fact, some critics argue that funding is now spread too thin, and that academic science would be strengthened if, for example, half as many investigators received twice as much support each since, as is the case, only a small number of scientists do truly first-rate work. In the short-run, the federal government might improve the quality of the research it supports by concentrating its funds more heavily on fewer investigators.

However, the Commission believes there are several reasons for supporting the present distribution. Having a somewhat greater number of centers of scientific research enlarges the pool of talent to work on both the more revolutionary and the more routine lines. First-rate research proposals can come from unexpected quarters. Funding a broad spectrum of projects, not all of which meet the very highest standard of excellence, may be a necessary cost to make sure that no potentially first-rate research is overlooked.

In attacking a common problem, geographically separate groups of researchers in a given field use slightly different approaches—choosing particular aspects to emphasize, and using different techniques. This richness and diversity of scientific method, and the constant process of feedback among the various groups resulting from it, makes the entire enterprise more productive.

Every additional institution with an ongoing research program becomes an additional recruiter for scientific talent. While most of the leading researchers are found at a relatively small number of institutions, they, themselves, receive their undergraduate and graduate training at a much larger set of colleges and universities.

Finally, the current distribution is probably the minimum dispersion of funds necessary in a democracy to maintain public and Congressional support for scientific research. A much narrower distribution would make it difficult to preserve institutions such as peer review.

Basic Research versus Applied Research

One of the trends feared by university administrators and researchers is Congressional questioning of the need for more basic research, the public doubt that there is social benefit from every advance in scientific understanding, and the increasing desire to use federal dollars actually to serve social goals and specific public needs rather than "simply to satisfy the curiosity of scientists at taxpayers' expense."

Most of the nation's research and development is conducted in industrial and government laboratories, tailored to specific needs and targeted for swift completion. Only a small fraction of this is performed at universities and supported there by federal dollars. What universities provide is an atmosphere particularly well-suited to basic research that advances theoretical understanding but does not aim to answer immediate needs. Well over half of all basic research conducted in the U.S. is in the academic setting. The federal government pays for the greater part of it in order to maintain a healthy research establishment, producing a broad steady stream of contributions to fundamental knowledge.

The choice of what basic research to support cannot be based on a weighing of costs against results. The time lag between scientific discovery and ultimate application is often great. Economic benefits can frequently be shown to result, after the fact, but it is extremely difficult to predict beforehand which projects will yield practical applications, what they will be, or how soon they will materialize.

In the past few years a trend has developed to treat basic research at universities as a commodity purchased to meet specific federal needs, rather than an activity sponsored because of its intrinsic value to our society. The Mansfield Amendment, a rider on the Department of Defense 1970 Authorization Act, prohibited the funding of military research projects that did not have a "direct and apparent relationship to a specific military function or operation." Although the wording of the amendment was softened considerably in the following year, it has had a lasting effect on fundamental research supported by the Department of Defense, and to a lesser extent, by other agencies as well.

A notable example of strongly mission-oriented research is the "war on cancer," supported by more than $4 billion of NIH funds in the past eight years, despite the reservations of many scientists who argued that the fundamental scientific understanding to provide the leverage for the most constructive work on cancer was lacking.

Academic researchers have themselves contributed to the current federal emphasis on applied research by overselling their ability to yield rapid practical applications in an effort to increase Congressional appropriations. Thus they have reinforced, rather than resisted, the natural tendency of Congress to seek immediate and tangible results.

The Commission concluded that the present trend is undesirable, that it is appropriate for the country to continue to support basic research with no clear relation to the missions of federal agencies, and that Congressional pressure to target research programs at specific goals is incompatible with the country's need for a vigorous program of basic research.

The Chiles Act (the Federal Grant and Cooperative Agreement Act of 1977) directs all federal agencies to use assistance grants rather than procurement contracts when their goal is to support or stimulate activities with broad public purposes. The relevant sections of the Act make no specific mention of basic research but the Office of Management and Budget, charged with implementing the Act, plans to treat most federally sponsored research as a form of assistance to be funded through grants. This may create difficulties for agencies such as the Department of Defense in funding basic research. Nevertheless, the Commission believes that by making it possible to move away from the practice of treating research support as a form of procurement, the Act is a step in the right direction.

In our opinion, there are real advantages in having a plurality of funding sources. That no one small body of government officials makes all the decisions on how much money to spend on various fields of research reduces the risk of having an unbalanced program. Also, the funding agencies have overlapping interests so that an investigator with a meritorious proposal may find another source of support if a particular agency cannot accommodate the proposal. Finally, year to year fluctuations in a single agency's appropriations have less effect on the overall research budget when several agencies have funds available. We believe that the multiplicity of funding sources has benefits that outweigh their primary inefficiency—the duplication of proposals.

Excessive Financial Accountability

Academic research is now held to a tighter standard of accountability in all respects than in years past. The increasing tendency on the part of federal agencies to treat basic research as if it were a commodity purchased in order to satisfy needs at the lowest price leads to an insistence on documentation in great detail of how every dollar that supports research is spent. Federal auditors are now unwilling to approve reimbursements that are not sufficiently precisely documented or those considered to be not closely enough related to the actual conduct of research. They also want to standardize both federal oversight and university accounting practices.

The Commission believes that federal agencies are carrying this too far. An investigator's work on a particular research project is not perfectly separable from work on other projects, on teaching, or on faculty committees. Auditors cannot distinguish between costs allocable to research and those that are not with perfect precision. The government is, or at least ought to be, engaged in supporting a socially worthwhile activity, not purchasing a product. The investigator's research interest usually provides a sufficiently powerful incentive for maximum effort. Moreover, failure will be reflected in the quality of the results and will weigh against the investigator in the peer review of subsequent proposals.

Academic administrators and researchers must recognize, for their part, that it is entirely appropriate for the government to oversee academic research expenditures, and that as recipients of public funds, they are accountable to the public for their use. The fact that the process may sometimes interfere with the researcher's desire for flexibility or the university's desire for autonomy does not alter the legitimacy of the oversight.

In the past, universities enjoyed relatively lax enforcement of regulations governing the handling of federal research funds. Cost transfers (discussed below) are prohibited by federal regulations, but they were frequently used with the tacit approval of funding agencies. Some universities still do not have accounting and control systems adequate to ensure that research dollars are actually used for the purposes intended by the funding agencies. In a few cases, unrelated expenditures were charged against research grants. Such practices are no longer acceptable to federal regulatory authorities, and universities must institute systems of accounting and control capable of detecting and preventing their occurrence. The use of federal research funds for unauthorized purposes, no matter how infrequent, cannot be tolerated.

While excessive oversight creates a costly burden of paperwork for both the academic institution and the federal government, consuming time and financial resources that could otherwise be spent on research, the greatest cost is its effect on the research process itself. A characteristic of the best basic research is the emergence of promising new leads in the course of a project. The investigator should have the flexibility to follow such leads by redirecting the research effort.

Inflexible oversight requires the investigator who unearths a new lead to interrupt research in order to seek approval for the necessary changes in expenditures, to lay down a new trail of documentation and perhaps, later on, to justify the change in plans to federal auditors. If the process consumes too much time and energy, the investigator may decide to stick to the original line of inquiry even though new leads are passed up that promise to be more productive. Financial oversight is entirely self-defeating when it has this result.

The Commission is convinced that the relationship between research universities and the federal government is adversely affected by present auditing procedures and that they frequently impose real burdens on individuals and institutions. Therefore, in Recommendation 3 we propose a new process that will reduce the paperwork, increase efficiency on all sides, and improve the relationship.

Level of Funding

The level of federal funding, more than any other factor, determines how much research can be undertaken and how rapidly scientific understanding will advance—in short, how large and fruitful the national scientific enterprise will be.

It is extremely difficult to determine just how much the federal government should spend on basic research, or what constitutes adequate support for academic science. Like health care and national defense, research can absorb almost unlimited resources and there is no obvious way to measure what the public gains for an increment in its investment. Twenty years ago, there was wide agreement among the scientific community, Congress, and the public that the nation was not investing enough in science. In 1960, a statement by the President's Science Advisory Committee (The Seaborg Report) could recommend that:

> Simply in terms of economic self-interest our proper course is to increase our investment in science just as fast as we can, to a limit not yet in sight.

Today, with annual federal expenditures for basic research in the vicinity of $4.5 billion, it is difficult to defend such a strong statement, either to the Executive branch and the Congress, or to a public whose enthusiasm for science and technology has waned.

The scientific and academic communities strongly believe that the federal government should be spending substantially more than it now does. They often propose that research funding should be large enough to support all investigators capable of first-rate work. In practice this offers little guidance to policy-makers—first, because it does not answer the question of how generously to fund those investigators, and second, because their numbers are sure to increase in response to increased appropriations.

Congress has clearly made the political judgment that the overall level of federal research expenditures should remain substantially unchanged for the immediate future. In the absence of unforeseen shifts in national priorities, the Commission sees no compelling reason to seek a major change in the current level: in absolute terms, academic science now receives generous federal support. Nor is it clear that the annual growth rate of the 1950s and 1960s should serve as a benchmark for current policy.

Ultimately the Executive Branch and Congress make these decisions in the same way that they set funding levels for any other federal program. The scientific community and the funding agencies can and should try to influence these outcomes, and the political judgment of the Executive and the Congress on funding levels may differ from that of scientists, but we cannot conclude that the political judgment is wrong.

Decisions on how to allocate federal research funds among the various fields of research are also difficult. Peer review can govern the selection of competing proposals within the same discipline, but it cannot provide a basis for choosing between a proposal for research in physics and one in biology. Inevitably, non-technical considerations will enter into the allocation of federal funds among the various fields of science. These issues are fundamentally political, and the budget and appropriations processes of government are the only ways to make such trade-offs among competing claims for public dollars.

Having weighed all these considerations, the Commission concluded that funding for academic research should incorporate a modest degree of long-term real growth in expenditures, and that the national research enterprise should be protected from unnecessary fluctuations in funding levels from one year to the next.

The cost of performing a particular experiment rises from year to year, but not much faster than the cost of other goods. Research, however, does not perform the same experiment year after year. Scientific understanding is ever-expanding. Knowledge gained from current efforts opens up new possibilities. The next step in research, because it probes more deeply, almost always requires more sophisticated equipment than the last. As a result the cost of research escalates more rapidly than the cost of most other activity.

Modest real growth in academic research funding insures adequate resources for allocation to new ideas on which most of the vitality of the scientific enterprise depends. While no rigid short-run connection exists between basic research and technological applications, there is nonetheless a fundamental long-run connection. In a competitive world in which the United States can no longer draw economic strength either as a holder of abundant raw materials or as a provider of a large supply of simple labor, it must depend increasingly on sophisticated technology as a significant ingredient in the growth of the economy.

RECOMMENDATIONS

Maintaining Peer Review

Recommendation 1

The present framework of research support—competitive awards to individual investigators, refereed by their peers, and a multiplicity of funding agencies—should remain the basic system of federal support for academic research.

The Sloan Commission believes that the system of federal support for academic research that evolved in the years following the end of World War II is still fundamentally sound and should be maintained. The Commission can find no better method than this competitive peer review process for deciding what research will be performed. Its effectiveness depends on the ability of the active scientists in each field to recognize and agree on what lines of research are most promising and which investigators produce the best work. Peer review has frequently been criticized, especially in the Congress, as an "old boys' network" that allows established researchers to approve each others' proposals without sufficient regard for scientific merit. However, we are convinced by recent studies conducted by the National Science Board and the National Institutes of Health (NIH) that peer review is effective in selecting the best research for support, without bias toward any set of researchers or institutions.

These studies of the effectiveness of peer review were directed to the natural sciences, remarkable for the existence at any one time of a high degree of consensus among active workers in any field on what the important problems are and how they can most fruitfully be investigated. Schools of thought characterized by different answers to one or both of these questions are subjected to critical experimental testing.

The social sciences present a different picture. In many fields, there are wide divergences among practitioners on the fundamental question of the degree to which they are "scientific" and should copy the methodological model of the natural sciences. Humanistic scholarship is judged by even broader criteria showing persistent diversity of perspectives and methodologies. A review process that embodies this diversity is appropriate to much work in the social sciences as well.

The social sciences draw research funds from both the National Science Foundation (NSF) and the National Endowment for the Humanities (NEH). It is important that both NEH and NSF continue to fund the social sciences so that research on the "scientific" model is not the only kind receiving support in these fields.

Research and scholarship in the humanities is almost all supported by the NEH. It has supplanted private foundations and other private donors as by far the largest supporter of academic work in these areas. However, unlike the NSF, on which it was modelled, the NEH has a broader, more popular orientation. Only one-third of its budget sponsors scholarship and research; the rest supports efforts to promote greater public understanding of the humanities, and of American history and culture in particular. There is a sharp division of opinion over how much of the NEH's resources should be used to create a wider appreciation of our cultural heritage and how much for scholarly research. That issue is outside the scope of our report.

The actual mechanisms of peer review vary among the several granting agencies. Both the National Institutes of Health and the National Science Foundation—the largest supporters of basic research—do it in a formalized way, the NIH more so than the NSF. Those agencies which support mostly applied research, but considerable basic science as well, often rely less on formalized systems of peer review, and use advisory committees of scientists to get the same kind of evaluations.

Financial Oversight: Institutional Compliance and Federal Restraint

Recommendation 2

Academic administrators and researchers should comply fully with financial oversight of federally sponsored research, and they should tighten internal management and accounting procedures to improve their ability to account for the expenditure of federal research funds.

Federal regulators and auditors should use flexibility in the exercise of financial oversight, and they should recognize that efforts to document fully and precisely how every federal dollar is spent are often unproductive.

Cost Transfers. An example of a common university practice in the past that is now unacceptable is provided by so-called "cost transfer." Investigators frequently transferred funds into a research project, either from a second project or from a non-research account, when a project was temporarily short of funds or without funding. The funds borrowed from another account were usually repaid by a later offsetting cost transfer, but sometimes not. On occasion, investivators transferred unused funds out of a project that was about to be terminated rather than returning them to the funding agency.

In virtually all cases, the aim of the investigator in making cost transfers was to make the fullest possible research use of federal funds. Since the effect of a cost transfer is to substitute the investigator's judgment for the decisions of peer reviewers and the funding agencies on the amount of money provided each project, such transfers are now prohibited by federal regulation.

The prohibition is reasonable when the two projects are on completely unrelated topics, or when one of the accounts involved in the cost transfer is not a research project. But when the two projects are closely related—for example, when two agencies share the funding of what is essentially the same project—the prohibition on cost transfers creates an artificial barrier to the efficient use of federal funds, and it serves no useful end.

Two projects which are distinct but related present a borderline case. If the relationship is sufficiently close, and if the same group of investigators are involved in both projects, then the prohibition should be lifted.

The National Science Foundation is now testing a new form of research grant, the Master Grant Agreement, which delegates to the university the authority to make unlimited cost transfers among all grants within a given department. The premise of the experiment is that work of different investigators within a single department is related closely enough to justify cost transfers.

The NSF experiment also provides considerable savings in paperwork by aggregating all grants within a given department into a single master grant for the purpose of financial oversight. We see great promise in this approach, and we call on all funding agencies to look closely at the results of the experiment.

Effort Reporting. The limited success of university administrators in reaching agreement with federal regulators on standards for financial oversight is well-illustrated by the recent revision of the Office of Management and Budget (OMB) Circular A−21. This defines the direct and indirect costs of academic research and governs their reimbursement. OMB consulted extensively with representatives from higher education, yet the positions of OMB and research universities remain far apart. The revised version of A−21 has been criticized in the strongest possible terms by many university presidents and administrators. They argue that it provides for more extensive financial oversight and less complete reimbursement of costs than is appropriate for academic research—a criticism that we share.

The outcome of the revision might have been more nearly acceptable to both sides if the university presidents had approached OMB in the early stages of the revision and attempted to negotiate the standards of oversight. Instead they simply reacted negatively to OMB drafts. The presidents, with their broad responsibility for the affairs of the university and their knowledge of how both the support and the regulation of research affect the university as a whole, are in the best position to undertake such negotiation. We believe that establishing such a dialogue early in the process of developing federal oversight policy offers the best chance to arrive at mutually acceptable policies, and we call upon university presidents to take a more active and constructive role.

One of the most contentious issues of OMB Circular A−21 is effort reporting. This is required of all investigators receiving salary reimbursement from federally sponsored research projects. Each investigator, or a supervisor with first-hand knowledge, must report periodically the share of total effort spent on the project, so that federal auditors can see if it matches the percent of salary included in the research project's budget, and reduce the salary reimbursement if it falls short. This after-the-fact certification of effort generates considerable resentment and friction among university investigators and administrators, in part because of the volume of paperwork it produces, and in part because they believe that the information they are asked to produce, and then to justify to federal auditors, is meaningless. Many investigators believe that the partitioning of activity that effort reporting seeks to record simply does not take place, and they routinely report levels precisely equal to the figures given in their research proposals. This arouses auditors' suspicions that the investigators are concealing lower levels than justified by salary reimbursement, and leads to government efforts to disallow the entire reimbursement.

The Commission is not convinced of the need for detailed effort documentation. Given a choice between methods of effort documentation, we prefer a system which sets commitments or targets before the fact for a researcher's participation in a research project and requires adherence to them, rather than one which attempts to measure participation after the fact. This is much closer to the spirit in which investigators undertake projects, and can provide accountability for the level of effort with less paperwork, friction, and dispute than after-the-fact certification of effort.

Such an approach is embodied in the monitored workload method of effort reporting developed by the Committee on Government Relations of the National Association of College and University Business Officers, and adopted with some changes by OMB as an alternative to after-the-fact certification of effort in the recent revision of Circular A−21.

University administrators have not expressed great interest in switching over to the monitored effort workload system, despite its apparent advantages. Over the years, they have devised ways of dealing with after-the-fact certification and the way in which it is audited, and they have a natural tendency to resist change, reinforced by their opposition to a few specific provisions in the OMB version. Nevertheless, we believe monitored workload is a substantial improvement that university administrators should seriously consider adopting, while pursuing further refinements in the standards and procedures of financial oversight.

Recommendation 3

Responsibility for financial oversight of all academic research grants and contracts, regardless of the source of funding or the recipient, should be transferred to a new Office of Inspector General, attached to the National Science Foundation but reporting directly to the National Science Board.

Reform of Procedure. The Commission believes that the efficiency of the present process of federal financial oversight of academic research must be improved. The burdens on both investigators and administrators need to be reduced. We recommend the development of a corps of federal auditors thoroughly familiar with the nature of scientific research and with the operation of research universities.

At present, financial oversight for about 80 percent of all federal research grants and contracts awarded to colleges and universities is performed by the audit agency of the Department of Health and Human Services (HHS), in accordance with the rule that the agency funding the most research at an institution has cognizance for financial oversight there.

HHS auditors are well-trained in cost accounting, but they often have little experience in dealing with research institutions, receive limited training to familiarize them with auditing of academic research, and typically are assigned to a particular institution for a short time.

Cost accounting at a university—even a university with excellent accounting controls—is quite different from that used by profit-making institutions, and is likely to appear foreign and chaotic to an auditor who is accustomed to dealing with easily identifiable cost centers and close administrative control over personnel.

Since sponsored research is only a small part of HHS's total program or of its oversight responsibilities, its auditors must be trained to deal with a wide variety of institutions and activities and do not develop the familiarity with research oversight necessary for its smooth and efficient operation. The experience of the few research universities audited by the Defense Contracts Audit Agency (DCAA) demonstrates the possibilities. They do not share the complaints of the majority, and find the process well-managed, though rigorous.

We believe that the National Science Foundation is in the best position to assume responsibility for auditing academic research. It understands the research process thoroughly and its total span of activity is small enough to allow it to give enough attention to auditing responsibilities.

In order to maintain a clear separation between the award and administration of research grants by the NSF and the financial oversight of these (and other agencies') grants by the Inspector General's Office, the two should operate as independent bodies, each reporting directly to the National Science Board. The DCAA might well provide some auditors to a new agency for its core staff.

We recommend that all auditors assigned to the Inspector General's Office go through a period of training to familiarize them with the accounting practices of research universities, and that the Office maintain some continuity in the audit team assigned to each institution for successive audits. These provisions are aimed at further improving the familiarity of federal auditors with academic research. We recognize that familiarity with research universities can foster an identification of the auditor's interests with those of the institution. We think that this tendency, if held well short of capture of the regulator by the regulated, is not necessarily a drawback; it could reduce the tension of the oversight process and improve its overall effectiveness. We note that the Internal Revenue Service has oversight procedures fairly close to those proposed here, and it finds that these practices do not subvert its auditing process.

Level of Funding

Recommendation 4

The Administration and the Congress should set long-term targets for basic research spending with provision for modest real growth, and implement these targets with multi-year authorizations for all federal agencies that fund basic research, in order to achieve more stability in the funding of academic research.

Need for Modest Real Growth. Basic research serves as a kind of overhead activity, a necessary ingredient in the growth of our economy. In these terms, the scale of the research enterprise is measured not by its absolute size, but by its size relative to the economy as a whole. If the share of gross national product invested in basic research diminishes, then its role in supporting the economy also diminishes. And the cost of failing to maintain an adequate science base, upon which growth and technological innovation depend, is likely to be greater than the cost of spending somewhat more on basic research than can be strictly demonstrated to be necessary.

Therefore, as the economy expands, our investment in basic research should at least grow to keep pace. This translates to a long-term rate of real growth between two and three percent annually—roughly equal to the growth in academic research funding that we have experienced over the past five years.

The Commission believes it is important for federal support of the humanities and humanistic social sciences, also to grow in real terms. There is a unity in all research and scholarship that transcends disciplinary boundaries and methodological differences. The university is an ideal place for basic research, precisely because knowledge in all fields is pursued for its own sake rather than for practical results. A narrow focus on natural science, based on practical consideration, even if self-imposed, will ultimately dampen the intellectual curiosity that sustains research and higher education as a whole.

Importance of Stable Funding.   The suddenness of the cessation of funding growth in 1969, and the fluctuations in levels since then, contributed at least as much to the financial squeeze affecting academic science as the halt in growth itself. Even when the aggregate funding level remains roughly constant, the funds available to some agencies and to some fields of science decrease as other agencies and disciplines receive a larger share. Congress, the funding agencies, and the scientific community should try to agree on long-term targets for funding levels and adhere to them over a period of several years. Whatever the rate of growth ultimately settled on, the gain in planning certainty for researchers would be beneficial. This requires the relevant committees in Congress to coordinate their deliberations in an unaccustomed way. The effort to achieve such coordination will be justified by its benefits.

We therefore recommend the adoption of five-year authorizations for all federal research programs to introduce stability into the funding process. The Office of Science and Technology Policy should formulate a comprehensive five-year budget plan, consulting with the various funding agencies, the Office of Management and Budget, and the Congressional Budget Office in order to develop proposed levels that meet with general approval. These proposals should then serve as the basis for five-year authorizations for each agency, as well as a guidepost for annual appropriations.

Several funding agencies already receive multi-year authorizations for research and development, and the Office of Science and Technology Policy is already empowered to coordinate R&D expenditures in the budget process. Thus the recommendation does not represent a major departure from the way in which research funding levels are now set, and by itself will not guarantee stability. The critical ingredient is an Executive and Congressional commitment to set and abide by long-term targets for research funding.

Stability for the Individual Investigator.   Stability is also important at the level of individual research projects. Currently grants made by the major funding agencies to individual investigators are usually for one to five years with relatively pro-forma annual renewals during that period. At the end of the grant period, the investigator must submit a new proposal. If it is rejected the project is abruptly terminated.

The system of step funding developed within the Department of Defense, and subsequently adopted by the National Aeronautics and Space Administration (NASA), is a considerable improvement. Under it, funding is provided for a number of years, but at declining levels toward the end of the grant. The investigator files annual renewals, just as before. Periodically, he or she submits a proposal to have additional years of full funding inserted into the sequence. This goes through the normal peer review procedure. At every stage, the investigator is assured of funds to phase out the project in an orderly fashion over several years, if the extension is denied. This assurance would be subject to the standards imposed by the annual renewal process and, of course, the constraints of the agency's annual appropriation.

New Emphases and Reallocations

The next group of recommendations (5 through 8) are ones the Commission proposes because of the end of growth in federal funding of basic research and scholarship. During the period of rapid growth, the project grant or contract that supports joint work undertaken by a small group of investigators emerged as the primary mechanism of funding. At that time, universities found it easy to finance many other necessary research activities that did not easily fit into the project mold. The ever-increasing volume of project grants made it possible for universities to find the money for graduate and postgraduate fellowships, for equipment purchase, and for other expenditures that today are very difficult to support. The Commission believes it is now necessary to shift some resources away from projects toward these other purposes in order to provide balanced support for academic research. These new emphases concern the flow of trained manpower and the preservation of universities' capability to do basic research. They include: insuring a steady flow of students into graduate study and postdoctoral research, supporting language and area studies, constructing and improving laboratories and equipment, helping academic libraries, and providing some general discretionary research funds.

Recommendation 5

The National Science Foundation and the National Institutes of Health should join in funding a new National Postdoctoral Fellowship Competition, which would annually award 1,000 fully portable fellowships in all fields of science, each for two years of support and renewable for a second two-year period. Further, each of the major funding agencies should fund a small number of new National Research Fellowships for young researchers in the next stage of their careers. We propose the eventual creation of 300 such fellowships, each carrying five years of support, for research on university campuses, at Federally Funded Research and Development Centers, or at intramural federal laboratories.

Scientific Manpower. A serious scientific manpower problem is developing. The health of the scientific enterprise requires a steady flow of talented young people into graduate study and postdoctoral research. Barring unforeseen and unlikely developments, such as a dramatic increase in federal funding for academic research, the prospects for academic employment over the next fifteen or so years will be sufficiently bleak to discourage many of the brightest young people. This has the likely consequence of loss of vitality and creativity in the ongoing corps of scientists, insufficiently renewed by a continuing influx of young talent.

Throughout the 1950s and early 1960s, the dramatic growth in federal funding of research, combined with growth in enrollments, encouraged many universities to expand their faculties in natural science departments rapidly. As a result a large number of tenured faculty positions are now filled by relatively young scientists, and the rate of attrition through retirement is, and will remain for some time, lower than normal. At the same time, the decline in undergraduate enrollments will reduce the number of teaching positions available.

The consequences are already being felt—promising young scientists face drastically reduced prospects and the academic job market will become even tighter in the future. The manpower problem is more serious in some fields, such as physics and pure mathematics, than in others, such as engineering and psychology, but almost none will be entirely unaffected. The problem will persist at least until the late 1990s when both enrollments and retirement rates are expected to return to normal.

Recently, between ten and fifteen thousand Ph.D. recipients have been hired each year as college or university faculty. In the next dozen or so years, this number will decline sharply, perhaps dropping to as low as 3,500. The proportion of Ph.D.'s getting faculty appointments averaged 50 percent until recently; it is now about 30 percent, and may decline to as low as 10 percent.

We do not have a clear understanding of all the factors that influence career choices of young scientists. But, willingness to enter graduate schools and to join the more junior ranks of academic researchers depends in part on opportunities for rewarding research careers in government, industry, or non-profit institutions outside higher education. However, the same funding trends that have reduced federal support for academic scientists have also reduced research opportunities in other sectors.

Providing short-term support for new Ph.D.'s can provide some relief, until enrollments and job prospects recover fifteen or so years from now. We consider the current manpower problem to be sufficiently pressing to justify shifting some resources away from traditional research projects in order to support young researchers in the first few years of their careers.

The proposed National Postdoctoral Fellowship Competition would support 1,000 new fellows each year, about 4,000 fellowships once the program reaches maturity. There are now close to 9,000 postdoctoral fellows, most supported by project grants and contracts of their faculty advisors, and many of the new awards would simply displace such fellowships. However, the proposed National Postdoctoral Fellowship should be far more attractive to young scientists. Awarded directly through a national competition, it would give them a degree of freedom to develop their own research topics and methods at institutions of their own choosing, a more well-defined and prestigious status within the universities, and longer tenure than is now enjoyed by most postdoctoral fellows.

The most promising would compete for an additional five years of support from a National Research Fellowship Competition to be run along similar lines. Together, these two programs would offer those contemplating research careers a greater chance to do research, at modest levels of support, for as many as nine years. Those who emerge from the last step of this abbreviated career track would still face a depressed market, but we believe that they would then have skills and experience to help them find worthwhile employment: academic research positions for some, and government, non-profit sector, or industrial jobs for others.

The proposed National Postdoctoral Fellowship Competition would cost about $60 million annually in fellowship stipends, and the National Research Fellowship Competition would cost another $30 million; this assumes annual stipends of $15 and $20 thousand respectively. An additional $10 million should be budgeted for research allowances, to be allocated among fellowship recipients by the awards committee. Universities would be expected to augment their fellows' research allowances. Both programs should be funded by rebudgeting current programs within each agency, with no increase in overall appropriations.

Undergraduate Research Support. Colleges that are primarily undergraduate institutions play a significant role in the flow of new talent into science, by producing a large number of students who go on to Ph.D. programs. Research at the college level is generally different from that performed at leading universities, but if talented young people are to choose research careers and receive the training that equips them to pursue those careers, they need teachers actively investigating some research questions and thus better able to point out the gaps in current knowledge, the problems of designing good experiments, and the diversity of science.

The colleges have a hard time encouraging research because of geographic isolation, the heavy teaching loads of their faculty, and limited financial resources. Research facilities and equipment, as necessary to them as to major universities, are often scarce and out-of-date, yet virtually no federal funds for plant and equipment are awarded to baccalaureate colleges.

In fiscal year 1977, primarily undergraduate institutions received $85 million in federal research funds; only 3 percent of the national total for academic research. Yet those funds play a critical role in maintaining research programs at undergraduate colleges. If the desire to concentrate funds on established research-producing universities is allowed to encroach upon the support of research at undergraduate institutions, many liberal arts colleges will not be able to offer training to prepare students for graduate studies in the sciences, and the number of colleges that can attract undergraduates with strong science interests will diminish.

Some expenditures are directed specifically to recruiting, by supporting the involvement of undergraduates in research. In fiscal 1979, the National Science Foundation spent $2.9 million on two programs which supported research by about 1,500 undergraduates at about 175 colleges and universities. This funding has declined in recent years—it totalled $5 million in 1972—and only Congressional intervention has prevented the Foundation from ending both programs. Support of undergraduate research has an important role to play in infusing new talent into the scientific enterprise and developing the research skills of promising young students. We believe this support should be maintained.

Language and Area Studies. For the past twenty years, the federal government has funded academic research and graduate fellowships in foreign language and area studies centers in universities and colleges. Funding was authorized under the National Defense Education Act of 1958, to ensure a supply of trained specialists on the grounds of national security. The Departments of Defense and State and the intelligence agencies needed the services of experts fluent in the languages who understood the history and cultures of countries throughout the world.

Expenditures reached a peak in the late 1960s, when 106 centers received federal funds. Since then, the number of centers decreased to 80, and the average level of support, measured in constant dollars, declined by 60 percent. The number of fellowships awarded annually declined from more than 2,500 to about 800 in the same period. Funding by private foundations—primarily the Ford Foundation, whose support once equalled that of the federal government—has declined to almost zero.

The need for expert knowledge of foreign languages and cultures is as great today as it was ten years ago, but the current level of support in these fields may not provide a sufficient reserve of knowledge and trained manpower required for national defense, foreign affairs, and international trade. The need for federal intervention is greatest in the case of those regions of the world which generate the least interest within universities and the least outside demand for experts. Without federal assistance, universities may neglect relatively obscure countries, and knowledge of their languages and cultures—knowledge that could be critically important in the future—may be lost.

A Presidential Commission on International Education (the Perkins Commission) has just reported on foreign language and area studies, among other topics. Its recommendations provide the basis for a careful federal review of manpower policies in this area.

Recommendation 6

A new competitive program of Research Facilities Grants should provide $50 million annually for laboratory facilities and equipment.

Laboratory Plant and Equipment. In pure mathematics and theoretical physics, it is still possible to do research with little more than pencil and paper. In most disciplines, however, research requires space in laboratories and access to elaborate equipment and instrumentation, the cost of which escalates rapidly as the state of scientific knowledge and the level of inquiry advance. Investigators with only modestly equipped laboratories are unable to undertake the most important and productive experiments.

Federal obligations to academic institutions for the construction of new laboratories and the purchase of laboratory equipment fell from a peak of $126 million in fiscal 1965 to $24 million in fiscal 1976—a decline in real terms of 89 percent. Many universities have fallen far behind in maintaining up-to-date facilities, and for the first time since before World War II one hears American scientists speaking enviously of the laboratories and instrumentation available in Europe. We therefore recommend that a total of $50 million be divided between the National Science Foundation and the National Institutes of Health in each of the next five years, for a program of Research Facilities Grants to upgrade research laboratories and equipment at universities and colleges. Awards should be made on the basis of a peer-reviewed grant competition, but the criteria used to make awards should be broad enough to encompass the goal of supporting research at undergraduate institutions, as well as at major research universities.

Recommendation 7

Academic research libraries should receive increased support for collection development and preservation.

Research Libraries. Academic libraries are the basic resource for research and scholarship in the humanities and social sciences, one that is rapidly becoming more costly and complex. The annual cost of maintaining a major research library is now about $10 million and is increasing by more than 10 percent each year. There is widespread agreement that this rate of growth in library expenditures cannot be sustained, and widespread fear that universities are running out of time to bring library costs under control.

The great strength of academic research libraries lies in the comprehensiveness of their collections and in their ability to continue to provide the publications needed through new acquisitions. The rising cost of buying and cataloging new books and periodicals forces libraries to become more selective in their acquisition policies. In the future, only a very few will have the resources to maintain strong, self-contained collections in every discipline. For the most part, collection development and management will have to become more of a cooperative venture, with each library concentrating on areas of particular strength and relying to a greater extent on other libraries for infrequently requested publications.

Strained budgets also make it difficult for libraries to find the resources to protect their collections from physical deterioration. Since the mid-nineteenth century, most books have been printed on paper with a high acid content. The acid, combined with moisture in the atmosphere, can make them unusable within fifty years. In many libraries, the number of volumes needing attention runs as high as 30 percent of total holdings. Preserving these collections requires expenditures that colleges and universities cannot afford.

Air conditioning of stacks would slow the process of deterioration; it is costly. But volumes already in an advanced state of deterioration need individual treatment: either de-acidification of the paper or transfer to other forms of storage such as microfilm. If preservation resources are to be used efficiently, cooperation is needed for each library to decide where its efforts should be concentrated.

The principal obstacles to greater cooperation are organizational rather than financial. Federal appropriations in support of academic libraries, authorized by Title II of the Higher Education Act, totalled $19 million in fiscal year 1979, of which roughly $4 million supported inter-library cooperation. Additional funds or services are provided by the Library of Congress, the National Endowment for the Humanities, and several private foundations. Capital expenditures for preservation require no inter-library cooperations; we, therefore, see no reason to delay an increase in federal expenditures for this purpose. Where cooperative activities are concerned, however, what is needed now is not an immediate infusion of new money, but rather the development by colleges and universities of institutional arrangements to promote greater sharing of resources and division of collection responsibilities. The development of those arrangements, described in the following paragraphs, is well underway. As it proceeds, it will become possible to use effectively an investment of additional federal funds for collection development and preservation.

In an effort to hold down operating expenses and increase efficiency, universities and colleges recently began to make use of centralized computer networks to facilitate the acquisitions process. Since 1968, the Library of Congress has had machine-readable bibliographic data on all of its acquisitions. This allows colleges and universities to identify a requested book, and to obtain the information needed to catalog it quickly and inexpensively.

A few academic libraries operate their own computer systems, but the great majority are members of one of three networks: the Ohio College Library Center, linked to several smaller regional networks; the Research Libraries Information Network; and the Washington Library Network. These provide on-line access to the Library of Congress bibliographic data, and data provided by member libraries where that volume can be found, thereby creating a master file of the holdings. Finally, the networks provide on-line access to additional, specialized data bases and abstracting services to aid library staff, and in some cases individual researchers, in conducting bibliographic searches.

These capabilities make bibliographic networking an ideal vehicle for facilitating the process of sharing library resources: for expanding inter-library loan programs, organizing cooperative programs for collection development, designating particular libraries as repositories of little-used books and periodicals, and coordinating preservation efforts. Some progress has been made but their full potential will not be realized until the three principal networks are linked together so that each library has access to all of the records. There is a natural tendency for academic research libraries to resist any cost-saving arrangements that may sacrifice the completeness of their collections. This tendency will be more easily overcome when each library is assured the rapid and dependable access to all materials, whatever their location, that a comprehensive bibliographic network can provide.

Two of the principal networks—The Research Libraries Information Network and the Washington Library Network—recently agreed to share their bibliographic data. The Ohio College Library Center—the oldest and largest network with approximately 2,600 members—has not yet agreed. However, a Bibliographic Service Development Program has been organized by the Council on Library Resources, with $5 million in funding provided by seven foundations and NEH, for the expressed purpose of solving the technical and organizational problems involved in fully linking all three networks.

The funds now available, from public and private sources, should be sufficient to bring about the creation of an integrated national bibliographic network. Once accomplished, federal support for academic libraries under Title II of the Higher Education Act should be increased to and maintained at its full authorized level of $25 million. The increase—some $6 million annually above 1979 funding—should be used to develop individual collections that can serve the needs of many libraries, and to fund a national preservation program.

The collection development program would award grants, usually to libraries with unique collections in specific fields, but in some cases to free-standing organizations such as the proposed National Periodicals Center. Grants could be used both to finance new acquisitions and to generate and merge into the national network bibliographic and other data, so that those collections will be maximally accessible to all college and university libraries.

The preservation program would support research on techniques that will increase the speed and lower the cost of preserving library materials. However, most of the funds should support the preservation efforts of individual academic libraries, using the resources of the national bibliographic network to set preservation priorities.

Recommendation 8

Every funding agency should provide funds for general research support, equal to 7 percent of the direct costs of each research grant and contract awarded.

Need for General Research Funds. The four forms of funding discussed above—traditional project grants, research fellowships, research facilities grants, and library assistance—will still fail to provide support for all research activities within a university. Resources will still be needed to support promising junior faculty who have not yet established their reputations, to assist in building research projects to the point where they can attract federal support, and to fill in the gaps left by federal grants that do not quite cover the full costs of the research that they support. We believe that providing a small amount of general research funds for these purposes will strengthen academic science, even if it means that slightly fewer projects can be supported.

We therefore recommend that every research grant and contract awarded to a university or college should carry with it an additional amount equal to 7 percent of the project's modified total direct costs, to be used in support of research, and so accounted for.

The central university administration is in a better position than any single department to decide which departments and institutes are most in need of general research funds. Accordingly, part of the funds should go directly to the department or center in which the research associated with the funds takes place, but part should be allocated among departments and centers by the central administration. Universities should not be allowed to spend any general research funds on indirect costs of research, or on any unrelated costs. General research funds should come from the funding agency's current budget, with no increase in overall appropriations.

Federal Restraint in Regulating Potentially Hazardous Research

Recommendation 9

In regulating potentially hazardous research, the federal government should not impose rigid and exceedingly detailed rules, or remove responsibility from those now evaluating hazardous research at the local level, including the researchers themselves, when they are effective in protecting the public health and safety, the welfare of human subjects of research, or the safety of laboratories.

The issues involved in regulation of potentially hazardous research are complex. They have been well-demonstrated recently in the case of recombinant DNA research. The basis for regulation is traditional, and eminently reasonable: public health and safety. Problems arise because of conflicts in judgment about what the risks are. At a higher level there are conflicts about whose opinions and judgments deserve credit. In this case, the consensus of the relevant scientific community was followed, and the adoption of wider and more stringent regulations was forestalled. Such problems will continue to arise, and will continue to be resolved by the political process. Where scientific opinion is divided, the results will always be displeasing to some experts. The federal government should refrain from enacting laws or issuing regulations that attempt to deal with all such issues in one broad stroke.

In the case of the complex of regulations involving experimentation with human subjects there are genuine conflicts of value involved, as well as problems of judging risks in light of imperfect knowledge. How the conflicting value of the knowledge that researchers wish to gain and the privacy and personal welfare that potential subjects wish to preserve can be balanced is not an issue for scientists alone to resolve. It is our judgment that the federal requirement that sponsored projects involving research on human subjects must be approved by Institutional Review Boards (IRBs) with mixed membership does provide an adequate voice to non-scientists in deciding this kind of issue.

However, the Department of Health and Human Services is now revising its regulations governing human subjects research to implement the recommendations of a recent national commission. Those recommendations would extend the requirements for informed consent and for IRB review far beyond the original focus on research that poses physical risks to subjects. They include much of behavioral and social science research as well. They would also give HHS greater authority to dictate the procedures used by IRBs and would require them to lay down an audit trail to justify their decisions to federal regulators. Both the extension of scope of review, and the preemption of IRB authority would make the review process much more cumbersome, yet no more effective in safeguarding the welfare of human research subjects. The Commission believes this is an unnecessary and undesirable extension.

Regulations governing the use of hazardous substances in the research laboratory can be imposed without unreasonably constraining academic research, as evidenced by the wide acceptance of federal standards on the handling of radioactive materials. However, some of the more recently developed regulations, such as those proposed by the Occupational Safety and Health Administration (OSHA) to cover the use of hazardous substances and potential carcinogens, do raise a problem.

The OSHA regulations were written primarily to deal with the use of hazardous substances in industrial processes, which involve vastly greater quantities of many fewer different substances than are typically encountered in a research laboratory. The regulations impose stringent requirements for monitoring the ambient levels of hundreds of substances, and they require detailed record-keeping of possible exposures and monitoring procedures.

The OSHA regulations create a burden of compliance that is far out of proportion to the risks presented by the use of hazardous substances in the research laboratory. The Commission believes that these regulations must be re-examined before they can reasonably be extended to govern the use of small research quantities of potentially harmful substances in academic laboratories.

Chapter 7

Government and the Education of Physicians

INTRODUCTION

B ecause academic medical centers have a large place in Amercan health care, they have attracted much government attention and a deep federal involvement. The government has been ready to use direct controls in dealing with medical schools that it has not used so far in any other part of the university.

Medical schools, their affiliated hospitals, and research centers produce the central resource of our health care system-physicians. They also are major centers of biomedical research, both basic and applied (clinical). In these respects, they are like other parts of the university: they train professionals and carry on research.

But academic medical centers have a function that has no parallel in the rest of higher education. They provide the public with a highly valued essential service. They account for nearly all of tertiary acute care hospital beds, and about one-third of all acute care beds. In many areas, university hospitals are the only places where certain complex medical procedures are performed.

In the United States, as in other industrialized countries, access to health care is increasingly viewed as a right, and the federal government has more and more taken the responsibility of insuring that it is provided. The government is now the largest single purchaser of health care: Medicare, Medicaid, other federal welfare programs, the End Stage Renal Disease program, and several smaller federal programs account for more than 40 percent of all acute care expenditures. In addition, the government pays for more than nine-tenths of the costs of biomedical research and one-third of the costs of constructing new medical and hospital facilities.

We now spend more on health care than any other nation, both per capita and as a share of gross national product. Further changes in government's responsibilities for health care are in the offing. Though it is impossible to predict just what form they will take, it is clear that we can look forward to increased federal responsibility, expenditure, and concern with academic medical centers.

1. Since its earliest form was research support, some of the federal involvement with medical education was parallel to that with universities in general. Federal support of biomedical and clinical research grew even more rapidly than that of other fields. Between 1958–59 and 1967–68, medical school budgets increased 2.8 times, funds for federal research programs increased 5.3 times, and federal training grants increased even more rapidly, growing 6.7 times. By 1968–69, more than half the full-time faculty members in medical schools received all or part of their salaries from federal grants and contracts.

This influx of federal money stimulated a spurt of growth in medical school faculties. During this period, when the number of undergraduate medical students increased only 17 percent, and the number of interns and residents about 40 percent, the total full-time faculty of the medical schools more than doubled, and the clinical faculty increased about two-and-a-half times.

2. The second strand of government activity, starting in 1963, was an effort to stimulate an increase in the output of physicians. In the previous decade the output had been growing at little more than 1 percent per year on the average, less than the rate of growth in population. The first Health Professions Education Act (1963) provided for educational loans to stu-

dents and construction grants for medical schools and their affiliated hospitals. Legislation in succeeding years (1965, 1968, and 1972) broadened these incentives, adding in 1972 direct cost of education supplements tied to enrollments (capitation) for schools increasing their number of graduates.

The same period saw the enactment of the first substantial federal payment programs for health care: Medicare and Medicaid. The profession and the medical schools, as well as federal officials, foresaw the consequent increase in the demand for physicians, and strongly supported an expansion of enrollments. The combination of federal incentive and support by the medical profession was effective; by 1978 the first year class reached 16,000, twice its 1962 number. In relation to population, the growth was 1.7 times.

Here again, as in the support of research, there was a parallel between what the federal government did in medical education, and what it had done earlier in the rest of the university. The National Defense Education Act (1958), passed as a response to Sputnik, used a mix of fellowships, loans, and cost-of-construction allowances to stimulate increased enrollments in undergraduate and graduate programs in science, engineering, and foreign languages. Five years later, legislation provided construction grants for new facilities as well. The parallel was there, but again the relative weight of federal dollars was greater in the medical center than in the rest of the university.

3. As the supply of medical places grew, demand for them grew even faster. In the late 1950s and early 1960s there were some 1.7 or 1.8 applicants for each of the roughly 8,500 places in the freshman class of U.S. medical schools. By 1975, the size of the freshman class had nearly doubled, but there were now 2.8 applicants for each place. In the last two years, the ratio decreased somewhat; in 1978–79 it was 2.2. With the greatly increased competition for places, the standards for admission have grown more stringent, and young men and women who would have been accepted a decade or even five years ago are now turned down. The choice becomes more and more difficult to make. It is widely agreed by medical school deans and admissions officers that at least twice the number of candidates admitted are capable of completing the present programs and becoming competent physicians. One consequence of the continued oversupply of applicants is that increasing numbers of

young American men and women go abroad for training, at admittedly inferior schools. The Autonomous University of Guadalajara in Mexico is the largest American medical school; its 2,600 American students form a student body twice as big as that of the largest U.S. school. The total number of Americans studying abroad is unknown, but probably exceeds 6,000.

NEW FOCUS OF FEDERAL POLICY

1. Despite the surge in demand, the rising costs of medical education and doubts about the need for even more physicians, brought an end to federal policies of expansion in the mid-seventies. In the Health Professions Assistance Act of 1976, the Congress shifted its focus from the total number of M.D.'s produced to their specialty training. The Act declared that "there is no longer an insufficient number of physicians and surgeons in the United States." At the same time, turning from aggregate numbers to distribution by specialty, the Act provided that schools had to train a certain proportion of their graduates for primary care rather than more specialized practice in order to continue to receive capitation. Finally, in another direct intervention into the internal workings of medical schools, the Act instructed each school to provide a certain (small) number of places in its third year class for Americans who passed Part I of the National Medical Boards after training abroad, again on pain of losing capitation. In these particulars, direct manpower planning had replaced the offer of incentives as the instrument used by the government in dealing with the medical schools. This was a novelty. There is still no parallel in the rest of the university. Meanwhile, funds for capitation were reduced, and current plans call for capitation to end entirely by 1982

However, planning and direct controls are by no means novel in government's dealing with the health care sector. Both hospitals and physicians have been the objects of federally legislated control and review programs aimed at reducing the cost of medical care, or at least limiting its rate of increase. Certificate of Need programs, administered by a network of Area Health Systems Agencies, were instituted to control building and equipment costs by preventing competitive expansions and duplication by hospitals in the same locality. Professional Standards Review Organizations were created to provide quality controls on physicians, eliminate unnecessary tests and surgical procedures, and reduce the length of hospital stays.

Almost all of what the government has done or is doing in the medical schools is simply part of this general sweep, aimed at controlling the cost of medical care and at the same time making care more widely available. Indeed, the chief basis for the change in federal policy on the production of M.D.'s from one that encouraged and paid for expansion to one that called for restriction was the belief that we both have enough physicians and that each new physician adds further to the costs of medical care. The strongest form of this belief is the "target-income hypothesis." This says that physicians have predetermined earning goals that depend on location, on type of practice, and on the conventional standards of their community of colleagues. By deciding on the frequency of patients' return visits, the number and character of tests prescribed, and so forth, doctors raise their earnings to this target. In this view, an increase in the number of physicians serving a given community, with a corresponding decrease in the average number of patients each one sees, results only in a compensating rise in the amount and cost of care that the average patient receives.

The strong form of this hypothesis is arguable, and the evidence inconclusive. Nonetheless, it is clear that "overdoctoring" can exist, especially in the context of specialty practice, and that unnecessary surgery and iatrogenic illnesses are not merely rare aberrations.

2. A number of aspects of the current provision of medical care insulate it from the ordinary economic working of the market place. The single most important is the institution of third-party payment—by insurors or the government—combined with the typical fee-for-service basis of physicians' charges. Under these arrangements, both patient and physician are shielded from the usual economic incentives governing market transactions. The patient has no reason to look for less costly providers and the physician has no incentive to be cost conscious in his choice of procedures. There are institutional elements in the patient–physician relation that work in the same direction. First is the inevitable ignorance of the average patient about the correct type, quality, or quantity of treatment appropriate to any particular problem. Once a patient consults a physician about a health problem, he or she has no independent basis for ques-

tioning the course of treatment. Second is what has been called the Principle of Medical Uncertainty. In any situation involving continuing illness, as long as there is one more thing that might be done—another consultation, a new drug, another treatment—both patient and doctor are inclined to do it. If the costs are covered by a third party neither has an incentive to consider the additional expense.

3. Government's attempt to influence the distribution of physicians between specialists and providers of primary or family care reflects its concerns with both the costs and availability of care, and their probably inconsistent goals of reducing cost while increasing availability. Specialty medicine is viewed as high-cost medicine, involving unusual problems, hospital practice, and high-technology equipment. In contrast, primary care is seen as dealing with everyday ills in an ambulatory setting. The increasing scientific sophistication of medicine and the great growth of clinical research helped stimulate a shift away from general practice to the specialties and subspecialties. In 1950, nearly two-thirds of the physicians in private practice in the United States were in general practice. By 1965, the proportion had fallen below four-tenths, and by 1973 below one-fifth. Specialty training grew longer, and the minimum length of post M.D. training that qualified a physician for certification in a specialty reached four years, with some surgical and neurological residencies extending to six or seven. Further, Medicare and Medicaid made possible the payment of salaries to residents, thus reducing the young doctor's financial sacrifice and at the same time increasing the share of training costs paid by the public. This change was a further stimulus to increasing the length of post M.D. training.

The growth of specialization has also been one of the elements leading to a highly uneven geographic distribution of doctors. Physicians are concentrated in and near large urban areas, and prefer to practice in academic medical centers, and in middle and upper income urban or suburban neighborhoods. Rural areas and poor urban neighborhoods are relatively underserved. This distribution reflects obvious economic forces. Neither thinly populated areas with little in the way of elaborate hospital facilities nor poor urban ghettos are attractive locations for practice so long as physicians can earn high incomes in locations both more attractive and better provided with the elaborate hospital resources used heavily in specialized medicine. In 1973, physicians were more than twice as plentiful in proportion to population in metropolitan as in non-metropolitan areas.

CONTINUING AND EMERGING PROBLEMS

1. The uneven distribution of physicians by specialty and location will continue as problems for both the cost and availability of medical care. Since the government seems to have chosen the instruments of planning and command to deal with these questions, the academic medical centers can look forward to even deeper involvement with government. The medical schools in the public universities may increasingly tie admission to a commitment to practice within the state for a period of time, as some already do. There is now substantial interstate movement of newly graduated M.D.'s going on to residencies; this movement will be constrained, with some disadvantages in terms of the matching of post-graduate training opportunities to the trainee's interests and capabilities. Further efforts by the government to affect the specialty distribution may reach more deeply into the medical curriculum, affecting programs for the M.D. degree, as well as post-graduate training in residencies.

2. The cost of medical education is likely to become a matter of greater concern. What many in government see as the problem of cross-subsidization—the extent to which research grants and patient-care revenues are used to meet the costs of instruction—is already much discussed. Among the 1978 amendments to the Social Security Act were provisions requiring hospitals to separate training costs from patient-care costs that were reimbursed from Medicare and Medicaid funds. The government's desire to constrain the rising costs of hospital care will lead to further stringencies in this respect. The efforts of auditing agencies to design accounting procedures aimed at the complete segregation of the costs of research from other institutional costs push in the same direction. These efforts are likely to affect undergraduate medical training—that is, of candidates for the M.D.—while those directed at reimbursements for patient-care costs will affect chiefly post-graduates—residents.

These developments, in addition to the end of capitation, are putting further pressures on medical schools to increase their tuitions. These now range from $3,000 per year to $12,500 in private medical schools; the median is about $5,400. Tuitions for in-state residents in the public schools range from $150 to $6,000 with a median of $1,750; for out-of-state residents the range is $750 to $14,500, with a median of $3,200.

Tuition covers the average cost of training in only a few schools. Estimating the costs of training candidates for the M.D. in the complex multi-activity setting of the academic medical center presents formidable problems of allocation. A study by the Institute of Medicine of the National Academy of Sciences in 1974 showed annual costs ranging from $6,900 per student per year to $18,650, with an average of $13,800. At today's prices, these figures would have increased to about $10,000, $27,000, and $20,000, respectively.

If these estimates are at all near the mark, colossal further increases in tuition would be required to replace the subsidies now supporting medical education, coming chiefly from the state, but with a still important share from the federal government. Or put conversely, the complete withdrawal of federal funds that help to support undergraduate medical education, especially those providing indirect help through research support and reimbursement for patient-care, would put medical schools in a difficult position. The private ones might be forced to triple their tuitions or close their doors.

3. Another persistent problem in the relations between government and the medical schools is minority admissions. Beginning at least a decade ago, the schools and the profession recognized that in the past, medical schools had discriminated against Black and other minority candidates. Acting on this recognition, and with assistance from the federal government, the schools, collectively through the Association of American Medical Colleges (AAMC), and individually, made a substantial effort to increase minority enrollment. The proportion of Black students among all freshmen rose sharply from about 2.5 percent in the 1950s and 1960s to 7.5 percent in 1975. In the 1950s, three-quarters of all Black students were enrolled in the two Black medical schools, Howard and Meharry. By 1975, more than 80 percent of the much larger number were spread throughout the predominantly white schools. Over the same period Black enrollments in all of higher education doubled, from under 5 percent to nearly 10 percent.

Affirmative action made this increase possible. A higher proportion of Black applicants than white ones were admitted, and less emphasis was placed on test scores and grade point averages. The Black students who were enrolled performed satisfactorily. They achieved lower scores, on the average, than white in Part I of the National Medical Board Examinations, taken by most students at the end of the first two years of medical school. But when they graduated as M.D.'s two years later, there was every indication that their skills and achievements as apprentice clinical practitioners were on the average of their white fellow students.

After 1975, the momentum of affirmative action programs slackened. Black enrollments fell slightly in proportion to the total; in 1978—79 they were 6.4 percent. The proportion of Black applicants accepted no longer exceeded substantially their share in the total applicant pool. The reasons for this change are not clear. The celebrated *Bakke* case, which challenged the affirmative action program of the University of California at Davis, filed in 1974, was decided adversely to the University by the California Supreme Court in 1976. This decision may have tempered the willingness of admission committees to overselect Blacks. The decline in the proportion of Black applicants may show that increasing numbers of able Black college graduates are now turning to professions requiring less lengthy and expensive training.

An end to the growth in the number of medical students, which both government and the schools are seeking, will sharpen this problem. The situation will be even more difficult if the number begins to decline. The puzzles and conflicts that affirmative action generates will increase, and the counterpressures of those in the majority who feel it is essentially discriminatory will become stronger.

4. The same problems may arise in relation to women. In the past, whether or not they were explicitly discriminated against by medical schools, women were certainly not encouraged to apply. In 1968, fewer than one applicant in ten was female. In the late 1960s and 1970s attitudes changed—many more women applied and were admitted. By 1976—77, women constituted about 25 percent of the freshman class in American medical schools, and about the same proportion of the appli-

cant pool. The end of enrollment growth may halt or even reverse these gains. And, as in the case of Blacks (and other minorities), if such a change occurs, it is likely that the government will press the question of illegal discrimination, either on its own motion, or under the stimulus of complaints from those aggrieved.

Another potentially serious problem of discrimination relates to age. The typical student entering medical school is twenty-two years old; just out of college. Very few candidates over twenty-eight are accepted; one element in the original rejection of Alan Bakke by the University of California at Davis was his age. The rationale of this policy is clear—a doctor who finishes training after forty will provide less medical service over his or her lifetime than one who finishes before thirty-five. A sharply limited number of medical school places are used more efficiently when they are allotted to younger candidates. Whether this rationale, based on averages, will withstand a legal challenge under the Age Discrimination Act by a rejected thirty-year-old candidate is questionable.

5. There are indications that the underlying situation of limitation of medical school places itself may become a matter of explicit policy concern. Limitations on the number of physicians trained are traditionally justified on two grounds: the necessities of training physicians to appropriate levels of knowledge and skill, and the high costs of expanding training capacity. Both reasons appear weak in present circumstances. The increasing number of highly qualified applicants to medical schools who are not admitted makes it plain that much larger numbers of physicians could be trained. While sudden increases in numbers of students in the present modes of training in medical schools might be difficult to handle, the fundamental teaching resources in both basic sciences and clinical subjects are abundant. The slackening in the demand for training in science in graduate schools leaves nearly every university with capacity to handle more students in those basic sciences that now occupy the first two years of medical training. Further, many colleges are able to provide all or part of this training; some are already doing so. The great expansion in the number and the increase in the quality of residency training programs in hospitals other than those directly staffed by the full-time clinical faculties of the medical schools provides the second needed element. These

same hospitals can offer the clinical clerkships that form the major part of the last two years of training.

More broadly, restricting the number of American-trained doctors in order to maintain quality seems inappropriate in the face of the large number of foreign-trained physicians who now form part of the current stock, and the increasing number of Americans going to schools abroad for training of admittedly inferior quality. The number of foreign-trained M.D.'s admitted to first-year residencies in the U.S. declined sharply in 1977: 600 as compared with 2,800 in 1976. Nonetheless, foreign-trained M.D.'s still accounted for 20 percent of all residents in training programs in 1977.

Problems stemming from pressure on the limitation of places are intensifying. Affirmative action of all kinds becomes difficult when the total number of places available is static or contracting. With the large number of qualified applicants, the selection process that decides who comes through the gate becomes harder to understand and justify. Reliance on "objective" criteria means that small differences in grade point averages and test scores are given a significance that cannot be justified in terms of outcomes. The fierce competition for grades and narrow focus on "appropriate" courses among undergraduates who plan to study medicine constricts their experience of college, depriving many of them of the liberalizing spirit of experimentation and inquiry that should be an important part of the humane education of any practicing physician.

Finally, whatever the peculiarities of the market for healthcare, the high and rising income of physicians says something to the economic observer. In 1949, the ratio of the median income of physicians in private practice to that of all male college graduates was 1.66 to 1; in 1966, 2.91 to 1; in 1975, 3.45 to 1, and in 1977, 3.72 to 1. Such figures in combination with the stringent limitation on the number of places, and the substantial state and federal support for academic medical centers, signal an unstable situation that is unlikely to continue without creating great pressures for change in some part of the structure that produces such results.

To look at the matter another way, the medical schools deplore their increasing loss of autonomy to government, especially the federal government. A substantial element in that loss is the growth of manpower planning and controls as instruments of federal health policy. The shortage of places in medical schools in relation to number of qualified applicants, and the extent of federal manpower controls in medicine are uncharacteristic of most other areas of professional education, and simply absent in the rest of the system. Veterinary medicine is most similar in respect to the relative shortage of places; dentistry much less so. In the last half-dozen years, there has been a surge of applications to law schools, and the proportion of candidates admitted has fallen sharply. The ratio has now turned up again somewhat, and since law school capacity can be expanded relatively quickly and cheaply, it is too soon to say whether the sharp drop was transient. In any event, there are no federal manpower policies outside the health professions that rely on direct controls.

Newly trained physicians are the most flexible element of the health care system's manpower. The smaller their numbers, the greater will be the struggle over who should determine how they are trained and what they do. Given their relative economic and political strengths, it seems unwise for the medical schools to expect to be the victors over the federal government in the struggle.

RECOMMENDATION

A National Commission on Higher Education in the Health Professions and its relations to health care should be created. It should be charged with a detailed examination of the whole system of education in the health professions, its relation to the way we now provide and pay for health care, alternate possible ways, and their implications for education.

An analysis of the problems of the whole health care system is beyond our scope. The intimate connection between medical education and the provision of health care that intensifies the difficulties of relations between government and academic medical centers makes it hard for our Commission to recommend ways of improving them. Yet any changes in government policies toward medical education must be made with some attention to their probable interaction with changes in the health care system.

Our recommendation is a way of recognizing the incompleteness of what we have said on this complex problem, recording our sense that it is of large enough continuing consequence to require a full study of its own. The issues involved are important not only to the kind and cost of health care offered Americans, but also to the future relationship of higher education and the government.

COMMENT

Comment by William Roth, joined by Ralph Dungan and Robert Ingersoll

I am concerned that in this otherwise excellent report, an area of highest cost to government—i.e., medicine, is given summary treatment. There is only one recommendation—and not a very original one at that. This is not because the Commission failed to consider the problems of medical education in some depth, but rather that a majority was ultimately confounded by its own inexpertise in so technical and complex an area. Its modesty was unfortunate. The medical associations, as well as the Department of Health, Education, and Welfare—on dubious economic and social grounds—have taken the position that there are enough doctors being trained in American universities. This in spite of the fact that thousands of academically qualified students are forced to seek medical education out of the country—often in inferior facilities, and then return to practice in America. In addition, thousands more foreign doctors, who should be serving the sick of their own less affluent countries, staff our hospitals. Although the Commission is not competent to evaluate all aspects of so large a question, it originally offered the suggestion that medical schools be allowed to determine their own class size—as do other professional schools, and not be limited by the accrediting bodies that approve its programs. This might be a small step in the direction of allowing medical schools the freedom to respond to the market. Finally, if there is to be a new commission on medical education, I would hope that its membership would include, in addition to doctors and administrators, consumers.

Chapter 8

Why Should We Care?

W hat is the public interest in the health of higher education? Is it the same as our concern with other large sectors of the economy that give jobs to many Americans and provide goods and services for many more? Millions of people and billions of dollars are involved. But the Commission believes that the social importance is greater than these, or any numbers, can measure.

Higher education now touches nearly half the young people in the United States. Democracy needs educated citizens and depends on many kinds of leaders. Nurturing them is a primary task of colleges and universities. Graduates assume the leading positions in every kind of organization in our highly organized society. They fill the ranks of the learned professions, old and new. They also serve as the technicians and specialists our urbanized, high-technology, high-mobility economy needs in increasing numbers.

Different programs and different institutions foster different kinds of individual growth. Some emphasize "education"—the broad development of the powers of observation, perception, reasoning, and reflection in a traditional framework of thought and body of knowledge. Some emphasize "training"—mastery of a range of specific techniques of knowing, learning, and doing. All institutions and programs include, or try to include, some minimum element of education as we have just defined it.

A college degree is not always needed for leadership positions in politics, business entrepreneurship, sports, and the performing arts. Experience and special gifts prepare some. But more and more, roads to the top begin at tollgates open only to those with certification by schooling.

Scholarship and research are a traditional major function of universities. In the United States today, the overwhelming proportion of fundamental research and scholarship in the natural sciences, social sciences, and humanities is carried out in academic settings. Work of the highest quality in basic science is done in industrial and government laboratories; significant contributions to the social sciences come from government agencies; independent libraries and museums are important to scholarship in the humanities. But the vitality and efficiency of these extra-academic institutions typically depend on a continuous interchange with the academic world, for both ideas and people.

Our material strength, health, and security rest firmly on the foundations laid by basic research in the sciences. The increased understanding of self and society gained from the social sciences and humanities is a vital ingredient in a society that places its reliance on democracy in the pursuit of social order and the adaptation and management of social change. Through its continuous dialogue with the minds of other times and places, humanistic learning also has a deeper role to play in shaping the educated and cultivated person.

At its best, the academy acts as our social memory, conscience, and imagination. It is the training ground and sanctuary for social and moral critics. Ours is an open and pluralistic society, committed to a democratic polity and some version of an egalitarian ideology. Competition is our dominant ethos in the world of ideas and ideals, just as in economics and politics. We have no established source of authoritative doctrine for any sphere of public or private life. The religious pluralism that was our early heritage has grown into a broad diversity of ideas on almost every subject.

In a society like ours, an institution which can plausibly claim that its members combine expert knowledge on almost any question, with a disinterested stance and a long view, has special authority. Of course, as individuals, academics are no more disinterested than other Americans, but they are not identified as a group with any single interest in the economic, political, or ideological marketplace. They are less likely than people in other occupations to be caught up in the dominant outlook of the moment, or to be bound by local or national viewpoints. Not the opinions of any one academic, or of any one group of them, but the range of ideas of the academic community, especially of that part of it critical of contemporary social arrangements, has a special place in the American process.

Independent critics with no institutional base are impressive and influential, and the role of art in all its forms is immeasurable. Churches and the press are equally important sources of social and moral criticism. But neither churches, which stand apart from the contentions of the marketplace, nor the press, which reflects them, has the authority of expert knowledge that is important to the academy's claim to protection and respect as critic.

Finally, the most important channel for social mobility we have in peacetime is provided by colleges and universities. Through them, many young people have opportunities for jobs with higher income and status than their parents had. While this has been an important role for at least a century, its significance increased dramatically in the last generation. The number of institutions tripled, and the variety of programs they offer increased greatly. As we have seen, because of low cost, wide distribution, and minimal entrance requirements, higher education is now broadly accessible to many millions who could not have considered it earlier.

The nature of jobs also changed: in relative terms, fewer are unskilled and semi-skilled, while the proportion of technical, semi-professional, and managerial ones increased. These changes amplify the importance of formal schooling as a requisite for occupations offering the best prospects for upward mobility.

The value of educational credentials in the job market differs greatly among types of institutions, particular ones, and levels of education. Yet, the parts of the whole system are interconnected enough to open possible paths from community colleges to distinguished professional schools.

In 1840, de Tocqueville could say:

> I think there is no other country in the world where proportionately to population, there are so few ignorant and so few learned individuals as in America.
>
> Primary education is within reach of all; higher education is hardly available to anybody.

Today, our "legitimate passion for equality," of which he also wrote, is putting higher education within reach of all who can make good use of it, with great benefit to many of us as individuals and to all of us as a nation. Through its recommendations, our Commission aims to continue the process in ways that protect the vital, unique contributions of colleges and universities to our country's needs.

Appendixes

Appendix 1

Studies Prepared for the Sloan Commission on Government and Higher Education

1. Background papers prepared by the Staff of the Sloan Commission on Government and Higher Education:

Deitch, Kenneth M., *Some Aspects of the Economics of American Higher Education*, November, 1977.

Deitch, Kenneth M., *Financial Aid: A Resource for Improving Educational Opportunities*, March, 1978.

Deitch, Kenneth M., *Pricing and Financial Aid in American Higher Education: Some Interactions*, July 22, 1978.

Deitch, Kenneth M., *When Does an Increase in the Cost of Education Lead to an Increase in a BEOG? A Note*, July, 1979.

Gruson, Edward S., *The National Politics of Higher Education*, January, 1978.

Gruson, Edward S., *International Education*, October, 1978.

Gruson, Edward S., *Developing Institutions: Background and Policy Alternatives*, December 14, 1978.

Gruson, Edward S., *Issues in Accreditation, Eligibility and Institutional Quality*, March 10, 1979.

Gruson, Edward S., *State Regulation of Higher Education in a Period of Decline*, April, 1979.

Levine, David O., *The Condition of Women in Higher Education: A Decade of Progress, An Uncertain Future*, January, 1979.

Lloyd-Campbell, Crystal C., *Adams v. Califano: A Case Study in the Politics of Regulation*, January, 1978.

Spero, Irene K., *Government and Higher Education: A Summary of 21 Institutional Self-Studies*, January, 1978.

White, Geoffrey, *Federal Support of Academic Research*, April, 1978.

White, Geoffrey, *National Youth Service and Higher Education*, October, 1978.

2. Studies commissioned for the Sloan Commission on Government and Higher Education (prepared during the academic year 1977–78):

Bailey, Cornelia W., *The Federal 504 Handicapped Access Regulations: A Case Study in Government-Higher Education Relations.*

Bowen, Howard R., *Socially-Imposed Costs of Higher Education.*

Brunner, Seth and Gladieux, Lawrence, *Student Aid and Tuition in Washington State: A Case Study of Federal/State Interaction*, CEEB.

Dresch, Stephen P. *A Market Responsive Model of Academic Personnel Flows: Implementation and Preliminary Policy Implications*, Institute for Demographic and Economic Studies, Inc., October 5, 1979.

Glenny, Lyman A. and Bowen, Frank M., *State Intervention in Higher Education.*

Hansen, Janet, *The State Student Incentive Grant Program: An Assessment of the Record and Options for the Future*, CEEB.

Hauptman, Arthur, *Student Grant Assistance in New York*, CEEB.

Kershaw, Joseph, *Government and Higher Education: A Survey of 21 Institutions* (summary paper for 21 institutional self-studies prepared for the Sloan Commission).

Moots, Philip R. and Gaffney, Edward M., *Government Regulation of Religiously Affiliated Higher Education.*

Orlans, Harold, *The Federal Regulation of Accrediting.*

Ramsden, Richard J., *Federal Student Assistance.*

Woodrow, Raymond J., *Federal Grants and Contracts to Colleges and Universities.*

3. State studies prepared for the Sloan Commission on Government and Higher Education (prepared during the summer and fall 1978):

Adamany, David, *State Government Regulation of Higher Education in California.*

Cope, Robert, *Observations on Washington State's System of Higher Education with Particular Attention to the Relationship between State Government and the Institutions.*

Hiett, Joe H., *Government and Higher Education in Florida—Part One: State Supported Student Financial Aid.*

Kershaw, Joseph, *Government and Higher Education in New York State.*

Petersen, Renee, *The State and Higher Education in Ohio.*

Stafford, Richard and Lustberg, Lawrence, *Higher Education in Massachusetts: Issues in Their Context.*

Stampen, Jacob, *Conflict, Accountability and the Wisconsin Idea: Relations between Government and Higher Education in Wisconsin, 1965 to 1978.*

Tolo, Kenneth W., *Higher Education in Texas: Student Aid and Governance.*

Trani, Eugene P., *Higher Education in Nebraska: A Report for the Sloan Commission on Government and Higher Education.*

Wharton, James, *Observations on Higher Education in Louisiana: Student Financial Aid and Governance.*

4. Institutional self-studies prepared for the Sloan Commission on Government and Higher Education (prepared during the summer of 1977).

Bernhardt, John, *Western Michigan University, Kalamazoo, Michigan.*

Bowker, Albert H. and Morgan, Patricia M., *The University of California, Berkeley and the Government.*

Bramlet, Linda and Marcus, Bruce, *A Self-Study on the Impact of the Federal Government on Rice University.*

Chambers, Charles M., *The Growing Influence of the Government on the Affairs of the University: A Study Prepared by the George Washington University, Washington, D.C.*

Dellapenna, Joseph W., *The Impact of the Federal Government on Villanova University.*

Farrell, W.J., *Government Impact on the University of Iowa.*

Garvin, David, *M.I.T. and the Federal Government: An Examination of the Effects of the Government Regulation and Research Support on Selected Parts of M.I.T.*

Hartley, John W., *Wellesley College: Case Study for the Sloan Commission on Government and Higher Education.*

Karlesky, Joseph J., *Federal Regulation at Franklin and Marshall College.*

Kershaw, Joseph, *The Federal Government and Williams College.*

Koerner, James D., University of Alabama: A Study in Bureaucracy.

LaPlante, Marilyn, *Impact of Federal Regulation on Higher Education: A Self-Study at Earlham College.*

McCabe, Robert H., Mehallis, George and Lorseri, Richard, *Impact of State and Federal Regulation and Reporting Requirements on Miami-Dade Community College.*

Office of Planning and Institutional Research, *Oregon State University Governmental Impact Study.*

Perlman, Daniel H., *Self-Study Report by Roosevelt University on the Impact of Government Programs and the Cost of Compliance with Government Regulations.*

Rollins,Richard A., *Impact: Bishop College and Government.*

Rosenzweig, Robert M., Wilkes, Christopher and Freedman, Nancy, *The Stanford University Medical Center and the Federal Government.*

Schoenherr, Charles W., *Sterling College, Sterling, Kansas.*

Copies of all the papers listed in Appendix 1 will be available through the ERIC system (ERIC, Suite 630, One Dupont Circle, N.W., Washington, D.C. 20036); with the exception of the Stephen P. Dresch commissioned study, which is available directly from IDES (IDES, 155 Whitney Avenue, New Haven, CT 06510).

Appendix 2

References, Source Materials and Basic Tables for Chapters 2 Through 7

CHAPTER 2—THE CONTEXT OF THE PROBLEMS

Table 1*   Average Enrollment in Public and Private Institutions in 1950, 1960, and 1975.

	1950	*1960*	*1977**
Total Enrollment (in thousands)	2,297	3,610	11,286
Total Number of Institutions	1,859	2,040	3,086
Average Enrollment	1,235	1,770	3,657
Private Enrollment (in thousands)	1,142	1,474	2,439
Number of Private Institutions	1,221	1,319	1,618
Average Private Enrollment	936	1,118	1,507
Public Enrollment (in thousands)	1,154	2,136	8,847
Number of Public Institutions	638	721	1,468
Average Public Enrollment	1,809	2,962	6,027

*Charles Andersen (editor), *A Fact Book on Higher Education: Second Issue/1976* (place of publication unlisted: American Council on Education, 1976) p. 76.80; and Charles Andersen (editor), *A Fact Book on Higher Education: Third Issue/1976*, p. 76.141.
**Grant and Lind, *Digest of Education Statistics 1979*, pp. 88 and 107.

Table 2*   Proportion of Enrollment in Selected Carnegie Categories in 1976.

Code of Classification	*Title*	*Percentage*
1	Doctoral-Granting Institutions	27.4
2	Comprehensive Colleges and Universities	28.4
3.1	Liberal Arts Colleges I	1.4
3.2	Liberal Arts Colleges II	3.4
4	Public Community Colleges	34.3
	Private Two-Year Colleges	1.4
	TOTAL	100.0

*The Carnegie Council on Policy Studies in Higher Education, *A Classification of Institutions of Higher Education*, Revised edition, (Place of publication unlisted: The Carnegie Foundation for the Advancement of Teaching, p. xii.

Table 3*   Current Fund Income, by Major Source, Public and Private Sectors and Total, 1976–77 (In Billions of Dollars and as a Percent of Total).

Source of Income	Public Sector		Private Sector		All Institutions	
	Amount	Percent	Amount	Percent	Amount	Percent
Tuition and Fees	3.9	13.3	5.2	36.6	9.0	20.7
All Government	18.9	64.5	3.2	22.5	22.1	50.9
Federal	4.4	15.0	2.8	19.7	7.2	16.6
State	13.0	44.4	0.3	2.1	13.3	30.6
Local	1.5	5.1	0.1	0.7	1.6	3.7
Endowment Earnings	0.7	2.4	0.1	0.7	0.8	1.8
Private Gifts, Grants and Contracts	0.7	2.4	1.4	9.9	2.1	4.8
Auxiliary Enterprises	3.1	10.6	1.8	12.7	4.9	11.3
All Other	2.0	6.8	2.5	17.6	4.5	10.4
TOTALS	29.3	100.0	14.2	100.0	43.4	99.9

*Grant, W. Vance and Lind, E. George, *Digest of Education Statistics, 1979,* (Washington, D.C.: U.S. Government Printing Office, 1979), p. 128.

Table 4*   Median Tuition-and-Fee Revenues as Percentage of
Educational-and-General Revenues per FTE Student, by Carnegie
Categories, 1974–75.

		1974–75	
Carnegie Category *(1)*		*Private* *(2)*	*Public* *(3)*
1.1	Research Universities I	23.5%	13.1%
1.2	Research Universities II	45.9	16.3
1.3	Doctoral-Granting Universities I	55.4	21.0
1.4	Doctoral-Granting Universities II	62.0	24.6
2.1	Comprehensive Universities & Colleges I	84.1	20.6
2.2	Comprehensive Universities & Colleges II	72.9	26.6
3.1	Liberal Arts Colleges I	69.7	NA
3.2	Liberal Arts Colleges II	68.3	NA
4.	Two-Year Colleges & Institutes	67.9	14.7

*Lanier and Andersen, *A Study of the Financial Condition . . .* , p. 29.

Table 5* **   Relationships Between the 18-Year-Old Population,
High School Graduates, and First-Time Degree-Credit Enrollment
in College, Selected Years, 1950−1978.

Year	High School Graduates 18-Year-Olds	First-Time Enrollment High School Graduates	First-Time Enrollment 18-Year-Olds
1950	.555	.427	.237
1952	.581	.445	.259
1954	.598	.490	.293
1956	.631	.505	.319
1958	.653	.513	.335
1960	.726	.495	.359
1962	.689	.535	.369
1964	.824	.535	.441
1966	.757	.516	.391
1968	.771	.603	.465
1970	.782	.615	.481
1972	.766	.579	.443
1974	.753	.611	.460
1976	.740	.615	.455
1978	.745	.604	.450

*Cartter, *Ph.D.s and the Academic Labor Market*, p. 50.

U.S. Bureau of the Census, *Statistical Abstract of the United States: 1976* (97th Annual Edition, Washington: U.S. Government Printing Office, 1976), p. 140.

Charles Andersen (editor), *A Fact Book on Higher Education: Second Issue/1976*, p. 76.102.

U.S. Bureau of the Census, *Current Population Reports*, Series P-25, No. 643, "Estimates of the Population of the United States, By Age, Sex, and Race: July 1, 1974 to 1976," (Washington: U.S. Government Printing Office, 1977), pp. 10, 12.

**18-Year-Olds: U.S. Bureau of the Census, *Current Population Reports*, Series P-25, No. 800, "Estimates of the Population of the United States, by Age, Sex, and Race: 1976 to 1978,: (Washington D.C.: U.S. Government Printing Office, 1979, p. 5).

High School Graduates: Over telephone from NCES.

First-Time (Degree-Credit) Enrollment: Estimated by a researcher at ACE.

Table 6*   Estimated Size of Particular Age Groups, 1978–2000
(in millions)

| | *Age Groups* | | |
	18	*18–21*	*18–24*
Year			
1978	4.23	17.11	28.98
1979	4.29	17.16	29.30
1980	4.21	17.12	29.46
1981	4.15	17.02	29.51
1982	4.09	16.87	29.36
1983	3.92	16.50	29.02
1984	3.70	15.99	28.48
1985	3.60	15.44	27.85
1986	3.52	14.87	27.08
1987	3.57	14.52	26.45
1988	3.65	14.47	25.97
1989	3.73	14.60	25.63
1990	3.43	14.51	25.15
1991	3.24	14.18	24.69
1992	3.17	13.69	24.24
1993	3.25	13.20	23.96
1994	3.20	12.97	23.59
1995	3.26	13.00	23.22
1996	3.36	13.18	22.86
1997	3.49	13.43	22.94
1998	3.65	13.89	23.35
1999	3.81	14.44	23.99
2000	3.91	14.99	24.65

*U.S. Bureau of the Census, *Current Population Reports*, Series P–25, No. 704, pp. 37–60.

CHAPTER 3—FEDERAL REGULATION

Crystal C. Lloyd-Campbell was responsible for gathering and analyzing the material for Chapter 2. She wishes to acknowledge the assistance of Charles Saunders, Elaine El-Khawas, Donna Shavlik, and Sheldon Steinbach of the American Council on Education; Bernice Sandler of the Association of American Colleges; Philip R. Moots and Edward M. Gaffney of the Center for Constitutional Studies, University of Notre Dame; Richard Beattie, Cynthia Brown, Patricia King, F. Peter Libassi, Arline Mendelson, and David Tatel of the Department of Health, Education, and Welfare; Peter J. Levine of the Department of Justice; Leonard Bierman, Ann Blackwell, and Karen Klaus of the Department of Labor; Wayne Horvitz and Nancy B. Broff of the Federal Mediation and Conciliation Service; Alan Palmer of the Federal Trade Commission; Theodore Habarth of the President's Reorganization Project; Fred Crossland, Robert Goldman, Harold Howe, II, Sanford Jaffe, and Mitchell Sviridoff of the Ford Foundation; Harold Swearer, Maurice Glickman, George Hicks, Henry Kucera, and Alfred H. Joslin of Brown University; Charles E. Bishop, M. Olin Cook, Patti Howe, and Walter L. Littlejohn of Arkansas; E.T. York, Jr., Dolores Auzenne, James Gardener, and John De Grove of Oklahoma; Sharon Beard and Jesse Stone of Louisiana; Albert Bowker, I. Michael Heyman, Bell Cole, William Shack, George J. Maslach, Rod Park, Richard Abrams, Sveltana Alpers, James Cahill, Diana Clemens, John M. Dillion, Helen Eckert, Sue Ervin-Tripp, Herma Hill-Kay, Laura Nader, John H.R. Polt, Elizabeth Scott, Neylan Vedros, and Margaret Wilkerson of the University of California; William Friday, Raymond Dawsen, William A. Johnson, and Jeffrey Orleans of the University of North Carolina; Cornelia W. Bailey; Barbara Bergman, University of Maryland; Margaret H. Bonz, Dartmouth College; David Breneman, the Brookings Institution; Stephan Burbank, University of Pennsylvania; Abram Chayes, Harvard Law School; Humphrey Doermann, the Bush Foundation; Harry Edwards, University of Michigan Law School; Carolyn Elliot, Wellesley; Jo Freeman, the Brookings Institution; Chester Finn, Senator Moynihan's

Office; Lili Hornig, Higher Education Research Service; Matina Horner, Radcliffe College; Jacqueline Mattfield, Barnard College; Walter McCann, University of Hartford; Jane McCarthy, Center for Mediation in Higher Education; Pauli Murray; Margot Polivy; Richard Rettig, Rand Corporation; Nancy Randolph, Harvard University; Mary Rowe, Massachusetts Institute of Technology; Michael I. Sovern, Columbia University; Richard Staples, Providence, Rhode Island; Sheila Tobias, Wesleyan University; and Brenda J. Wilson, Harvard Graduate School of Education.

While a student at Harvard Law School, Richard Yurko contributed substantially to this chapter.

REFERENCES

Page 53

Quoted from *Sweezy* v. *New Hampshire*, 354 U.S. 234, 263, (1957) (Frankfurter, J. concurring).

For comparative analyses of higher education systems and modes of government regulation see, Burton R. Clark, "The Insulated Americans: Five Lessons from Abroad," Change (November 1978) p. 24; "The Benefits of Disorder" Change (October 1976) p. 31; *Structures of Post-Secondary Education*, Yale Higher Education Program Working Paper YHEP 10, 1976 Yale University New Haven.

Pages 54-55

For a discussion of the philosophical and historical background of our egalitarian goals, see, J.R. Pole, *The Pursuit of Equality in American History*. (Univ. of California Press, Berkeley, 1978); Edward A. Purcell, Jr., *The Crisis of Democratic Theory* (Lexington, Univ. Press of Kentucky, 1973).

For background on the problems of agency administration of the equal opportunity laws, see generally, *Reorganization of Equal Employment Opportunity Programs; Background and Option Papers*, Task Force on Civil Rights Reorganization President's Reorganization Project, Washington, D.C. 1977; *A Preliminary Report on The Revitalization of the Federal Contract Compliance Program*, Office of Federal Contract Compliance Programs Task Force, U.S. Dept. of Labor, Washington, D.C. 1977, *The Federal Civil Rights Enforcement Effort—1977: To Eliminate Employment Discrimination: A Sequel*, and *The Federal Civil Rights Enforcement Effort—1974* Vol. V., *To Eliminate Employment Discrimination*, Reports of The U.S. Comm'n on Civil Rights (1977 and 1975); David Copus, "Long-term Problems in Title VII Enforcement," Internal memorandum, Special Investigation and Concilization Division, EEOC; Jan Vetter, *Affirmative Action in Faculty Employment under Executive Order 11246*, Report of The Committee on Grant and Benefit Programs of the Administrative Conference of the United States (1974).

For discussion on the developing judicial involvement in administrative agency activities and the changing character of "public law" see generally, R. Belton, "A Comparative Review of Public and Private Enforcement of Title VII of the Civil Rights Act of 1964" 31 Vand. L. Rev. 905 (1978); Note, "Judicial Control of Systemic Inadequacies in Federal Administrative Enforcement" 88 Yale L.J. 407 (1978); Paul Verkuil, "The Emerging Concept of Administrative Procedure," 78 Column L. Rev. 258 (1978); Owen M. Fiss, "The Supreme Court 1978 Term, Foreword: The Forms of Justice" 93 Harv. L. Rev. 1 (1979); Abram Chayes, "The Role of The Judge in Public Litigation" 89 Harv. L. Rev. 1667 (1976); Richard Stewart, "The Reformation of American Administrative Law" 88 Harv. L. Rev. 1667 (1975); Lawrence H. Tribe, "Structural Due Process" 10 Harv. CR−CL L. Rev. 269 (1975).

The Need for Regulation

Page 56

For information on black undergraduates, see James, R. Mingle, *Black Enrollment in Higher Education: Trends in the Nation and the South* (Atlanta, Southern Regional Education Board, 1978) and on woman faculty, see, *The Condition of Education*, National Center for Education Statistics (1978).

Page 57

On the impact of equal opportunity regulation in higher education see, *Making Affirmative Action Work in Higher Education: An Analysis of Institution and Federal Policies with Recommendations*, A Report of the Carnegie Council on Policy Studies in Higher Education; San Francisco (1975) at pps. 53−54; *Climbing the Academic Ladder: Doctoral Women Scientists in Academia*, Comm. on the Education and Employment of Women in Science and Engineering, Comm'n on Human Resources, National Research Council, National Academy of Science 1979, Chapters 3 and 4; Patricia A. Graham, "Expansion and Exclusion: A History of Women in American Higher Education," 3 Signs 759 (Summer 1978) at 722−723; Special Subcommittee on Education of the Committee on Education and Labor, U.S. House of Representatives, *Hearings on Federal Higher Education Programs Institutional Eligibility, Civil Rights Obligations Hearings*, Part 2B, 93rd Congress 2nd Sess. (1974), pp. 1271−1418; and *Opportunities for Women in Higher Education, Their Current Participation, Prospects for the Future and Recommendations for Action*, A Report of the Carnegie Commission on Higher Education (1973).

Page 58: Particular Problems in Regulating Higher Education

The Age Discrimination in Employment Act Amendments of 1978 P.L. No. 95–256, 92 Stat. 189, extended the mandatory retirement age to 70. The amendments which took effect January 1, 1979 will become effective for tenured employees in higher education July 1, 1982.

For information on employment of minorities and women in higher education see generally, Roy Radner and Charlotte Kuh, *Preserving a Lost Generation*, Carnegie Council on Policy Studies in Higher Education, 1978; National Center for Education Statistics, *Salaries, Tenure, and Fringe Benefits of Full-Time Instructional Faculty in Institutions of Higher Education*, 1977–78 Report; National Center for Education Statistics, *Projections of Education Statistics to 1968–87*, 1978. More information on women in higher education is contained in, David O. Levine, "The Condition of Women in Higher Education," paper for the Sloan Commission on Government and Higher Education, January 1979.

Recent research indicates that Black faculty now command a premium in the academic marketplace. See, R.B. Freeman, "The New Job Market for Black Academicians," 30 Ind. and Lab. Rel. Rev. 161, 168–79 (1977); W. Williams, "Higher Education and Minority Opportunities," 7 Howard L.J., 545, 552 (1978); see also, "A Proposal for Reconciling Affirmative Action with Nondiscrimination under the Contractor Anti-discrimination Program," 30 Stan. L. Reve. 803, 814–815 (1978). A premium salary paid to Black male professors may alter the statistics of academic salaries at an institution to the point that non-minority professors may have a valid Equal Pay Act complaint. See Ester Greenfield, "From Equal Pay to Equivalent Pay: Salary Discrimination in Academia," 6 J. of Law and Education, 41, 42 (1977).

Page 58

"Pattern and practice" employment discrimination actions and Executive Order, "workforce underutilization" determinations are based on a statistical analysis of the employer's workforce compared to the relevant labor pool. See, Title VII, of the 1964 Civil Rights Act 42 U.S.C. §2000(e) et seq. (as amended 1972); EEOC guidelines on Employee Selection Procedures, 29 CFR §1600 ff. (1979) and Exec. Ord. 11, 246 (30 Fed. Req. 12, 319 (1965) as amended, 32 CFR 14, 303 (1967), and 41 C.F.R. §§60–2.11–.12 (1977).

For judicial interpretation of these regulations and the relevant statistical analysis see *United Steelworkers of America v. Weber*,   U.S.   , 99 S.Ct. 2721, 2725, and 99 S.Ct. 2732, fn* (Blackmun, J., concurring); *Hazelwood School District v. United States*, 433 U.S. 299 (1977); *International Brotherhood of Teamsters v. United States*, 431 U.S. 324 (1977); *Albemarle Paper Co. v. Moody*, 422 U.S. 405 (1975);

Franks v. Bowman Transportation Co., 424 U.S. 747 (1974); *Griggs v. Duke Power Co.*, 401 U.S. 424 (1971).

The similarity of the problems of academic and upper echelon employment is noted in, Thomas Reed Hunt and George Pazuniak, "Special Problems in Litigating Upper Level Employment Discrimination Cases," 4 Delaware J. of Corporate Law 114 (1978), at pps. 147, 149–152; "A Proposal of Reconciling Affirmative Action with Nondiscrimination under the Contractor Antidiscrimination Program," op. cit., 815 (1978).

On the issue of utilization analysis in higher education, see draft memorandum of William C. Bowen, "Utilization Analyses and Goals and Timetables," July 20, 1976, p. 4–5, submitted to the Federal Advisory Committee on Affirmative Action in Employment at Institutions of Higher Education, Robben Fleming, Chairman; *Making Affirmative Action Work in Higher Education*, op. cit., at pps. 56–59 and "Excerpts from University of North Carolina Memorandum," Jan. 17, 1975, pp. 240–242. One commentator has suggested that the *Griggs* statistical disparity standard is appropriate where the discrimination issue involves *promotion* of *incumbent* employees, but not where the group is "a large shifting, ill-defined, potentially limitless and endlessly manipulable group of *would-be* employees, as in *Davis.*" See B. Lerner *"Washington v. Davis*: Quantity, Quality and Equality in Employment Testing," The Supreme Court Rev. pp. 263, 270 (1976). See also, *Scott v. University of Delaware*, 455 F. Supp. 1102 (D.C. Del. 1978) where the plaintiff challenged the Ph.D. requirement as discriminatory because it "has a disparate impact on blacks which is not justified by the legitimate needs of the University," at p. 1123.

Another aspect of this "qualification" problem is contained in the OFCCP affirmative action guidelines relating to contractor workforce analysis. "Employee specifications cannot set higher qualification standards than those of the *lowest* qualified incumbent," 41 C.F.R. §60–2.24(f)(5)(1974) (emphasis added). This lowest common denominator rule could mean that an institution that wished to "upgrade" its faculty would be held to its present standards until the "lowest qualified incumbent" retired!

The courts have not required a showing by the plaintiff of superiority, but only minimal competence to meet the competency standard. See *Powell v. Syracuse University*, 580 F. 2d 1150, 1155 (CA 2 1978):

... [P]roof of competence sufficient to make out a *prima facie* case of discrimination under Title VII was never intended to encompass proof of superiority or flawless performance.*** In the context of this case, Ms. Powell has demonstrated that she possesses the *basics* necessary for the performance of her job and has thereby made out a *prima facie* showing of competence. (emphasis added).

On the particular problems of employment selection and tenure systems see, *Sweeney v. Board of Trustees of Keene State College*, 569 F. 2d 169 (CAL 1978) where it stated:

> Fact-finding biased in either direction can lead to socially harmful results: harm to the woman who is discriminated against without redress; harm, on the other hand, to a university and its students and to more qualified applicants, if a lifetime job or promotion is conferred by the court upon a woman who would have been passed over had she been a male. 569 F. 2d 169, 180 (Campbell, J., concurring)

Page 59. On faculty dossiers and balancing public interest and private rights see Clark, "The Dossier in Colleges and Universities" in Wheeler, *On Record: Files and Dossiers in American Life*, (1969) and David W. Leslie, "Legal Protection for Privacy," in *Protecting Individual Rights in Higher Education*, 1977. See also, "Draft Presidential Decision memorandum" for the Privacy Policy Coordinating Committee, National Telecommunications and Information Administration, U.S. Dept. of Commerce, pps. 2–3 (1978).

The relevant statutes are: Freedom of Information Act, 88 Stat. §6, 5 U.S.C. §552, Privacy Act of 1974, 88 Stat. 1095, 5 U.S.C. §552(a); see also, Family Educational Rights and Privacy Act, 20 U.S.C. §§1232 g–i and see, e.g., the executive order regulations 41 CFR §60–1. 43 CFR §60–60.3 (1974).

One example of the case-by-case approach to this problem involved the University of California; see, *Department of Health Education and Welfare, and Department of Labor v. University of California*, ALJ Opinion September 1979, OFCCP No. 5239475, where the hearing officer noted the special problems involving academic employment records and permitted the institution to submit edited data.

Page 60. The importance of the collegial structure in governance of academic institutions has been acknowledged by the Supreme Court; see *NLRB v. Yeshiva University*, _____ U.S. _____ , 100 S.Ct. 48 L.W. 4175, (1980). Compare, *NLRB v. Wentworth Institute*, 515 F. 2d 550 (CA 1, 1975).

For a discussion of the legal significance of these distinctions see Kahn, "The NLRB and Higher Education: The Failure of Policy-Making Through Adjudication," 21 UCLA L. Rev. 63, 68 (1973).

Page 61

Few academic employment discrimination cases are actually "won" by the plaintiffs. Of 44 higher education cases reviewed, only 7 resulted in court decisions that awarded plaintiff relief. See Time Charts of Administrative and Judicial Proceedings in Higher Education Employment cases, *infra*. For a good picture of the tensions created for grievants in academia see, Joan Abramson, *The Invisible Woman*, (San Francisco: Jossey-Bass Publishers, 1975).

On standards of academic quality, see Special Subcommittee on Education of the Committee on Education and Labor, *Hearings on Federal Higher Education Programs*, Institutional Eligibility, *op. cit.* at 1244, statement of Lilli S. Hornig, Executive Director, Higher Education Resource Services, Brown University; and *Making Affirmative Action Work in Higher Education, op. cit.* pages 129−133. For a contrary view, see Richard A. Lester, *Antibias Regulation of Universities* (New York 1974).

The Present Regulatory Apparatus-How it Functions

Pages 62−63

On the intent requirement as an element of the constitutional equal protection standard, see *Columbus Board of Education v. Penick,* ____ U.S. ____ , 99 S.Ct. 2941 (1979); *Dayton Board of Education v. Brinkman,* ____ U.S. ____ , 99 S.Ct. 2971 (1979); *Village of Arlington Heights v. Metropolitan Housing Development Corp.*, 429 U.S. 252 (1977); *Washington v. Davis*, 426 U.S. 229 (1976).

The Court has noted that:

> Determining whether invidious discriminatory purpose was a motivating factor demands a sensitive inquiry into such circumstantial and direct evidence of intent as may be available. The impact of the official action 'whether it bears more heavily on one race than another,' *Washington v. Davis*, 426 U.S. at 242−may provide an important starting point. Sometimes a clear pattern, unexplainable on grounds other than race, emerges from the effect of the state action even when the governing action appears neutral on its face. (Citations omitted). *Village of Arlington Heights v. Metropolitan Housing Authority*, 429 U.S. at 266.

> ... [A] constitutional issue does not arise every time some disproportional impact is shown. On the other hand when the disproportion is ... dramatic ... , it really does not matter whether the standard is phrased in terms of purpose or effect.

Washington v. Davis, 426 U.S. 242, 254, n. 20 (Stevens, J., concurring). But see, *Personnel Administrator v. Feeney*, 99 S.Ct. 2282 (1979) and "The Supreme Court, 1978 Term," 93 Harv. L. Rev. 60, 137, 138 (1979).

For discussion of the statutory standards for discrimination, see *Board of Education of the City Sch. Dist. of New York v. Harris*, _____ U.S. _____ , 100 S.Ct. 363 (1979); *Griggs v. Duke Power Co.*, 401 U.S. 424 (1971) (under the statute, Title VII, disparate treatment on the basis of some suspect classification (such as race or sex) is presumptive evidence of discriminatory intention).

Even under the statutory standards however, intention may become a relevant issue. When an alleged discriminatory practice is "facially neutral" evidence of disparate impact presents a prima facie case of discrimination.

> A ... prima facie showing is not the equivalent of a factual finding of discrimination, however. Rather, it is simply proof of actions taken by the employer from which we infer discriminatory animus because experience has proved that in the absence of any other explanation it is more likely than not that those actions were bottomed on impermissible considerations. When the prima facie showing is understood in this manner, *the employer must be allowed some latitude to introduce evidence which bears on his motive.*** ... (T)he District Court was entitled to consider the racial mix of the work force when trying to make the determination as to motivation. *Furnco Construction Corp. v. Waters*, 438 U.S. 567 at 579−80 (1978) (emphasis added).

See also, *Board of Trustees of Keene State College v. Sweeney*, U.S. , 99 S.Ct. 295 (1978), where the Court states:

> While words such as "articulate," "show," and "prove," may have more or less similar meanings depending upon the context in which they are used, we think that there is a significant distinction between merely "articulat[ing] some legitimate, nondiscriminatory reason" and "prov[ing] absence of discriminatory motive." ... [W]e make it clear that the former will suffice to meet the employee's prima facie case of discrimination. *Id.* at 295 and 296, fn. 2.

For a discussion of the Executive Order Program, see Office of Federal Contract Compliance Program Task Force, U.S. Department of Labor, *A Preliminary Report on the Revitalization of the Federal Contract Compliance Program*, September 16, 1977, p. xix. The recent case of *United Steelworkers of America v. Weber*, _____ U.S. _____ , 99 S.Ct. 2721 (1979) held that voluntary affirmative action undertaken by a government order program did not violate the discrimination standards of Title VII.

Pages 63—64

There is a complete listing of the equal opportunity laws affecting higher education (showing the procedural jurisdictional and remedial relief available) at Annex B, pages 246—252.

In May, 1978 President Carter's proposed Reorganization Plan No. 1 of 1978, (43 Fed. Reg. 19807 (1978)) for consolidating some of the responsibility for enforcement of the equal employment opportunity programs was approved. This reorganization plan was phased in over the course of two years. By July 1979 the *three* agencies chiefly responsible for enforcement of the employment opportunity laws were: EEOC, Department of Labor/OFCCP (Executive Order Program); and the Department of Justice. This consolidation of enforcement responsibility eliminates some of the confusion in the area of employment, but it does not affect enforcement of the educational program equal opportunity laws, such as Titles VI, IX and §504. As noted in the text the office of Civil Rights in the Department of Health, Education and Welfare has primary responsibility for enforcing these programatic equal opportunity laws in colleges and universities. OCR's enforcement responsibilities will be shifted to the new Department of Education 180 days after the Secretary of Education takes office, or sooner, at the President's discretion. See Pub. Law 96—88, 96 Cong. 2nd Sess. (October 17, 1979).

Pages 64—65

For information on the orientation of EEOC see R. Belton, "A Comparative Review of Public and Private Enforcement of Title VII of the Civil Rights Act of 1964," *op. cit.* at 914, 917. EEOC does have authority to bring "pattern and practice" suits, but it has not used this authority effectively. In the past the agency focus on individual complaints was a product of its statutory duty to make an investigation of every complaint. See, 42 U.S.C. 2000(e)—5. See also, David Copus, "Long-Term Problems in Title VII Enforcement," *op. cit.*; R.W. Walker, "Title VII: Complaint and Enforcement Procedures and Relief and Remedies," 7 B.C. L. Rev. 495 (1966). The differing approach of OFCCP is noted in *A Preliminary Report on the Revitalization of the Federal Contract Compliance Program, op. cit.*, at pp. 5, 7, 13—16, 30 (1977).

The Department of Justice also illustrates this problem of differing procedural styles resulting in differentiated enforcement of the laws. Since 1972, the Department of Justice has exclusive authority to litigate *public* sector Title VII employment cases and suits against federal contractors under the Executive Order program. 42 U.S.C. 2000(e)—5. The Department has concentrated on race discrimination cases and has not "adequately addressed" the problems of sex discrimination in employment, *The Federal Civil Rights Enforcement Effort—1977: To Eliminate Em-*

ployment Discrimination: A Sequel op. cit. at pps. 246–247, 272–273 (1977).

For information on the problems caused by decentralized structure see *"Reorganization of Equal Employment Opportunity Programs; Background and Option Papers" op. cit.* pps. A40–41; *Federal Civil Rights Enforcement Effort—1977; To Eliminate Employment Discrimination— A Sequel op. cit.* pps. 82–87; *Preliminary Report on Revitalization of the Federal Contract Compliance Program, op. cit.* at 21, 60.

Inexperience or unappropriate background is noted in the Civil Rights Comm'n Report *op. cit.* at p. 151. See also Office of the Secretary of HEW, *Vacancy Announcement #79–533–B*, Opportunity for Equal Opportunity Program Specialist, Opening Date 12/27/78, Closing Date 1/11/79. As reported by an official in Region 1, at one pre-award compliance investigation conducted by OFCCP at a prestigious private university, none of the agency's on-site personnel had had any prior experience with higher educational institutions.

Pages 66–67

Both research and student aid funds are subject to fund cut-off actions; See, *Adams v. Califano*, 430 F. Supp. 118 (1977); *Bob Jones University v. Johnson*, 396 F. Supp. 597 (1974); *In the Matter of Hillsdale College*, ALJ Dec. 8/23/78. Currently the public university system of North Carolina faces possible termination of Federal funds in connection with enforcement of Title VI, and a private college in Texas faces a cut-off of student aid funds in connection with alleged fiscal mismanagement. The University of California, the University of Michigan, and others, have faced fund termination threats in connection with the federal contract compliance program.

Part of the conflict of interest lies in the fact that one federal agency may be the grant-making or contracting agency, while another is responsible for assuring compliance with equal opportunity laws or Executive Orders. Contradictory and diverse pressures result. Under the pressure of an impending contract or contract renewal institutions may agree to "affirmative action" clauses in their contracts which they believe are inappropriate or unrealistic. See, T. Morgan, "Achieving National Goals through Federal Contracts: Giving Form to An Unconstrained Administrative Process," 1974 Wis. L. Rev. 301 (1974).

Furthermore the pressure of time (the agency has only 30 days to make a pre-award compliance review) merges investigation and agency determinations. Thus the traditional line between prosecutor and judge collapses.

In a recent action involving the University of North Carolina, HEW announced that it was going to *initiate* formal administrative hearing proceedings under Title VI and *simultaneously* announced that all federal grants and contracts to the system would be referred to HEW and that some contracts (estimated from 23 to 65 million dollars) would be deferred prior to hearing. See, HEW Press release May 2, 1979. North Carolina brought suit to enjoin such action and the federal district court granted the injunction stating:

> Yet the fact remains that HEW's deferral power, exercised in the manner described, constitutes a continuing threat to the stability of the University system. ***We are left with an image of Gulliver being held down while the Lilliputians fasten thousands of strings around his limbs. No litigant should have to battle a Kafkaesque bureaucracy in which it is beckoned to the administrative hearing or negotiation table while being pressured into compliance through the threat of "deferrals" which are part and parcel of the original controversy.

See *State of North Carolina v. Department of Health, Education and Welfare*, No. 79–217–Civ. 5 (DC F. Dist. NC) June 8, 1979.

Three Case Histories

Pages 67–69: The Case of John Doe, Student

The statutes referred to are: 42 U.S.C. §2000(d) (1976) (Title VI of the 1964 Civil Rights Act); 42 U.S.C. §6101 ff. (1975) (Age Discrimination Act); 29 U.S.C. §794 (1976) (Section 504, Rehabilitation Act); 28 U.S.C. §793 (1973) (Section 503—employment of handicapped); 38 U.S.C. §2011 (1974) (Vietnam Era Veterans); and 29 U.S.C. §621–636, as amended (1978) (Age Discrimination in Employment).

The two courts referred to in the text are: *Kaplowitz v. University of Chicago*, 387 F. Supp. 42 (N.D. Ill., 1974); *Cannon v. University of Chicago*, 559 F.2d 1063 (1977), U.S. _____ , 99 S.Ct. 1946 (1979) (reversed and remanded on different issue).

On the private right of action, see, *Cannon v. University of Chicago*, *op. cit.* (Title IX). Since Title IX is modelled after Title VI, the decision has some impact on the question of whether or not there is a private right of action under Title VI as well. But see, *Regents of the University of California v. Bakke*, 438 U.S. 265 (1978) (four Justices assumed a private right of action under Title VI in this case, four Justices declined to decide the issue and one Justice denied a private right of action under Title VI) see also, *Lau v. Nichols*, 414 U.S. 563 (1974). And see, *Southeastern Community College v. Davis*, _____ U.S. _____ , 99 S.Ct. 2361 (1979) (§504 of the Rehabilitation Act of 1973).

See also, Annex B, pages 246–252.

Only the Age Discrimination Act, 45 C.F.R. §90.43(d), 90.50, 44 Fed. Reg. 33768 (1979) requires exhaustion of administrative remedies prior to bringing a civil suit in the courts. But see, *Cannon v. University of Chicago, op. cit.*

The recent case, *Southeastern Community College v. Davis, op. cit.*, does not appear to reach the type of *physical* access problem noted in the text. In that case the Court held that "an otherwise qualified person [who may not be excluded from participation in an educational program] is one who is able to meet all of a program's requirements in spite of his handicap." (*Id.* at 2367). However, the basis for the Court's decision in *Davis* was that Section 504 did not require "fundamental alterations" in *curriculum* to meet the needs of handicapped students. "Section 504 imposes no requirement upon an educational institution to lower or to effect substantial modifications of standards to accommodate a handicapped person." *Id.* at 2369, 2370. Furthermore the Court felt that an interpretation of the regulations which required extensive curriculum modifications— "beyond those necessary to eliminate discrimination against otherwise qualified individuals . . . would do more than clarify the meaning of §504. Instead they would constitute an unauthorized extension of the obligations imposed by the statute." (*Id.* at 2369). However, modification of physical facilities to meet the needs of otherwise qualified handicapped students does appear to be an instance "where an insistence on continuing past requirements and practices might arbitrarily deprive genuinely qualified handicapped persons of the opportunity to participate in a covered program." *Id.* at 2370.

Statistical evidence of differential impact in testing programs may be a hypothetical question in the context of higher education but has been decisive in other educational situations. See, McClung, *Competency Testing Programs: Legal and Education Issues*, 47 Ford L. Rev. 651 (1979); also *Hobson v. Hanson*, 408 F. 2d 175 (D.C.C.A. 1969); also, *Larry P. v. Riles*, 343 F. 2d 963 (CA 9 1974), permanent injunction issued, #C−71− 2270 RFP, (U.S. Dist. Ct. N.D. Calif., October 16, 1979) (enjoining use of I.Q. Tests as a basis for placement in "stigmatizing" educable mentally retarded category by school authorities).

On the issue of federal funding see, *Bob Jones University v. Johnson*, 396 F. Supp. 597 (D.C. S.C. 1974) which held institutional eligibility for continued receipt of federal student financial aid is conditional on compliance with federal equal opportunity laws and regulations (Title VI). See also, In the *Matter of Hillsdale College*, ALJ decision, HEW 8/23/78, (refusal to sign assurance of compliance form under Title XI not evidence of non-compliance until specific violation of statute or regulations shown), *reversed*, HEW Civil Rights Reviewing Authority, XIX Chronicle of Higher Education, No. 10, p. 16 (Nov. 5, 1979).

Examples of other recent cases involving non-discrimination in student programs are:

Student Admission: *Cannon v. University of Chicago, op. cit.*; *Davis v. Southeastern Community College, op. cit.*; *Regents of the University of California v. Bakke, op. cit.*

Student government: Uzell v. Friday, 401 F. Supp. 775, 547 F.2d 801 (CA. 4, 1977); *cert. granted*, vacated, 46 L.W. 3803 (1979); 591 F.2d 997 (CA 4, 1979).

Academic credit: Wayne State University v. Cleland, 440 F. Supp. 806 (E.D. Mich., 1977), *aff'd.* in part, *rev'd.* in part, 590 F.2d 627 (CA 6, 1978).

Student dismissal: Board of Curators of the University of Missouri v. Horowitz, 435 U.S. 78 (1978).

Pages 69–72: The Case of Associate Professor Robert Roe and Mary Moe

On the tenure issue, see, e.g., *Scott v. The University of Delaware*, 455 F. Supp. 1102 (D.C. Del. 1978); *Kunda v. Muhlenberg College*, 463 F. Supp. 294 (E.D. Pa. 1978) (*aff'd* ___ F.2d ____ (CA 3 1980). For an example of recent cases on promotion and contract renewal, see *Board of Trustees of Keene State College v. Sweeney*, 99 S.Ct. 295 (1979), *remand*, 604 F.2d 106 (CA 1, 1979); *Powell v. Syracuse University*, 580 F.2d 1150 (CA 2, 1978) *cert. denied*, 47 L.W. 3369 (1978).

For examples of state laws and actions, see e.g., Mass. Gen. Laws, c. 151B. *Mass. Electric Co. v. Mass. Commission Against Discrimination*, 375 N.E.2d 1192 (1978); *General Electric Co. v. Gilbert*, 429 U.S. 125 (1976). See also, *Smith College v. Mass. Commission Against Discrimination*, 380 N.E.2d 121 (1978), *Wheelock College v. Mass. Commission Against Discrimination*, 355 N.E.2d 309 (1976).

Pages 72–75

Adams v. Califano, 433 F. Supp. 118 (D.C.D.C. 1977). The full history of the case is: *Adams v. Richardson*, 351 F. Supp. 636 (D.C.D.C. 1972, as amended; 1973); *Adams v. Richardson*, 356 F. Supp. 92 (D.C.D.C. 1973); *Adams v. Richardson*, 480 F.2d 1159 (C.A.D.C. 1973); *Adams v. Califano*, 430 F. Supp. 118 (D.C.D.C. 1977). The four *Adams* cases will be referred to as "the Adams case."

Maryland brought suit against the agency; see *Mayor and City Council of Baltimore v. Mathews and Mandel v. HEW*, 571 F.2d 1276 (C.A. 4 1978) (per curiam, withdrawing opinions issued in 562 F.2d 914 (C.A. 4 1977) because of death of one of the circuit judges prior to issuance of opinion), *cert. den'd*, 99 S.Ct. 184 (1978).

For a detailed case study of the Adams case, with particular emphasis on higher education systems in North Carolina, see Crystal Lloyd-Campbell, "Adams v. Califano: A Case Study in the Politics of Regulation," Sloan Commission on Government and Higher Education, Working Paper, Revised March 1979.

For the consent decree setting timetables for agency actions see: *Adams v. Califano*, Civ. No. 3095–70, *Women's Equity Action League v. Califano*, Civ. No. 74–1720 (D.C.D.C. December 29, 1977).

For cases illustrating equal educational opportunity based on a unitary structure in compulsory education see *Columbus Board of Education v. Penick*, 99 S.Ct. 2941 (1979); *Keyes v. School Dist. No. 1*, 413 U.S. 189 (1973); *Swann v. Charlotte-Mecklenburg*, 402 U.S. 1 (1971); *Green v. County School Board*, 391 U.S. 430 (1968).

In connection with the *Adams* cases it is interesting to note that in 1975, five years after the *Adams* suit was started, an organization of Black educators (NAFEO) filed an amicus brief in support of HEW, in opposition to the plaintiffs' (NAACP–LDF) "immediate integration" request. NAFEO said the Black colleges had historically fulfilled a "crucial need" and should continue to play an important role in Black education. The court acknowledged their concerns by noting that desegregation might "place a greater burden" on Black colleges, or eliminate existing opportunities for Black students. He ordered HEW to set guidelines for higher education desegregation which took "into account the importance of Black colleges *and at* the *same time*, comply with the congressional mandate." *Adams v. Califano*, 430 F. Supp. at 120 (emphasis added). In practice, of course, this is a difficult tight-rope to cross. Achievement of goals for increased access by Black students into traditionally white colleges and universities, may shift Black students at the expense of Black colleges. The ability of the traditionally Black institutions to attract new students (white or Black) is hampered by this past history and the charges by civil rights leaders and others that "Black schools are educationally bankrupt" and deny equal educational opportunity. See, D. Bell, Jr., "Serving Two Masters: Integration Ideals and Client Interests in School Desegregation Litigation," 85 Yale 470, 479 (1976); See also, J.H. Wilkinson III, *From Brown to Bakke: The Supreme Court and School Integration, 1954–1978* at 187–189 (1979). See also, Randolph, "Academic Irony: Black Colleges Seeking to Stay Black Undergo Pressure to Integrate, The Wall Street Journal, March 19, 1979 at 1.

James S. Coleman, author of *Equality of Educational Opportunity*, (a report for the U.S. Department of Health, Education, and Welfare, Office of Education, (Washington, D.C.: National Center for Education Statistics, 1966) appears to have had second thoughts about his earlier conclusions. In 1975, Professor Coleman reassessed his original conclusions and concluded that mandatory desegregation had more negative than positive effects. As he stated recently: "This belief in the inherent inferiority of an all-black school has a curiously racist flavor." See, Lorenzo Middleton, "The Effects of School Desegregation: The Debate Goes On," The Chronicle of Higher Education, Vol. XVII, No. 10, November 6, 1978; and James S. Coleman, letter to the editor, The Chronicle of Higher Education, Vol. XVII, No. 15, December 11, 1978.

See also Frederick Mosteller and Daniel Patrick Moynihan, *On Equality of Educational Opportunity*, (New York: Random House, 1972); Christopher Jencks, *Inequality*, (New York: Harper & Rowe (1972)).

The Commission's Recommendations For Reform

Page 75

For a discussion of the general issues of government regulation and reform see *American Bar Association Commission on Law and the Economy, Federal Regulation: Roads to Reform* (Exposure Draft) (Washington, D.C.: American Bar Association, 1978); Freedman, James O., *Crisis and Legitimacy: The Administrative Process and American Government.* (Cambridge: Cambridge University Press, 1978); Theodore J. Lowi, *The End of Liberalism*, (New York: W.W. Norton & Co., Inc., 1969); Roger G. Noll, *Reforming Regulation* (Washington, D.C.: The Brookings Institution, (1971); John Rawls, *A Theory of Justice* (Cambridge: Harvard University Press/Belknap Press, 1971); Charles L. Schultze, *The Public Use of Private Interest* (Washington, D.C.: The Brookings Institution, 1977); and Roberto Magabeira Unger, *Law in Modern Society* (New York: The Free Press, 1976).

Representative literature on the issue of government regulation of higher education is: Walter C. Hobbs, *Government Regulation of Higher Education* (Cambridge: Ballinger Publishing Co., 1978); Chester E. Finn, Jr., "Federal Patronage of Universities in the United States: A Rose by Many Other Names?" *Minerva*, Vol. XIV, No. 4, Winter 1976–77, pp 496–529; Robert A. Scott, "The Hidden Costs of Government Regulation," *Change*, Vol. 10, No. 4, April 1978, pp. 16–23.

Pages 76–78

In connection with the recommendation for a meaningful self-assessment process see Paul T. Hill, *A Study of Local Education Agency Response to Civil Rights Guarantees*, Rand Corp. Publication, January, 1979.

Other Federal Regulation Affecting Higher Education

Pages 85–86

For example the Fair Labor Standards Act of 1938, was amended in 1966 to apply to hospitals and institutions of higher education; Fair Labor Standards Amendments of 1966, Pub. L. No. 89–601, 80 Stat. 836. The Old Age Assistance Program, instituted pursuant to the Social Security Act of 1935 was extended to include non-profit educational institutions, two-thirds of whose employees voted for coverage in a referendum. Social Security Act Amendments of 1950, §204(e), 64 Stat. 477, 535. Because the votes were so overwhelmingly for coverage, Congress eliminated the referendum requirement in 1960. Social Security Amendments of 1960, §105(a), Pub. L. No. 86–778, 74 Stat. 924, 942.

For a discussion of the institution administrative costs involved in government regulation see C. Van Alstyne and S. Coldren, *The Costs of Imple-*

menting Federally Mandated Social Programs at Colleges and Universities, Policy Analysis Service—Special Report (Washington, D.C.: American Council on Education, June, 1976), p. 15, and see J.A. Kershaw, "Government and Higher Education, A Survey of 21 Constitutions," Sloan Commission of Government and Higher Education, October, 1977.

The Business Roundtable in connection with the accounting firm of Arthur Anderson undertook of study of the costs of regulation in business organizations; see *Cost of Government Regulation,* Study for the Business Round Table (NY 1979).

Conclusion

Pages 88—89

The quoted material is from *Brown v. Board of Education,* 347 U.S. 483, 493 (1954).

ANNEX A

A GUIDE TO EQUAL OPPORTUNITY/
NONDISCRIMINATION LAWS AND
REGULATIONS

A non-technical summary of the equal opportunity/nondiscrimination laws mentioned in Chapter 3 and analyzed in the charts below.

Title VII: (42 U.S.C. §2000(e) et seq.) Part of the Civil Rights Act of 1964, this title deals with discrimination in employment generally. It prohibits discrimination in nearly every aspect of employment, from the decision on whom to hire to the salary paid, fringe benefits granted, and working conditions provided. Originally, educational institutions were exempt from the requirements of Title VII; but the exemption was eliminated by an amendment in 1972, and now educational institutions are subject to the provisions of the Act.

Under Title VII, discrimination based on race, color, religion, national origin, and sex is declared illegal.

Title VI: (42 U.S.C. §2000(d) et seq.) Another part of the Civil Rights Act of 1964, this title focuses on discrimination in programs supported by federal funds. In contrast to the employment provisions of Title VII, Title VI excludes most employment issues and trains the regulatory eye on the benefits being provided to the recipients of the program. Either segregation (or other separate treatment) or unequal distribution of benefits (ranging from the opportunity to receive benefits at all to the level and character of those benefits) may constitute a violation of Title VI.

Discrimination on the basis of race, color, and national origin is prohibited by Title VI.

Title IX: (20 U.S.C. §1681 et seq.) This title was part of the Education Amendments of 1972 and is limited to sex discrimination* in *educational* programs receiving federal funds. As a programmatic statute modelled after Title VI of the Civil Rights Act of 1964, Title IX is generally consid-

---

*Title IX also prohibits discrimination on the basis of blindness, but this form of discrimination is now subject to the more comprehensive provisions of Section 504.

ered to apply to discrimination in educational programs, not employment. Like Title VI, Title IX prohibits denial of or differential in benefits, but in this instance based on sex. However, admissions decisions at all undergraduate private institutions and single-sex public institutions are exempted from this ban on discrimination.

Title IX applies only to sex discrimination and only to educational institutions.

Executive Order 11246: (30 Fed. Reg. 12319 (1965)) A very different provision from the three outlined above, the Executive Order was promulgated by the President in 1965 and requires that, in addition to not discriminating, all employers who contract with the government take "affirmative action" to ensure proper representation of minorities and women (the latter added in 1967) in the employer's work force. The executive Order, then, is an employment (as opposed to a programmatic) directive which arises out of the contract relationship between government and contractor.

The Executive Order applies to race, color, religion, national origin, and sex.

Equal Pay Act: (29 U.S.C. §206(d)) A relatively specific employment provision, this 1963 legislation does not speak in terms of discrimination; rather, it requires equal pay for equal work and bans any salary distinction for performance of similar work duties based on sex. Although it applies to all employ*ers* covered by the Fair Labor Standards Act, professional employ*ees* were not covered by the Act until 1972.

Again, the Act makes sex-based salary distinctions illegal.

Section 503: (29 U.S.C. §793) Part of the Rehabilitation Act of 1973, this section parallels Executive Order 11246 in requiring affirmative action by employers with government contracts to hire and promote handicapped persons.

Section 504: (29 U.S.C. §794) Another section of the Rehabilitation Act of 1973, this parallels the programmatic nature of Title VI. Section 504 prohibits discrimination on the basis of handicap in all federally assisted educational programs.

Architectural Barriers Act: (42 U.S.C. §4151 et seq.) Together with Section 502 of the Rehabilitation Act of 1973 (29 U.S.C. 792), this 1968 Act requires that buildings financed by federal grants or loans be accessible to the handicapped.

Age Discrimination in Employment Act (ADEA): (29 U.S.C. §621 et seq.) This 1967 Act prohibits employment discrimination against persons 40–70 years old, including mandatory retirement programs. It was not until 1974 that the Act was extended to public sector employees and only in 1978 that the Act's coverage extended to employees 65–70 years old.

Age Discrimination Act (ADA): (42 U.S.C. §6101 et seq.) Another programmatic provision modelled after Title VI, this 1975 Act prohibits discrimination on the basis of age (*not* limited to persons 40–70 years old) in any educational program receiving federal funds or assistance.

Vietnam Era Veterans Readjustment Assistance Act: (38 U.S.C. §2012 et seq.) This 1974 employment provision requires affirmative action to employ and promote Vietnam veterans by government contractors. Modelled after Executive Order 11246, the affirmative action requirement is an element of the employer's government contract.

Fair Housing Act: (42 U.S.C. §3601 et seq.) Passed in 1968, this act prohibits housing discrimination based on race, national origin, religion, and sex in housing financed with federal aid or by state and local agencies receiving federal assistance.

Sections 799A and 845: (42 U.S.C. §§16) These sections of the Public Health Service Act prohibit sex discrimination in admissions by schools of medicine, schools of nursing, and schools in other health-related fields receiving federal assistance under the Act.

In addition to the laws noted above, there are several other laws which have been subject to a century of judicial interpretation pertaining to present equal opportunity/nondiscrimination efforts. It is best simply to quote them in pertinent part:

14th Amendment: (U.S. Const. Amend. XIV §2) "No State shall . . . deny to any person within its jurisdiction the equal protection of the laws."

42 U.S.C. §1981: "All persons . . . have the same right . . . to make and enforce contracts . . . and to the full and equal benefit of all laws and proceedings for the security of persons and property as is enjoyed by white citizens, and are subject to like punishment, pains, penalties, taxes, licenses and exactions of every kind and to no other."

42 U.S.C. §1983: "Every person who, under color of any statute, ordinance, regulation, custom or usage, of any State or Territory, subjects, or causes to be subjected, any citizen of the United States . . . to the deprivation of any rights, privileges, or immunities secured by the Constitution and laws, shall be liable to the party injured in action at law, suit in equity, or other proper proceeding for redress."

ANNEX B—CHARTS

Procedural and Jurisdiction
Chart of the Equal Opportunity/
Nondiscrimination Laws

Procedural Regulations of the
Antidiscrimination Statutes

Annex B: Procedural and Jurisdictional Chart of the Equal Opportunity/Nondiscrimination Laws.

	Age	Color	Handicap	Natl. Origin	Race	Religion	Sex	Veteran	Employment
Title VII		X		X	X	X	X		X
Title VI		X		X	X	X			X
Title IX			Blindness only				X		?
11246		X		X	X	X	X		X
Equal Pay Act							X		X
§503			X						X
§504			X						X
Arch. Barriers and §502			X						
Age Discrimination in Employment	X								X
Age Discrimination Act	X								X
Vietnam Era Veterans Act								X	X
§1981		X			X				X
§1983	?	X	X	X	X	X	X		X
5th Amendment 14th Amendment			Could be any with varying levels of judicial scrutiny						X
Fair Housing				X	X	X	X		
§§799A and 845 of the Public Health Service Act							X		X

Procedural Regulations of the Antidiscrimination Statutes.

Statute [1]	Admin. Agency	Pre-hearing Conciliation	Agency Remedies After Hearing	Agency Action on Behalf of Complainant	Private Cause of Action?	Exhaustion of Admin. Remedies Required?	Court Remedies	Special Regulations for Higher Education
Title VII 42 U.S.C. §2000 (e)-(o) 17 1972	EEOC	Yes, if EEOC finds reasonable cause after investigation.	None. (No final hearing authority) Referral to DOJ for public institutions.	EEOC may sue on behalf of complainant. EEOC may initiate pattern and practice suit.	Yes	Yes [2]	General equitable remedies. [3] (hereinafter (G.E.R.).	Recordkeeping regulations 29 C.F.R. §§1602.47 - 1605.55
Equal Pay Act 29 U.S.C. §206 (d) 1966/1972 [4]	EEOC [5]	Not required; most disputes settled voluntarily.	None	EEOC may sue on behalf of complainant.	Yes, if EEOC does not file suit.	No	G.E.R./ fines and imprisonment after criminal prosecution for willful violations.	None
Age Discrimination in Employment Act §9 U.S.C. 621-634 1967/1974 [6]	EEOC [5]	Required before EEOC files suit.	None	EEOC may sue on behalf of complainant.	Yes, if EEOC does not file suit.	No, however individual must give EEOC 60 days notice before filing suit.	G.E.R.	None

Executive Order 11246, as amended 1965	DOC/ OFCCP	Encouraged, but not mandatory. OFCCP refers all *individual* complaints to EEOC for processing in accordance with EEOC, Title VII procedures.	Cancel, terminate, or suspend contracts; debarment of contract from further contracts.	May refer to Department of Justice for suit. The Department of Justice may also initiate suit after an independent investigation.	No, but an individual may sue to compel agency enforcement proceeding.	N/A	Department of Justice may sue for G.E.R. Also, contracts may have judicial review of agency decisions.	No, however, 3 memoranda by OCR in 1974 and 1975 are still in effect.
§503 of the Rehabilitation Act of 1973 29 U.S.C. §793, 1973	DOL/ OFCCP	Yes	Termination or suspension of the contract; debarment from future contracts.	Director of OFCCP may seek judicial action.	No, but an individual may sue to compel agency to initiate enforcement proceeding.	N/A	G.E.R. Judicial review of agency decisions to impose sanctions on contractors.	None
Vietnam Era Veterans Readjustment Assistance Act 38 U.S.C. §2012, 1974	DOL/ OFCCP	Yes	Termination of contract; withholding of progress payments to contractor; debarment from future contracts.	May refer to Department of Justice for suit.	No, but an individual may sue to compel agency to initiate enforcement proceedings.	N/A	G.E.R., Contractors may have judicial review of unfavorable agency decisions.	None

Procedural Regulations of the Antidiscrimination Statutes. *(continued)*

Statute[1]	Admin. Agency	Pre-hearing Conciliation	Agency Remedies After Hearing	Agency Action on Behalf of Complainant	Private Cause of Action?	Exhaustion of Admin. Remedies Required?	Court Remedies	Special Regulations for Higher Education
Title VI 42 U.S.C. §2000 (d) – (d) 6 1964	HEW/OCR[7]	Yes	Termination of funds.	May refer to DOJ for suit.	Yes[8]	No	G.E.R., Judicial review of final agency decisions.	None
Title IX 20 U.S.C. §§1681-1686, 1972	HEW/OCR[7]	Yes	Termination of funds.	May refer to DOJ for suit.	Yes[8]	No	G.E.R., Judicial review of final agency decisions.	45 C.F.R §§86.21-86.23
§504 of the Rehabilitation Act of 1973. 29 U.S.C. §794, 1973	HEW/OCR[7]	Yes	Termination of funds.	May refer to DOJ for suit.	Yes[8]	No	G.E.R., Judicial review of final agency decisions.	45 C.F.R. §§86.41-86.47
Age Discrimination Act 42 U.S.C. §6101-6107, 1975	HEW/OCR[7]	Yes, the regulations also require mediation.	Termination of funds.	May refer to DOJ for suit.	Yes	Yes[9]	G.E.R., Judicial review of final agency decisions.	None

§§799A–845 of the Public Health Service Act 42 U.S.C. §216, 1971	HEW/OCR[7]	Yes	Termination of funds.	May refer to DOJ for suit.	Yes[8]	No[8]	G.E.R., Judicial review of final agency decisions.	Applies only to medical and nursing schools. 45 CFR Part 83
Fair Housing Act 42 U.S.C. §§3601–3619, 1968	HUD	Yes	N/A	Yes. The Attorney General may institute a pattern and practice suit for equitable relief.	Yes	No	G.E.R.	None
Architectural Barriers Act, 42 U.S.C. 4151–4156 (1968) and 502 of the Rehabilitation Act of 1973	GSA. The Architectural and Transportation Barriers Compliance Board was created in 1973 to insure compliance with the Act.	Yes	Withhold or suspend funds with respect to buildings not in compliance.	No	No	No	Judicial review of final Board Orders.	None

Notes to Annex B.

1. Dates refer to year the statute was made applicable to higher educational organizations.

2. Administrative remedies are exhausted if, after the expiration of 180 days from the date the complaint was filed, the agency has reached no final decision or has made a "no action" determination.

3. General equitable remedies include backpay, and injunctive relief, i.e., reinstatement, hiring, altered seniority systems, training, or other remedial programs, recruitment, wage increases, award of attorney's fees, and other relief including continuing court oversight.

4. The Equal Pay Act was applied to "hourly" or "non-exempt" employees of colleges and universities in 1967. In 1972, coverage under the Act was extended to include administrative and faculty personnel of such organizations.

5. The authority to enforce the Equal Pay Act and the Age Discrimination in Employment Act was transferred from the Department of Labor to the EEOC on July 1, 1979. EEOC has said that they will follow the investigation and enforcement procedures previously established by the Wage and Hour Division of the Department of Labor. The interpretations of the Act, however, which were previously issued by the DOL are currently being reviewed by the EEOC.

6. The ADEA has applied to private institutions since its passage in 1967. In 1974, the coverage of the Act was extended to include public institutions.

7. There will be an Office for Civil Rights within the recently created Department of Education that will take over the responsibility for enforcing the statute formerly exercised by OCR within the Department of Health, Education and Welfare.

8. The Supreme Court held in *Cannon v. University of Chicago*, 99 S. Ct. 1946 (1979), that individuals had a private right of action under Title IX. In the light of *Cannon, Regents of the University of California v. Bakke*, 98 S. Ct. 2733 (1978), *Lau v. Nichols*, 414 U.S. 563 (1974), and *Southeastern Community College v. Davis*, 99 S. Ct. 2361 (1979), it seems likely that Title IX and §504 will be held to provide similar private rights of action.

(End of Annex B)

Table 1.   Complaints of Employment Discrimination in Higher
Education Analysis of Administrative Agency and Judicial Action
(44 Cases; See List Following Table 2).

1. Type of Action:
   Individual   35
   Class   9

2. Form of Discrimination*:
   Race   16
   Sex   32

   (*4 Complaints alleged both race and sex discrimination.)

3. Practice Challenged*:
   Promotion   23
   Non-Reappointment   23
   Salary   15
   Tenure   15
   Hiring   7

   (*Many plaintiffs challenged more than one practice.)

4. Number of Statutes Alleged to Have Been Violated:

Number of Statutes	Cases	Number of Statutes	Cases
1	17	4	4
2	10	5	2
3	9	6	2

5. Number of Administrative Agencies or Courts to Which Complaints
   Were Made:

Courts and/or Agencies	Complaints	Courts and/or Agencies	Complaints
1	10	4	8
2	18	5	1
3	7		

6. Agencies to Which Complaints Were Made:

Agency	Number of Complaints
EEOC	23
State or Local Agency	11
DOJ	4
HEW	2
OFCCP	2
DOL	1

7. Outcomes (As of 12/31/79):
   For Plaintiffs   5
   For Defendent Institutions   24
   Decision Pending   15

Table 2.   Distribution of Times Elapsed Between Stages of
Proceedings in Cases Involving Allegations of Race and Sex
Discrimination (41 Cases).

1. First Complaint Within Institution for First Court Complaint:

Less than 1 year	6
1 – 2 Years	12
2 – 3 Years	6
3 – 4 Years	3
4 – 5 Years	4

2. First Complaint Within Institution for First Court Decision on the Merits:

Less than 1 year	1
1 – 2 Years	5
2 – 3 Years	8
3 – 4 Years	11
4 – 5 Years	4
5 – 6 Years	8
6 – 7 Years	2
More than 7 years	2

3. First Complaint Within Institution to Latest Court Decision on the Merits:

Less than 1 year	0
1 – 2 Years	4
2 – 3 Years	3
3 – 4 Years	10
4 – 5 Years	8
5 – 6 Years	10
6 – 7 Years	4
More than 7 years	2

4. First Administrative Agency Complaint to First Court Complaint:

Less than 1 year	6
1 – 2 Years	7
2 – 3 Years	3
3 – 4 Years	5

5. First Administrative Agency Complaint to First Court Decision on the Merits:

Less than 1 year	2
1 – 2 Years	2
2 – 3 Years	8
3 – 4 Years	5
4 – 5 Years	3
5 – 6 Years	4
6 – 7 Years	1
More than 7 years	1

Table 2. continued

6. First Agency Complaint to Latest Court Decision on the Merits:

Less than 1 year	1
1 – 2 Years	2
2 – 3 Years	4
3 – 4 Years	4
4 – 5 Years	6
5 – 6 Years	6
6 – 7 Years	2
More than 7 years	1

7. First Court Complaint to First Court Decision on the Merits:

Less than 1 year	7
1 – 2 Years	14
2 – 3 Years	4
3 – 4 Years	3
4 – 5 Years	1

8. First Court Complaint to Latest Court Decision on the Merits:

Less than 1 year	3
1 – 2 Years	11
2 – 3 Years	10
3 – 4 Years	1
4 – 5 Years	4

ALPHABETICAL LIST OF ALL FACULTY AND PROFESSIONAL EMPLOYMENT DISCRIMINATION CASES INVOLVING COLLEGES AND UNIVERSITIES

1. *Al–Hamdarii v. State University of New York*, 438 F. Supp. 299 (1977)
2. *Berry v. University of Texas*, HEW Docket No. CC−10. (1971, 1979)
3. *Carrion v. Yeshiva University*, 535 F.3d 722 (1976)
4. *Citron v. Jackson State University*, 456 F. Supp. 3 (1977)
5. *Clap v. Lehigh University*, 450 F. Supp. 460 (1978)
6. *Clark v. Atlanta University* 15 FEP 1139 (1976)
7. *Craig v. Alabama State University*, 451 F. Supp. 1207 (1978)
8. *Cramer v. Virginia Commonwealth University*, 586 Fed 297 (1978)
9. *Cussler v. University of Maryland*, 430 F. Supp. 602 (1977)
10. *Davis v. Weidner*, 421 F. Supp. 594 (1976)
11. *Dyson v. Lavery*, 417 F. Supp. 103 (1976)
12. *Egelston v. State University College at Genesco*, (1976)
13. *EEOC v. Tufts Institution of Learning*, 421 F. Supp. 152 (1975)
14. *Faro v. New York University*, 502 F.2d 1229 (1974)
15. *Green v. Board of Texas Tech University*, 474 F.2 594 (1973)
16. *Hanshaw v. Delaware Technical and Community College*, 405 F.Supp. 292 (1975)
17. *Hill v. Nettleton*, 455 F. Supp. 514 (1978)
18. *Huang v. College of the Holy Cross*, 436, F. Supp. 639 (1977)
19. *Jawa v. Fayetteville State University*, 426 F. Supp. 218 (1978)
20. *Johnson v. University of Pittsburgh*, 435, F. Supp. 1328 (1977)
21. *Keyes v. Lenoir Rhyne College*, 552 F. 2d 579 (1977)
22. *Kunda v. Muhlenburg College*, 463 F. Supp. 294 (1978)
23. *Labat v. Board of Higher Education of the City of New York*, 401 F. Supp. 753 (1975)
24. *Lewis v. Chicago State College*, 299 F. Supp. 1357 (1969)
25. *Mecklenburg v. Montana State Board of Regents*, 13 FEP 462 (1976)
26. *Moore v. Kibbie*, 400 F. Supp. 1367 (1975)
27. *Morpurgo v. Board of Higher Education of the City of New York*, 400 F. Supp. 1135 (1977)
28. *Mosby v. Webster College*, 563 F.2d 901 (1977)
29. *Pace College v. Commission on Human Rights*, 38 NY 2d 28 (1975)
30. *Pendrell v. Chatham College*, 370 F. Supp. 494 (1974)
31. *Perham v. Ladd*, 436 F. Supp 1101 (1977)
32. *Peters v. Middlebury College*, 409 F. Supp. 857 (1976)

33. *Powell v. Syracuse University*, 580 F. 2d 1150 (1978)
34. *Presseisen v. Swarthmore College*, 442 F. Supp. 593 (1977)
35. *Rackin v. University of Pennsylvania*, 386 F. Supp. 992 (1974)
36. *Scott v. University of Delaware*, 455 F. Supp 1102 (1978)
37. *Sime v. Trustees of California State University and Colleges*, 526 F. 2d 1112 (1975)
38. *Smith College v. MCAD*, 380 NE2 121 (1978)
39. *Stevens v. Junior College District of St. Louis, St. Louis County*, 548 F. 2d 779 (1977)
40. *Sweeney v. Board of Trustees of Keene State College*, 569 F. Supp. 169, (further proceedings December 1979)
41. *United States v. University of Maryland*, 438 F. Supp. 742 (1977)
42. *Wagner v. Long Island University*, 419 F. Supp. 618 (1976)
43. *Wheelock College v. MCAD*, 355 NE 2d 309 (1976)
44. *Van de Vate v. Bolling*, 379 F. Supp. 925 (1974)

CHAPTER 4—THE ROLE OF THE STATES

Edward S. Gruson was responsible for gathering and analyzing the material for Chapter 4. He wishes to acknowledge the effort, capacity, candor, and contribution of David Adamany, Robert Cope, Joe H. Hiett, Joseph Kershaw, Renee Petersen, Richard Stafford and Lawrence Lustberg, Jacob Stampen, Kenneth W. Tolo, Eugene P. Trani, and James Wharton who prepared the studies of state government and higher education for the Commission.

In Washington, Lois Rice and her associates Lawrence Gladieux and Janet Hansen were consistently available for advice and explanation about historical, legislative and executive actions. I am very grateful. Irene Spero was consistently acute, perceptive and essential in staffing the Washington office. From the higher education associations, Charles Saunders, Jerry Roschwalb, John Mallen, Jack Tirrell and John Phillips were generous with their time, experience and good spirit.

REFERENCES

Page 95

For a comprehensive review of trends in state support of higher education see: Ruyle, J.H. and Glenny, L., *State Budgeting for Higher Education: Trends in State Revenue Appropriations from 1968 to 1977*, (Center for Studies in Higher Education, University of California, Berkeley, 1978). For the years before and after the Berkeley study see the compilations prepared annually by Chambers, M.M., *Appropriations: State Tax Funds for Operating Expenses of Higher Education*, (Office of Research and Information, National Association of State Universities and Land-Grant Colleges, Washington, D.C.).

Table 1. Historical Growth of State Higher Education Agencies (Cumulative Totals).

State Higher Education Agency	1930	1950	1960	1969	1976
Voluntary	0	3	5	4	0
State-wide governing board	10	15	15	16	19
Regulatory coordinating agency	1	2	5	15	19
Advisory coordinating agency	0	1	5	13	10
None	0	0	0	0	2

Source: Adapted from Glenny, L. A. and Bowen, F. M., *State Intervention in Higher Education*, Sloan Commission on Government and Higher Education, November 1977, p. 20.

Table 2. Patterns of State Coordination of All Public Institutions of Higher Education.

A No Overall Coordination (2)	B Coordination by Consolidated Board (19)	C Regulatory Coordinating Agency (19)	D Advisory Coordinating Agency (10)
Delaware	Alaska	Colorado	Alabama
Vermont	Arizona	Connecticut	Arkansas
	Florida	Indiana	California
	Georgia	Illinois	Maryland
	Hawaii	Kentucky	Michigan
	Idaho	Louisiana	Minnesota
	Iowa	Massachusetts	Nebraska
	Kansas	Missouri	New Hampshire
	Maine	New Jersey	Washington
	Mississippi	New Mexico	Wyoming
	Montana	New York	
	Nevada	Ohio	
	North Carolina	Oklahoma	
	North Dakota	Oregon	
	Rhode Island	Pennsylvania	
	South Dakota	South Carolina	
	Utah	Virginia	
	West Virginia	Tennessee	
	Wisconsin	Texas	

Source: Adapted from Carnegie Foundation for Advancement of Teaching, *The States and Higher Education*, San Francisco, Jossey-Bass, 1976, p. 90.

Pages 97–98

For background on the development and problems of state higher education boards or agencies see: Berdahl, Robert O., *Statewide Coordination of Higher Education*, (American Council on Education, Washington, D.C., 1971); Millard, Richard M., *State Boards of Higher Education*, (American Association for Higher Education, Washington, D.C., 1976); and Glenny, L.A. and Bowen, F.M., *State Intervention in Higher Education*, (Sloan Commission on Government and Higher Education, November, 1977). Also, Berdahl, Robert O., "Secondary and Postsecondary Education: The Politics of Accommodation," in E.K. Mosher and J.L. Wagoner, Jr., editors *The Changing Politics of Education: Prospects for the 1980s*, (Berkeley: McCutchan Publishing Corporation, 1978).

Page 99

For views of the nature and consequences of retrenchment see: Mortimer, K.P. and Tierney, M.D., *The Three R's of the Eighties: Reduction, Reallocation and Retrenchment*, (The Pennsylvania State University, Center for Postsecondary Education: American Institute for Research). Interesting studies are underway at Southern Regional Educational Board. See their *Developing Guidelines for Statewide Policy in Cases of Merger, Reorganization or Closure of Institutions*, (Atlanta, Georgia: 1979, mimeograph). Also, the reports of the Minnesota Higher Education Coordinating Board, especially, *Planning for Fluctuating Enrollments: A Working Paper for the Annual Meeting of Postsecondary Governing Boards, December 1977.*

Pages 100–101

The incidents in Ohio are reported on in Petersen, Renee, *The State and Higher Education in Ohio*, (Report prepared for the Sloan Commission on Government and Higher Education, Cambridge, 1978). The quote is from Trani, Eugene P., *Higher Education in Nebraska*, (Report prepared for the Sloan Commission on Government and Higher Education, Cambridge, September, 1978, p. 29).

Pages 101–102

See Stafford, Richard and Lustberg, Lawrence, *Higher Education in Massachusetts: Issues in Their Context*, (Report prepared for the Sloan Commission on Government and Higher Education, Cambridge, 1978). Also, Lustberg, Lawrence S., *The Founding of Community Colleges in Massachusetts: A Study of Issues in Political Sociology*, Harvard University, Cambridge, April 1979, p. 165, unpublished senior thesis).

Pages 102–105

For reviews of the processes presently used in academic program reviews see: Barak, Robert J. and Berdahl, Robert O., *State Level Academic Program Review*, (Education Commission of the States, Denver, 1978); and Folger, John K., editors, *Increasing the Public Accountability of Higher Education*, (San Francisco: Jossey-Bass, 1977). For a brief summary of the issues in Wisconsin's experience with academic program reviews see: Stampen, Jacob O., *Conflict, Accountability and the Wisconsin Idea: A Report Prepared for the Sloan Commission on Government and Higher Education*, (Cambridge: November, 1978).

Pages 105–108

The most thorough review of the financing of public institutions of higher education is presented in a series of volumes by Lyman A. Glenny and his associates published by the Center for Research and Development in Higher Education at the University of California, Berkeley. For tantalizing circumscribed suggestions of changes in policy directions see the publication of the Minnesota Higher Education Coordinating Board cited above. For a good review of a complex series of formulas in one state see Tolo, Kenneth W., *Higher Education in Texas: Student Aid and Governance*, (Report prepared for the Sloan Commission on Government and Higher Education, Cambridge, October, 1978). Note also, Renee Petersen's report cited above and Wharton, James, *Observations of Higher Education in Louisiana: Student Financial Aid and Governance*, (Report prepared for the Sloan Commission on Government and Higher Education, Cambridge, 1978).

Pages 108–109

Although trends vary from state-to-state and among regions, data provided by the Policy Analysis Division of the American Council on Education suggest that state funding for Public Research Universities I and II has lagged behind the rate of growth of funding for other parts of the public sector. Most of the studies of state systems of higher education prepared for the Sloan Commission indicate that legislators and the executive perceive that teaching is "sacrificed" for research in the flagship institutions. See especially, Hiett, Joseph H., *Government and Higher Education in Florida*, (Report prepared for the Sloan Commission on Government and Higher Education, Cambridge, October, 1978); Trani, Eugene P., *op. cit.*; Tolo, Kenneth W., *op. cit.*; Petersen, Renee, *op. cit.* See also Millet, John D., *Politics in Higher Education*,(Tuscalousa, Alabama: University of Alabama Press, 1974). A variant on this theme can be found in Kershaw, Joseph, *Government and Higher Education in New York State*, (Report prepared for the Sloan Commission on Government and Higher Education,

Cambridge, 1978). Kershaw suggests that it may not be possible in New York state to support four major university centers at the highest level of quality. For the point of view of a scholar in a system which discourages research (California State Universities and Colleges) see: Adamany, David, *State Government Regulation of Higher Education in California*, (Report prepared for the Sloan Commission on Government and Higher Education, Cambridge, December, 1978).

Pages 109—111

For a summary of some of the less attractive behavior of institutions of higher education see: "What Assurance Does the Office of Education's Eligibility Process Provide," (General Accounting Office, Washington, D.C., January 17, 1979). Also see Bailey, S.K., *Academic Quality Control: The Case of College Programs on Military Bases*, (Washington, D.C.: American Association for Higher Education, January, 1979); Gruson, E.S., *Issues in Accreditation, Eligibility and Institutional Quality*, (Discussion paper prepared for the Sloan Commission on Government and Higher Education, Cambridge, March, 1979). For a review of state licensing activities, among others, see: Jung, S.M., et al., *Final Technical Report: A Study of State Oversight in Postsecondary Education*, (American Institute for Research, December, 1977). Model legislation was proposed in Education Commission of the States, *Task Force on Model State Legislation for Approval*

Table 3.   Summary of Faculty Bargaining Decisions.

	4-year Campuses			2-year Campuses			Grand Total
	Public	Private	Total	Public	Private	Total	
American Association of University Professors	24	25	49	5	1	6	55
American Federation of Teachers	70	18	88	119	6	125	213
National Education Association	46	13	59	183	2	185	244
A.A.U.P.-N.E.A.	4	0	4	7	0	7	11
Independent and Other	19	11	30	46	1	47	77
Total	163	67	230	360	10	370	600
Bargaining Rejected	22	38	60	14	3	17	77

Source: *Chronicle of Higher Education*, July 26, 1978. Data reported as of May 15, 1978.

of Postsecondary Educational Institutions and Authorization to Grant Degrees, Report. (Denver: Education Commission of the States, 1973).

Pages 112–114

The prediction comes from Mayhew, Lewis B., *Legacy of the Seventies*, (San Francisco: Jossey-Bass, 1977). A summary of faculty bargaining decisions and distribution by Carnegie Classification of institutions of higher education are given in Tables 3 and 4.

The following table summarizes the distribution of faculty unions by sector and Carnegie Classification; it also shows the number of institutions which have rejected faculty unionization in 1978.

Table 4.

Carnegie Classification	Bargaining Unit Accepted		Bargaining Unit Rejected	
	Public	Private	Public	Private
Research University I	2	2	2	7
Research University II	9	0	1	3
Doctorate-Granting University I	7	2	3	4
Doctorate-Granting University II	2	3	0	0
Comprehensive Universities and Colleges I	52	15	8	1
Comprehensive Universities and Colleges II	28	9	6	2
Liberal Arts Colleges I	0	1	4	0
Liberal Arts Colleges II	2	16	8	0
2-Year Campuses	360	10	3	14
Specialty	59	18	0	0

See also Lee, B.A., *Collective Bargaining in Four-Year Colleges*, (AAHE–ERIC, Higher Education Report, No. 5, 1978, Washington, D.C., American Association for Higher Education, 1978); and Garbrinio, J.W., "State Experiences in Collective Bargaining," in *Faculty Bargaining in Public Higher Education*, (San Francisco: Jossey-Bass, 1977). See also Begin, J.P., *Due Process and Collegiality Under Faculty Grievance Mechanisms: The Cost of Rutgers University*, (New Brunswick, New Jersey: Institute of Management and Labor Relations, Rutgers University, 1977; Finkin, M.W., "Grievance Procedures," in Duryen, E.D., Fisk, R.S., and associates, editors, *Faculty Unions and Collective Bargaining*, (San Francisco: Jossey-Bass, 1973).

Pages 115-119

These pages draw heavily from the reports prepared in ten states on the relations between state government and public higher education.

Page 115

The quote is from Adamany, David, *op. cit.*, (p. 166).

Page 116

The experience in Wisconsin is from Stampen, Jacob O., *op. cit.*, (p. 78); for the incidents in Washington see: Cope, Robert G., *Observations on Washington State's System of Higher Education*, (Report prepared for the Sloan Commission on Government and Higher Education, Cambridge, December, 1978, p. 14, *et seq.*).

Pages 116-117

Adamany, David, *op. cit.*, (pp. 166-167). The Senior Vice President of the University of Wisconsin is quoted in Stampen, Jacob O., *op. cit.*, (pp. 98-99).

Page 117

On some of the management problems in colleges and universities see: Jenny, Hans H., *Higher Education and the Economy*, (ERIC Higher Education Research Report, No. 2, 1976, Washington, D.C., American Association for Higher Education, pp. 47-52).

Pages 118-119

The quotes referring to the California study are found in Adamany, David, *op. cit.*, (pp. 189-90). The final quote is from Jenny, Hans H., *op. cit.*, (p. 49).

CHAPTER 5—FINANCIAL AID

Chapter 5—Financial Aid

Kenneth M. Deitch was responsible for gathering and analyzing the material for Chapter 5. He wishes to thank the host of people who have shared their knowledge and experience with him. It should be clear that acknowledgement in no way indicates that the person agrees with the views expressed in this chapter. It is rather, an expression of thanks and appreciation. In this spirit, thanks are owed to Robert Atwell, Arthur Beroz, David Breneman, Congressman Barker Conable, Sheldon Cohen, Sal Corallo, Carol Cox, Richard Dix, Humphrey Doermann, Stephen P. Dresch, Arthur Doyle, Virginia Fadil, Alfred B. Fitt, Carol Frances, Joseph Froomkin, R. Jerold Gibson, Lawrence Gladieux, Fred Glimp, Bette Hamilton, George Hanford, Janet Hansen, Robert Hartman, Arthur Hauptman, Helge Holst, John C. Hoy, Joseph Kane, Joseph Kershaw, Kurt Kendis, Leo Kornfeld, Martin Kramer, Charlotte Kuh, Theodore J. Marchese, Arthur Marmaduke, Dallas Martin, Richard M. Millard, Rexford Moon, Frank Morris, David S. Mundel, James Nelson, Susan Nelson, Michael O'Keefe, Douglas Palmer, John D. Phillips, Roy Radner, Richard J. Ramsden, Lois D. Rice, David Riesman, Kenneth Rossano, Michelle Scott, Hayden Smith, Marshall Smith, Patricia Smith, Jacob O. Stampen, John E. Tirrell, William Van Dusen, Abbott Wainwright, Thomas Wolanin, and Kenneth E. Young.

REFERENCES

Page 124

For a history of the landmark legislation known as the Educational Amendments of 1972 see Gladieux, Lawrence E., and Wolanin, Thomas R., *Congress and the Colleges: The National Politics of Higher Education* (Lexington: Lexington Books, 1976).

Pages 124—126

On the subject of access to higher education see: The Carnegie Commission on Higher Education, *New Students and New Places: Policies for the Future Growth and Development of American Higher Education* (New York: McGraw-Hill Book Co., 1971); Humphrey Doermann, *Toward Equal Access* (New York: The College Entrance Examination Board, 1978); Ferrin, Richard I., *A Decade of Change in Free-Access Higher Education* (New York: The College Entrance Examination Board, 1971); Leslie, Larry L., *Higher Education Opportunity: A Decade of Progress* (Washington, D.C.: The American Association for Higher Education, 1977); The Panel on Financing Low-Income and Minority Students in Higher Education, *Toward Equal Opportunity for Higher Education* (New York: The College Entrance Examination Board, 1973); Willingham, Warren W., *Free Access Higher Education* (New York: The College Entrance Examination Board, 1973); For another view of the consequences of wide access in higher education see: Freeman, Richard, *The Declining Economic Value of Higher Education and the American Social System* (U.S.A.: Aspen Institute for Humanistic Studies, 1976).

Pages 126—132

On the issues raised by the question "who should pay for higher education?" see: The American Association of State Colleges and Universities, Low Tuition FactBook: *Eight Basic Facts About Tuition and Educational Opportunity* (Washington, D.C.: AASCU, 1976); The Carnegie Commission on Higher Education, *Higher Education: Who Pays? Who Benefits? Who Should Pay?* (New York: McGraw-Hill Book Co., 1970); The Carnegie Council on Policy Studies in Higher Education, Low or No Tuition: *The Feasibility of a National Policy for the First Two-Years of a College* (San Francisco: Jossey-Bass, 1975); Committee on Economic Development, Research Policy Committee, *The Management and Financing of Colleges* (New York, Committee for Economic Development, (1973); The Staff of the Carnegie Commission on Higher Education, *Tuition: A Supplemental Statement on Higher Education on "Who Pays? Who Benefits? Who Should Pay?* (Berkeley, California: The Carnegie Foundation for the Advancement of Teaching, 1974); Young, Kenneth E., (editor) *Exploring The Case for Low Tuition in Public Higher Education* (Place of publication unlisted: American Association of Community and Junior Colleges, National Association of State Universities and Land-Grant Colleges, 1974). For a discussion of the "independent" student see: College Scholarship Service of the College Entrance Examination Board, *Who Pays? Who Benefits? A National Invitational Conference on the Independent Student* (New York: College Entrance Examination Board, 1974); Hanson, David J., *The Lowered Age of Majority: Its Impact on Higher Education*, Washington,

D.C.: Association of American Colleges, 1975); Nelson, Janet E., Rice, Lois D., Jacobson, Edmund C., and Van Dusen, William D., *Who is the Independent Student? A Study of the Status and Resources of Independent Students*, (Prepared by the New York Office of the College Entrance Examination Board for the Office of Planning Budgeting and Evaluation of the United States Office of Education, Department of Health, Education, and Welfare, 1976); Nelson, Janet E., Van Dusen, William D., Jacobson, Edmund C., *The Willingness of Parents to Contribute to Postsecondary Educational Expenses*, (Prepared by the College Entrance Examination Board under contract to the Office of Planning, Budgeting and Evaluation, Postsecondary Programs Division, United States Office of Education, no date). An overview of the current status of the federal financial aid programs is offered in: Carnegie Council on Policy Studies in Higher Education, *Next Steps for the 1980s in Student Financial Aid: A Fourth Alternative* (San Francisco, and other cities: Jossey-Bass, 1979).

Pages 137—140

For discussion of the "half-cost" rule see: Ramsden, Richard J., "The Basic Educational Opportunity Grant Program One-Half Cost: An Analysis" (Hanover, New Hampshire: Consortium on Financing Higher Education, November 6, 1975, mimeographed), Hartman, Robert W., "Federal Options for Student Aid" in David W. Breneman and Chester E. Finn, Jr., editors, with the assistance of Susan C. Nelson, *Public Policy and Private Higher Education* (Washington, D.C.: The Brookings Institution, 1978). For discussion of alternatives to half-cost see: "Testimony of Michael O'Keefe, Department of Health, Education, and Welfare, before the Subcommittee on Postsecondary Education of the House Committee on Education and Labor" May 16, 1979.

Pages 141—143

For a review of need analysis and its problems see: College Scholarship Service, *CSS Need Analysis: Theory and Computation Procedures for the 1979—80 FAF* (New York: College Entrance Examination Board, 1978). Also see: *Next Steps . . .* (op. cit.); and Nelson, Janet E., "Measuring Need vs. Meeting Need" *The College Board Review* (No. 94, Winter 1974—75).

Pages 144—145

For education benefits under social security see: Congress of the United States, Congressional Budget Office, *Social Security Benefits for Students* (Washington, D.C.: U.S. Government Printing Office, 1977). For veteran's educational benefits see: Rashkow, Ilona "Veteran's Educational Benefits: 1944—1978" (Congressional Research Service, Library of Congress, November 10, 1976, Revised November 28, 1976).

Pages 145–147

On the issues of retention see: Astin, Alexander W., *Preventing Students from Dropping Out* (San Francisco: Jossey-Bass, 1977). For some information on the historically Black colleges see: Williams, Mary Carter, *Profile of Enrollment in the Historically Black Colleges* (Management Information Systems, Institute for Services to Education, Spring 1978); Galambos, Eva C. *Black College Graduates and the Job Market* (Atlanta, Georgia: Southern Regional Education Board, 1976); and Galambos, Eva C., *Racial Composition of Faculties in Public Colleges and Universities* (Atlanta, Georgia: Southern Regional Education Board, 1979).

Pages 150–157

The subject of lending is analytically complex. For an introduction see: Rice, Lois D., editor, *Student Loans: Problems and Policy Alternatives* (New York: College Entrance Examination Board, 1977). The topic of income-contingent lending is treated in: Johnstone, D. Bruce, with the assistance of Stephen P. Dresch, *New Patterns for College Lending: Income Contingent Loans* (New York and London: Columbia University Press, 1972); and Beroz, Arthur, *A Proposal for a United States Student Assistance Agency* (October 1977, mimeographed). President John Silber of Boston University has also pursued this topic in: Silber, John B., "The Tuition Dilemma" in the *Atlantic Monthly* (Volume 242, No. 1, July, 1978). The various annual reports of Sallie Mae, the Student Loan Marketing Association, provide a good picture of that institution's activities.

Pages 157–159

The campus-based programs are discussed in: Ramsden, Richard J., "Federal Student Assistance," (Report to the Sloan Commission on Government and Higher Education, Cambridge, October, 1977). A massive work on aspects of the subject is found in: Homles, Robert Bradford, *An Examination and Analysis of Selected Aspects on the Allocation Procedures for the Campus-Based Federal Student Financial Aid Programs* (Submitted at the University of Michigan, 1977). For information on the state programs see the annual survey published by the National Association of State Scholarship and Grant Programs. The 10th Annual Survey was for 1978–79. Joseph D. Boyd, Executive Director of the Illinois State Scholarship Commission has been the principal person preparing the document. For federal-state relations in financial aid see: Smith, Patricia and Kent, Laura, editors, *The Impact of the Basic Grant Program on the States* (Report of a Seminar held February 1, 1977, Washington, D.C.: American Council on Education, Policy Analysis Service, August, 1977). There follow two references of particular interest to a reader wishing to learn more about financial aid in general. The Student Financial Assistance

Study Group, *Recommendations for Improved Management of the Federal Student Aid Programs: A Report to the Secretary* (U.S. Department of Health, Education, and Welfare, June, 1977); and Froomkin, Joseph, *Needed: A New Federal Policy for Higher Education* (Institute for Educational Leadership, Washington, D.C.: The George Washington University, October, 1978.

Table 1*   Percentage of Support from Major Sources for Paying Students' Charges for College, by Level of Family Income, for Freshmen in 1975.

Source	*Family Income*		
	Under $8,000	*$8,000– 19,999*	*$20,000 and over*
	Percent		
Parents or Family	18.6	36.8	62.9
Total Grants	48.4	21.0	7.1
Total Self-support	30.2	39.7	27.8
From: Work	16.3	20.3	14.6
Borrowing	6.9	8.2	3.8
Savings	7.0	11.2	9.4
Other	2.8	3.5	2.2
Total	100.0	100.0	100.0

*Leslie, *Higher Education Opportunity: A Decade of Progress*, p. 26.

Table 2*   Selected Characteristics of Recipients of Aid and of Programs, for Five Title IV Programs, 1976–77.

	Total (unduplicated count)**	BEOG Program	SEOG Program	CWS Program	NDSL Program	GSL Program
Number of Recipients	1,937,000	1,411,000	432,000	698,000	757,000	695,000
Public Institution Percent	72.6	79.9	63.3	64.1	61.4	56.0
Private Institution Percent	27.4	20.1	36.7	35.9	38.6	44.0
Total	100.0	100.0	100.0	100.0	100.0	100.0
Minority Percent	34.9	43.0	39.1	29.3	25.7	17.0
Nonminority Percent	65.1	57.0	60.9	70.7	74.3	83.0
Total	100.0	100.0	100.0	100.0	100.0	100.0
Status						
Dependent Undergraduate Family Income						
Less than $6,000	22.8	30.0	24.4	19.2	14.9	8.0
$6,000–$7,499	10.1	13.5	11.0	8.9	6.9	5.5
$7,500–$11,999	17.8	19.6	20.5	18.4	17.8	12.9
$12,000–$14,999	12.2	8.6	12.0	16.5	16.5	16.8
$15,000 or more	9.0	3.3	6.6	11.5	14.5	23.8
Independent Undergraduate	24.0	24.9	25.6	20.5	21.6	18.4
Graduate Students	4.0	—	—	5.0	7.8	14.6
Total	100.0	100.0	100.0	100.0	100.0	100.0
Average Award ($)		$820	$550	$670	$750	$1,380

*Frank J. Atelsek and Irene L. Gomberg, *Estimated Number of Student Aid Recipients, 1976–77* (Washington: American Council on Education, 1977), pp. 12, 14, 15.

**Excludes GSL.

Table 3* Percentage of Recipients of Aid Having Selected Characteristics, by Program, 1974-75.

Characteristics	Total** (unduplicated count)	Recipients					
		BEOG	SEOG	SSIG***	CWS	NDSL	GSL
Total Recipients	1,584,000	543,000	350,000	302,000	575,000	749,000	669,000
Status							
Dependent Undergraduates: Family Income							
Less than $7,500	33.3	53.5	54.3	34.8	38.5	30.8	13.5
$7,500–$11,999	24.8	25.3	22.4	27.5	25.9	24.7	18.2
More than $11,999	19.1	7.3	5.3	25.2	17.2	21.4	37.3
Independent Undergraduates	18.0	14.0	18.1	12.5	14.5	17.0	15.6
Graduate Students	4.8	—	—	—	3.9	6.1	15.4
Total	100.0	100.0	100.0	100.0	100.0	100.0	100.0

* Atelsek and Gomberg, *Student Assistance* . . . , p. 18

** The Guaranteed Student Loan Program is not included.

*** The SSIG program began operating only in 1974–75. There were some problems in the data and Atelsek and Gomberg indicate that the reported number of SSIG recipients is inflated.

Table 4* Median Educational and General Revenues per FTE Student, by Selected Carnegie Category and Control, Current Dollars, 1974–75.

Carnegie Category	1974–75	
	Private	Public
(1)	(2)	(3)
1.1 Research Universities I	$12,688	$5,689
1.2 Research Universities II	6,165	4,220
1.3 Doctoral-Granting Universities I	4,912	3,433
1.4 Doctoral-Granting Universities II	3,493	2,462
2.1 Comprehensive Universities & Colleges I	2,561	2,411
2.2 Comprehensive Universities & Colleges II	2,680	2,432
3.1 Liberal Arts Colleges I	3,724	NA
3.2 Liberal Arts Colleges II	2,837	NA
4. Two-Year Colleges and Institutes	2,175	1,915

*Lanier and Andersen, *A Study of the Financial Condition . . .* , p. 21.

Table 5* Estimated Beneficiaries and Outlays, Social Security Education Benefits, Fiscal Years 1977–1982.

Fiscal Year	Beneficiaries (thousands)	Benefits Paid (millions of dollars)
1977	841	1,622
1978	876	1,819
1979	900	2,017
1980	908	2,188
1981	911	2,344
1982	910	2,485

*Congress of the United States, Congressional Budget Office, *Social Security Benefits for Students* (Washington: U.S. Government Printing Office, 1977), p. 10.

Table 6* Enrollment of Veterans and Spending for Veterans' Training
Under G.I. Bill or Bills, Fiscal Years 1967–1979**

(1)	(2)	(3)	(4)
		Total Enrolled in	
	Total in	*Institutions of*	
	Training	*Higher Learning*	*Spending*
Fiscal Year	*(in thousands)*	*(in thousands*	*(millions of dollars)*
1967	468	339	252
1968	687	414	407
1969	925	529	615
1970	1,211	677	939
1971	1,585	917	1,522
1972	1,864	1,065	1,812
1973	2,126	1,181	2,513
1974	2,359	1,337	3,006
1975	2,692	1,696	4,165
1976	2,822	1,925	5,029
1977	1,938	1,220***	3,567
1978	1,447	912***	2,814
1979	1,237	779***	2,420

*Veterans Administration, Reports and Statistics Service, Office of the Controller, *Veterans Benefits Under Current Educational Programs Information Bulletin*, April 1977, p. 70.

The Washington Office of the College Board, "The Fiscal Year 1979 Federal Budget and the Outlook for Student Assistance Programs," February 3, 1978, p. 7.

Administrator of Veterans Affairs *Annual Report 1976* (Washington: U.S. Government Printing Office, date of publication unlisted), p. 196.

**For Fiscal Years 1978 and 1979 there is estimated to be a small number of trainees and a correspondingly small amount of spending under the Post-Vietnam Era bill in addition to the participation and spending under the Vietnam Era bill.

***Estimated assuming the proportion of trainees training in institutions of higher learning will be the same in 1977–1979 as it was in 1974–1976.

CHAPTER 6—FEDERAL SUPPORT
FOR ACADEMIC RESEARCH

Geoffrey White was responsible for gathering and analyzing the material for Chapter 6. He wishes to express his appreciation to the staffs of the National Science Foundation, the National Center for Educational Statistics, and the National Association of College and University Business Officers for their patience and courtesy in providing information and answering inquiries; Margaret Child, Milton Goldberg and Robert Yuill were particularly helpful in response to repeated requests; a number of officials both in the executive branches and on the Congressional staffs, Henry Kirschenmann, Thomas Kramer, Philip Kropatkin, Terry Lierman, John Lordon, Richard Malow, John Stewart and Ann Strauss, provided helpful comments; Harvey Averch, Harvey Brooks, Alexander Morin and Walter Rosenblith read early drafts of the chapter and made helpful comments; the members of the staff of the National Commission on Research, and particularly its Executive Director, Dr. Cornelius J. Pings, were helpful in providing information and in allowing Mr. White to attend a number of their meetings; and many individual scientists in both Massachusetts Institute of Technology and Harvard University made helpful comments on their own experiences with federal funding at various stages of the work.

REFERENCES

The principal source of the data cited in this chapter is the statistical reports of the National Science Foundation.

Pages 164–166

Figures on federal research funding are from the National Science Foundation's report *Federal Support to Universities, Colleges and Selected Non-Profit Institutions: Fiscal Year 1977*, (Federal Support) Table B–10.

Figures on basic research funding are from the National Science Foundation report *National Patterns of Research and Development Resources: 1953–1978/79*, (National Patterns) Table B–2.

Figures on academic research funding are from the National Science Foundation reports *Expenditures for Scientific Activities of Universities and Colleges: Fiscal Year 1977*, (Scientific Activities) Table B–7; and (National Patterns) Table B–1.

Figures on academic research funding are from National Patterns, Table B–1; Federal Support, Table B–1; and Scientific Activities, 1978.

Figures on the distribution of federal research grants and contracts are from Scientific Activities, Table B–22.

Page 173

The figure on annual federal expenditures for basic research is extrapolated from National Patterns, Table B–6.

Page 175

The two studies of peer review are *Peer Review in the National Science Foundation*, (National Academy of Sciences, 1978); and *Grants Peer Review*, (National Institutes of Health, 1976).

Page 185

The projections of Ph.D. hires are from Fernandez, Luis, *U.S. Faculty After the Boom: Demographic Projections to 2000*, (Carnegie Council on Policy Studies in Higher Education, p. 33).

Page 187

The figures on undergraduate institution research are from Federal Support, Table B–25, and from telephone conversations with National Science Foundation officials.

Page 188

The figures on language and area studies are from a background paper on international education prepared for the Sloan Commission.

Page 189

The figures on research and development plant are from Federal Support, Table B—1.

Page 189

The figures on library funding are from telephone conversations with Office of Education officials.

Table 1.   Federal Outlays for Research and Development.

Fiscal Year	A R&D + R&D Plant Outlays $M	B Total Budget Outlays $B	C A/B %	D GNP $B	 A/D %
1940	74	9.6	0.8	100.0	.07
1941	198	14.0	1.4	124.9	.16
1942	280	34.5	0.8	158.3	.18
1943	602	78.9	0.8	192.0	.31
1944	1,377	94.0	1.5	210.5	.65
1945	1,591	95.2	1.7	212.3	.75
1946	918	61.7	1.5	209.6	.44
1947	900	36.9	2.4	232.8	.39
1948	855	36.5	2.3	259.1	.33
1949	1,082	40.6	3.7	258.0	.42
1950	1,083	43.1	2.5	286.2	.38
1951	1,301	45.8	2.8	330.2	.39
1952	1,816	68.0	2.7	347.2	.52
1953	3,106	76.8	4.0	366.1	.85
1954	3,148	70.9	4.4	366.3	.85
1955	3,308	68.5	4.8	399.3	.83
1956	3,446	70.5	4.9	420.7	.82
1957	4,462	76.7	5.8	442.8	1.01
1958	4,991	82.6	6.0	448.9	1.11
1959	5,806	92.1	6.3	486.5	1.19
1960	7,744	92.2	8.4	506.0	1.53
1961	9,287	97.8	9.5	523.3	1.77
1962	10,387	106.8	9.7	563.8	1.84
1963	12,012	111.3	10.8	594.7	2.02
1964	14,707	118.6	12.4	635.7	2.31
1965	14,889	118.4	12.6	688.1	2.16
1966	16,018	134.7	11.9	753.0	2.13
1967	16,859	158.3	10.7	796.3	2.12
1968	17,049	178.8	9.5	868.5	1.96
1969	16,348	184.5	8.9	935.5	1.75
1970	15,736	196.6	8.0	982.4	1.60
1971	15,992	211.4	7.6	1,063.4	1.50
1972	16,743	231.9	7.2	1,171.1	1.43
1973	17,510	246.5	7.1	1,306.6	1.34
1974	18,326	268.4	6.8	1,413.2	1.30
1975	19,590	324.6	6.0	1,516.3	1.29
1976*	21,379	373.5	5.7	1,692.4	1.26

*Estimated.
Sources: NSF and Economic Report of the President, January 1977.

Table 2.   National Expenditures on Basic Research As a Percentage
of Gross National Product.

A Calendar Year	B Basic Research $M	C GNP $B	B/C %
1953	441	366	.121
1954	496	366	.136
1955	547	399	.137
1956	679	421	.161
1957	780	443	.176
1958	877	449	.195
1959	1,040	487	.214
1960	1,197	506	.237
1961	1,401	523	.268
1962	1,724	564	.306
1963	1,965	595	.330
1964	2,289	636	.360
1965	2,255	688	.371
1966	2,814	753	.374
1967	3,039	796	.382
1968	3,274	869	.377
1969	3,425	936	.366
1970	3,513	982	.358
1971	3,577	1,063	.337
1972	3,748	1,171	.320
1973	3,877	1,307	.297
1974	4,144	1,413	.293
1975	4,527	1,529	.296
1976	4,881	1,700	.283
1977	5,440	1,887	.288
1978	6,045	2,108	.287
1979	6,700	2,343	.286

Sources: NSF–National Patterns of R&D Resources, NSF 77–310, and
NSF 78–313, Economic Report to the President.

Table 3.   National Research and Development Expenditures By Performing Sector.

Total Research and Development

Performer	1958		1968		1978	
	$T	Percent	$T	Percent	$T	Percent
Federal Government	1,374	13	3,493	14	6,565	14
Industry	8,389	78	17,429	71	33,250	70
Colleges and Universities	456	4	2,149	9	4,585	10
Associated FFRDC's	293	3	719	3	1,375	3
Other Non-Profit Institutions	199	2	814	3	1,520	3
Total	10,711	100	24,604	100	47,295	100

Federal Research and Development

Performer	1958		1968		1978	
	$T	Percent	$T	Percent	$T	Percent
Federal Government	1,374	20	3,493	23	6,565	28
Industry	4,759	70	8,560	57	11,750	49
Colleges and Universities	254	4	1,573	11	3,075	13
Associated FFRDC's	293	4	719	5	1,375	6
Other Non-Profit Institutions	99	1	582	4	1,050	4
Total	6,779	100	14,927	100	23,815	100

(Table 3. continued overleaf)

Table 3. continued

Federal Basic Expenditure

Performer	1958		1968		1978	
	$T	Percent	$T	Percent	$T	Percent
Federal Government	126	26	410	18	975	23
Industry	43	9	180	8	225	5
Colleges and Universities	178	37	1,251	54	2,265	54
Associated FFRDC's	78	16	276	12	410	10
Other Non-Profit Institutions	53	11	197	9	315	8
Total	478	100	2,314	100	4,190	100

Total Basic Expenditure

Performer	1958		1968		1978	
	$T	Percent	$T	Percent	$T	Percent
Federal Government	126	14	410	13	965	16
Industry	295	34	642	20	975	16
Colleges and Universities	281	32	1,649	50	3,165	52
Associated FFRDC's	78	9	276	8	410	7
Other Non-Profit Institutions	97	11	297	9	520	9
Total	877	100	3,274	100	6,045	100

Sources of this and all following tables are the various serial publications of the National Science Foundation.

Table 4. Federally Financed Expenditures on Research and
Development At Colleges and Universities, Fiscal Years 1953–1978
(In Millions of Dollars).

Fiscal Year	Current Dollars	Constant 1972 Dollars
1953	138	234
1954	160	268
1955	169	277
1956	213	339
1957	229	352
1958	254	384
1959	306	453
1960	405	590
1961	500	722
1962	613	869
1963	760	1,048
1964	916	1,245
1965	1,073	1,433
1966	1,262	1,639
1967	1,409	1,775
1968	1,573	1,911
1969	1,595	1,850
1970	1,648	1,813
1971	1,724	1,803
1972	1,839	1,839
1973	2,038	1,952
1974	2,032	1,806
1975	2,288	1,836
1976	2,501	1,876
1977	2,717	1,909
1978	3,057	2,011

Table 5 (a).   Federal Obligations* in Support of Academic Science,
Fiscal Years 1963–1978 Current Dollars in Millions.

Fiscal Year	R&D	R&D Plant	Other Science Activities	University FFRDC's	Total Academic Science
1963	830	106	393	814	2,143
1964	976	101	452	862	2,391
1965	1,095	126	595	895	2,712
1966	1,252	115	797	918	3,082
1967	1,301	111	911	908	3,232
1968	1,398	96	855	936	3,286
1969	1,475	55	832	917	3,278
1970	1,447	45	696	961	3,149
1971	1,551	30	762	984	3,327
1972	1,853	37	709	1,077	3,676
1973	1,871	43	550	1,011	3,475
1974	2,085	29	623	1,083	3,820
1975	2,238	45	522	1,207	4,012
1976	2,422	24	513	1,444	4,403
1977	2,784	36	526	1,612	4,959
1978	3,354	34	591	NA	NA

*Obligations in a given year may be larger or smaller than expenditures in that year. Thus, the figures in Table 5 (a) and Table 5 (b) do not match exactly those in Table 4.

Table 5 (b).   Federal Obligations* in Support of Academic Science,
Fiscal Years 1963−1978 Constant 1972 Dollars in Millions.

Fiscal Year	R&D	R&D Plant	Other Science Activities	University FFRDC's	Total Academic Science
1963	1,144	146	542	1,123	2,955
1964	1,326	137	614	1,171	3,248
1965	1,462	168	794	1,195	4,620
1966	1,626	149	1,035	1,192	4,002
1967	1,639	140	1,148	1,144	4,071
1968	1,699	117	1,039	1,137	3,992
1969	1,711	63	965	1,064	3,803
1970	1,591	49	766	1,057	3,462
1971	1,623	31	797	1,029	3,480
1972	1,853	37	709	1,077	3,676
1973	1,792	42	527	968	3,328
1974	1,853	26	554	963	3,396
1975	1,796	37	419	969	3,221
1976	1,817	18	385	1,083	3,303
1977	1,956	26	370	1,133	3,485
1978	2,207	23	389	NA	NA

*Obligations in a given year may be larger or smaller than expenditures in
that year. Thus, the figures in Table 5 (a) and Table 5 (b) do not match exactly those in Table 4.

Table 6.   Federal Research and Development Obligations To Colleges and Universities, By Agency (In Millions of Dollars).

Fiscal Year	DOD	DOE	DHEW	USDA	NSF	NASA	Other
1955	67	15	27	20	7	—	4
1956	83	18	31	25	11	—	4
1957	83	20	64	30	18	—	4
1958	118	30	79	31	21	—	3
1959	127	29	110	32	43	10	5
1960	155	34	158	32	56	10	4
1961	158	43	221	33	64	18	3
1962	259	46	310	39	86	53	9
1963	211	58	350	41	108	78	9
1964	310	60	419	49	120	89	14
1965	292	74	474	58	134	124	32
1966	292	82	538	62	180	117	56
1967	280	90	628	64	209	124	68
1968	244	93	671	61	221	131	69
1969	279	103	667	64	192	122	69
1970	266	101	615	67	201	127	69
1971	249	96	696	75	217	129	91
1972	244	87	879	89	335	112	107
1973	233	85	904	94	349	103	104
1974	184	94	1,129	97	376	92	109
1975	191	119	1,192	111	397	100	116
1976	212	138	1,281	124	429	107	117
1977	267	187	1,436	142	477	114	150
1978*	439	222	1,701	176	552	128	189
1979*	473	249	1,807	196	706	128	205

*Estimated.

Table 7. Federally Financed Expenditures for On-Campus Scientific Research By Broad Field of Science.

Field of Science	In Millions of Dollars		
	FY 1954	*FY 1968*	*FY 1978*
Physical and Mathematical Sciences	48	319	479
Engineering	52	246	408
Life Sciences	34	725	1,625
Environmental Sciences	*	89	275
Psychology	5	49	64
Social Sciences	3	101	141
Other Sciences	1	44	66

Field of Science	In Percent of Total		
	FY 1954	*FY 1968*	*FY 1978*
Physical and Mathematical Sciences	34	20	16
Engineering	37	16	13
Life Sciences	24	46	53
Environmental Sciences	*	6	9
Psychology	4	3	2
Social Sciences	2	6	5
Other Sciences	1	3	2

Table 8.   Federally Financed Research and Development Expenditures of the Fifty Universities Receiving the Largest Amounts Fiscal Year 1978.

Rank	Institution	Federal R&D Expenditures ($ Million)	
United States Total		3,057	
1	Massachusetts Institute of Technology	102	
2	University of California, San Diego	84	
3	Stanford University	79	
4	University of Washington	75	
5	University of Wisconsin, Madison	69	
6	Harvard University	64	
7	Columbia University	60	
8	University of Michigan	58	
9	University of California, Los Angeles	58	
10	Cornell University	55	
Total 10 Largest Institutions		703	23%
11	Johns Hopkins University	54	
12	University of Minnesota	53	
13	University of Pennsylvania	52	
14	University of California, Berkeley	50	
15	Yale University	47	
16	University of California, San Francisco	47	
17	University of Chicago	44	
18	Pennsylvania State University	42	
19	University of Illinois, Urbana	42	
20	New York University	41	
Total 20 Largest Institutions		1,176	38%
21	University of Southern California	39	
22	University of Texas, Austin	39	
23	Washington University	38	
24	University of Rochester	36	
25	Purdue University	30	
26	University of Colorado	30	
27	Duke University	28	
28	University of Utah	28	
29	Yeshiva University	27	
30	Ohio State University	27	
Total 30 Largest Institutions		1,500	49%

Table 8. continued

Rank	Institution	Federal R&D Expenditures ($ Million)	
31	University of Alaska	27	
32	University of Miami	26	
33	University of California, Davis	25	
34	Texas A&M University	25	
35	Colorado State University	25	
36	California Institute of Technology	25	
37	Michigan State University	25	
38	Northwestern University	24	
39	University of North Carolina, Chapel Hill	23	
40	University of Arizona	22	
Total 40 Largest Institutions		1,747	57%
41	University of Iowa	21	
42	Baylor College of Medicine	21	
43	Case Western Reserve University	21	
44	University of Connecticut	21	
45	University of Pittsburgh	21	
46	University of Alabama, Birmingham	20	
47	University of Maryland, College Park	20	
48	University of Florida	20	
49	University of Hawaii, Manoa	20	
50	Georgia Institute of Technology	20	
Total 50 Largest Institutions		1,944	64%

CHAPTER 7—GOVERNMENT AND THE
EDUCATION OF PHYSICIANS

Carl Kaysen prepared Chapter 7 with the help of the research staff and particularly careful scrutiny by the physician members of the Commission, Drs. James Campbell and Robert J. Glaser. Drs. Albert Gellhorn, James Pitman, David Rogers, and John Sanson were always ready to discuss new ideas. We also wish to thank the officers and staff of the American Association of Medical Colleges who were helpful in providing access to their complete and systematic store of information. Drs. Stephen Beering, Theodore Cooper, Christopher Fordham, Richard H. Moy, Robert L. Van Citters, and Vernon E. Wilson helped with critical reactions to early drafts of the chapter. The late John Knowles was very generous with his time and comment.

REFERENCES

Page 197

For a review of the academic medical center, its history, and potential see: Rogers, David R., *American Medicine: Challenge for the 1980s* (Cambridge: Ballinger, 1978). See also Knowles, John, *Doing Better and Feeling Worse: Health in the United States*, (New York: W.W. Norton & Co., 1977); Finkenstein, Dr., *Medical Students, Medical Schools and Society During Five Eras*, (Cambridge: Ballinger, 1978); U.S. Department of Commerce, Bureau of the Census, *Statistical Abstract of the United States: 1978*, (Washington, D.C.: G.P.O., 1978). On the funding of biomedical research see Morgan, Thomas E. and Jones, Daniel D., *Trends and Dimensions of Biomedical and Behavioral Research Funding in Academic Medical Centers, 1964—74*, (Washington, D.C.: American Association of Medical Colleges, 1976).

Page 198

See especially Cambridge Research Institute, *Trends Affecting the U.S. Health Care System*, U.S. D.H.E.W., #HRA 230—75—0072, (Germantown, Maryland: Aspen, 1975). For the growth of medical school budgets see *Journal of the American Medical Association* (Vol. 210, No. 8, November 24, 1969). For the federal role in financing medical schools see Williams, A., Carter, G., et al., *The Effects of Federal Biomedical Research*

Programs on Academic Medical Centers, (Santa Monica: Rand, 1967) and *Report of the President's Biomedical Research Panel*, U.S. D.H.E.W., Pub. #OS 76–005, (Washington, D.C.: 1976), as well as AAMC, *Trends and Dimensions of Biomedical and Behavioral Research Funding in Academic Medical Centers, 1964–74*, (Washington, D.C.: 1976). For the growth of clinical and other faculty see "Medical Education in the United States," an annual supplement of the *Journal of the American Medical Association*, (Reproduced as Table 1, "Academic Medical Center Enrollments/Faculty, 1964–78"). On the growth of the supply of physicians see *Journal of the American Medical Association*, (Vol. 240, No. 26, December 22–29, 1978).

Pages 198–200

On the growth of regulation in medical education see LeRoy, L. and Lee, P., *Deliberations and Compromise: The Health Professions Educational Assistance Act of 1976*, (Cambridge: Ballinger, 1978). On the growth of enrollments see *American Association of Medical Colleges Yearly Applicant Studies*, (Washington, D.C.: AAMC, annually. On American students at foreign medical schools see Fields, Cheryl, "They'd Rather Be Back Home," *Chronicle of Higher Education*, (April 17, 1978).

Page 201

For an exposition of the "target-income hypothesis" see Reinhardt, Uwe, *Physician Productivity and the Demand for Health Manpower: An Economic Analysis*, (Cambridge: Ballinger, 1976). Among a number of studies of "overdoctoring" is Winberg, J., *Vermont Hospitalizations: 1973 Variations in Patient Stay*, (Public Health Service Grant, PHS RMO 303). See also Reinhardt, Uwe, *op. cit.*, and Bunker J., Barnes, B., and Mosteller, F., *Costs, Risks and Benefits of Surgery*, (New York: Oxford University Press, 1977), as well as *Trends . . . , op. cit.* On the concern for costs see Executive Office of the President, Council on Wage and Price Stability, *The Complex Puzzle of Rising Health Care Costs*, #52–003–00255–8, (Washington, D.C.: U.S. Government Printing Office, December 1976) and Low, Sylvia, A., *Blue Cross: What Went Wrong?*, (New Haven: Yale University Press, 1976); Lave, Judith R., Presentation for Cornell University Conference for Business Executives, Ithaca, New York, May, 1977. Also see Wildavsky, A., in John Knowles, *op. cit.*

Pages 201–202

On the principle of medical uncertainty see Califano, Joseph, "A Private Sector Perspective on the Problems of Health Care Costs," working paper (Washington Business Group on Health, April, 1977), and A. Wildavsky, *op. cit.* On the distribution of physicians among specialists and general practitioners see Dukerson, O.D., *Health Insurance*, (Homewood,

Illinois: Richard D. Irwin, Inc., 1968); U.S. Department of Health, Education and Welfare, Office of the Assistant Secretary for Planning and Evaluation, *Health, Education, and Welfare Trends, 1966—67 Edition*, (Washington, D.C.: U.S. Government Printing Office, 1968); American Medical Association, *Distribution of Physicians in the U.S., 1973*, (Chicago: 1974); also American Medical Association, *Physicians Distribution and Medical Licensure in the U.S., 1975*, (Chicago: 1976) and Wexler.

Pages 203—204

For figures on current tuitions (1979) see Association of Medical Colleges, *Medical School Admissions Requirements, 1979—80*, (Washington, D.C.: AAMC, 1979). On the costs of medical education see National Academy of Science, The Institute of Medicine, *The Cost of Education in the Health Professions*, #HRA PB 238—328, (Washington, D.C.: National Technical Information Service).

Pages 204—205

On minority admissions see Odegaard, Charles, *Minorities in Medicine: From Receptive Passivity to Positive Action*, (New York: The Josiah Macy Foundation, 1976) and Reitzes, Deitrich C., *Negroes and Medicine*, (Cambridge: Harvard University Press, 1958) and the annual applicant surveys published by the AAMC.

Pages 205—206

On the comparative performance of white and Black medical students see the AAMC annual applicant surveys, as well as Odegaard, *op. cit.*, and Wechsler, Henry, Dorsey, Joseph L., and Bovey, Joanne D., "A Follow-Up of Residents in Primary Care Programs in Massachusetts," *The New England Journal of Medicine*, Vol. 298, No. 1, January 5, 1978 and Institute of Medicine, *A Manpower Policy from Primary Health Care*, (Washington, D.C.: National Academy of Sciences, 1978); Feitz, Robert H., *The MCAT and Success in Medical School*, (Paper presented at Annual Meeting of American Educational Research Association, Chicago, April 15—19, 1974) and the Association of American Medical Colleges' *amicus curaie* brief in the *Bakke* case. For trends in the enrollment of women in medical schools the annual applicant surveys are the primary source. Also see Walsh, Mary Roth, *Doctors Wanted: No Women Need Apply*, (New Haven: Yale University Press, 1977) and Coste, Chris, "Women in Medicine," *New Physician*, (November, 1975). Data on the age distribution of applicants and matriculants of medical schools may be found in the annual applicant surveys of the American Association of Medical College.

Page 207

On curriculum articulation significant work has been done at the University of Illinois—Rush Presbyterian Hospital Medical Center and as part of the Sophie A. Davis Program at the City Center of New York. (Personal visits.) For the number of foreign-trained physicians practicing in the United States, see Weinstein, Bernard M., "The Foreign Medical Graduate Issue and U.S. Hospitals," *Journal of the American Medical Association*, Vol. 241, No. 9, March 2, 1979.

Pages 207—208

U.S. Department of Commerce, Bureau of the Census, Series P—60, selected Consumer Income Reports and data from *Medical Economics*, selected issues, 1946—78 on income of self-employed and incorporated physicians. See also Freeman, Richard B., *The Over-Educated American*, (New York: Academic Press, 1976).

Table 1.   Physician Manpower: Selected Years 1950—1973.

Year	Total Physicians[a]	Physicians Per 100,000 Total Population[b]	Non-Federal Physicians In Patient Care	Non-Federal Physicians In Patient Care Per 100,000 Civilian Resident Population[c]
1950	219,997	141	NA	NA
1955	241,711	142	NA	NA
1960	260,484	141	NA	NA
1965	292,088	147	237,482	123
1970	334,028	159	252,778	124
1973	366,379	171	272,850	131

Source: American Medical Association, Center for Health Services Research and Development, *Socioeconomic Issues of Health: 1974 Edition* (Chicago, Ill.: 1974), p. 120.

Notes: NA = Not Available.

[a]Includes inactive and address unknown as of December 31.

[b]Total population includes Armed Forces and their dependents in the U.S. and abroad; civilians in the 50 states, D.C., and U.S. outlying areas; and U.S. government and civilian employees and their dependents abroad.

[c]Excludes U.S. outlying areas (Canal Zone, Pacific Islands, Puerto Rico, and Virgin Islands).

Table 2.   Distribution of Non-Federal Physicians By Specialty: Selected Years 1963–1973.

Specialty	1963		1967		1969		1973	
	Number	Percent	Number	Percent	Number	Percent	Number	Percent
Total	253,226	100.0%	279,418	100.0%	293,397	100.0%	297,598	100.0%
General Practice	70,405	27.8	65,430	23.4	55,341	18.9	51,653	17.4
Medical Specialties	50,846	20.1	61,115	21.9	64,322	21.9	78,708	26.6
Surgical Specialties	65,017	25.7	75,286	26.9	76,303	26.0	85,343	28.5
Other Specialties[a]	66,958	26.4	77,587	27.8	97,431	33.2	81,894	27.5

Sources: American Medical Association, Department of Survey Research, Center for Health Services Research and Development, Distribution of Physicians, Hospitals, and Hospital Beds in the U.S., 1969, Vols. I and II (Chicago, Ill.: 1970); Selected Characteristics of the Physician Population, 1963 and 1967 (Chicago, Ill.: 1968), and Distribution of Physicians in the U.S., 1973 (Chicago, Ill.: 1974), p. 76.

[a] In 1963, 1967 and 1969, includes inactive physicians as well as specialists in psychiatry, radiology, pathology, etc. In 1973, inactive and not classified physicians are excluded.

Table 3.   Distribution of Non-Federal Physicians, By Location: 1973.

	Total	Metropolitan Areas[a]		Non-Metropolitan Areas	
	(100.0%)	*Number*	*Percent*	*Number*	*Percent*
Active non-federal physicians as of December 31, 1973	311,342	270,022	86.7%	41,320	13.3%
U.S. resident population (000) as of December 31, 1972	209,448	156,922	74.9	52,526	25.1
Physicians/100,000 population	148.6	172.1	—	78.7	—

Source: American Medical Association, Center for Health Services Research and Development, *Distribution of Physicians in the U.S., 1973* (Chicago, Ill.: 1974), pp. 15–16.
Note: — = Not Applicable.
[a]Includes 252 SMSA's (Standard Metropolitan Statistical Areas) and 43 "potential" SMSA's as defined by the U.S. Census Bureau.

Table 4.   Income of Physicians, Dentists, and All Professional Technical and Kindred Workers, 1939—1976.

| | *Median Net Income Of:* | | | |
| | *Office-Based Nonsalaried Physicians* | *Office-Based Nonsalaried Dentists* | *Male Professional, Technical and Kindred Workers[2]* | *Average Wages and Salaries for Full-Time Employees* |
Year				
1939	$ 3,263[1]		$ 1,809	$ 1,280
1947	8,744		—	2,612
1951	13,150		4,071	3,262
1955	16,107	$11,533	5,055	3,923
1963	25,050		7,182	5,349
1965	28,960		7,798	5,814
1967	34,740	22,850	8,882	6,307
1970	43,100	28,100	10,722	7,713
1972	46,780		12,097	8,760
1973	50,823		12,977	9,290
1974	54,140	30,500	13,391	9,991
1975	58,440		14,311	10,845
1976	62,799		—	11,623

1. For 1939, *Medical Economics* published an estimate of mean rather than median income. Median income is estimated by assuming that the ratio of median to mean income in 1939 is the same for *Medical Economics* data as it is for Department of Commerce data.

2. Data on male professional workers are used since data for all professionals are not available for the entire time period.

Source: Column 1: 1939-1967, *Medical Economics*, selected issues, 1946-1968; 1970 estimated from data on income of self-employed and incorporated physicians appearing in selected issues of *Medical Economics*; 1972-1976, data supplied to the Council on Wage and Price Stability by *Medical Economics*. Column 2: "Survey of Dental Practices" 1956, 1968, 1971 and 1975, American Dental Association. Column 3: 1939-1970, U.S. Bureau of the Census, *Historical Statistics of the United States*, 1976, p. 304; 1971-1975, U.S. Department of Commerce, Bureau of the Census, Current Population Reports, P-60, *Money Income of Families and Persons in the United States*, annual issues. Column 4: 1939-1972, *The National Income and Product Accounts of the United States*, 1929-74, Bureau of Economic Analysis, U.S. Department of Commerce Table 6.9; 1973-1976, *Survey of Current Business*, July 1977, Table 6.9.

Table 5.   Summary of Information on Applications to U.S. Medical Schools, 1967–77.

Year	Number of Applicants	Number of Applications	Number of Applications Per Individual	Number of Accepted	Number of Applicants Per Acceptance	Percent Accepted
1967–68	18,724	93,332	5.0	9,702	1.9	51.8
1968–69	21,118	112,195	5.3	10,092	2.1	47.9
1969–70	24,465	133,822	5.5	10,547	2.3	43.1
1970–71	24,987	148,797	6.0	11,500	2.2	46.0
1971–72	29,172	210,943	7.2	12,335	2.4	42.3
1972–73	36,135	267,306	7.4	13,757	2.6	38.1
1973–74	40,506	328,275	8.1	14,335	2.8	35.4
1974–75	42,624	362,376	8.5	15,066	2.8	35.3
1975–76	42,303	366,040	8.65	15,365	2.75	36.3
1976–77	42,155	372,282	8.83	15,774	2.67	37.4
1977–78	40,569	371,545	9.16	15,977	2.54	39.4

Source: AAMC Yearly Applicant Studies.

Note: Final data for the 1977–78 and the 1978–79 applicant pools has not yet been published.

Table 6. Minority and Women Representation In First-Year Medical School Classes 1968–69 to 1976–77.

	68–69	69–70	70–71	71–72	72–73	73–74	74–75	75–76	76–77
American Indians, Mexican Americans and Mainland Puerto Ricans									
No. Applicants	—	—	—	—	—	822	738	766	784
No. Enrolled	26	61	111	181	215	274	367	355	360
Black Americans									
No. Applicants	—	—	1,250	1,552	2,382	2,227	2,368	2,286	2,486
No. Enrolled	266	440	697	882	957	1,027	1,106	1,036	1,040
Women									
No. Applicants	2,097	2,289	2,734	3,737	5,493	7,210	8,695	9,560	10,244
No. Enrolled	887	948	1,256	1,693	2,300	2,786	3,275	3,647	3,858

Source: AAMC Annual Applicant Surveys.

Table 7.   Academic Medical Center Enrollment/Faculty 1964–1978.

Total For All Centers	Fiscal Year							
	1962-63	1963-64	1964-65[1]	1965-66[2]	1966-67	1967-68	1968-69	1969-70
Total student enrollment	66,864	69,929	67,606	76,170	79,625	86,082	91,046	92,678
Medical student enrollment	31,491 47%	32,001 46%	32,428 48%	32,835 43%	33,423 42%	34,538 40%	35,833 39%	37,669 41%
Medical student equivalents[3]	8,946 13%	9,726 14%	10,678 16%	11,315 15%	11,756 15%	14,178 16%	15,842 17%	14,144 15%
Graduate student enrollment	4,105 6%	4,707 7%	5,509 8%	7,056 9%	8,364 11%	8,693 10%	9,743 11%	9,095 10%
Interns and residents	17,673 27%	17,996 26%	18,991 28%	19,950 26%	20,330 26%	21,968 26%	23,462 26%	26,664 29%
Post-doctorals	4,649 7%	5,502 8%	NA	5,014 7%	5,752 7%	6,705 8%	6,166 7%	5,106 6%
Total full-time faculty	13,681	14,468	15,514	17,149	19,296	22,163	23,014	23,672
Clinical science faculty	8,965 66%	9,632 67%	10,381 67%	11,489 67%	13,292 69%	15,435 70%	15,916 69%	16,465 70%
Basic science faculty	4,716 34%	4,836 33%	5,133 33%	5,660 33%	6,004 31%	6,728 30%	7,098 31%	7,207 30%

1. 1965 enrollment data is from AMA–AAMC Liaison Committee on Medical Education Questionnaire, Part II.
2. Data for 1966 and succeeding years is from "Medical Education in the United States," 1964–74, an annual supplement of *Journal of American Medical Association.*
3. Theoretical number of other health science students instructed by medical faculty. This item is variably reported.

Table 7. continued

Total For All Centers	Fiscal Year							
	1970–71	1971–72	1972–73	1973–74	1974–75	1975–76	1976–77	1977–78
Total student enrollment	98,012	109,984	118,578	118,531	144,095	108,783	115,891	114,456
Medical student enrollment	40,487 41%	43,650 40%	47,546 40%	50,217 42%	54,074 38%	56,244 52%	58,266 50%	60,456 53%
Medical student equivalents[3]	15,012 15%	16,545 15%	20,368 17%	21,569 18%	38,971 27%	NA	NA	NA
Graduate student enrollment	10,016 10%	9,654 9%	10,601 9%	11,146 9%	12,460 9%	12,414 11%	13,736 12%	12,146 11%
Interns and residents	27,225 28%	31,728 29%	32,556 27%	35,599 30%	35,285 24%	37,288 34%	41,160 36%	38,783 34%
Post-doctorals	5,272 5%	8,407 8%	7,516 6%	NA	2,505 2%	2,837 3%	2,729 2%	3,071 2%
Total full-time faculty	26,504	29,469	33,550	34,394	36,336	39,390	41,394	44,762
Clinical science faculty	18,451 70%	20,902 71%	24,047 72%	24,513 71%	26,280 72%	28,602 73%	30,207 73%	33,059 74%
Basic science faculty	8,053 30%	8,567 29%	9,503 28%	9,881 29%	10,056 28%	10,728 27%	11,187 27%	11,703 26%

3. Theoretical number of other health science students instructed by medical faculty. This item is variably reported.

List of Tables, Appendix 2

Chapter 3

Chapter 4

Chapter 5

Chapter 6

Chapter 7

Acknowledgments

Many people assisted the Commission in many ways. Acknowledgments for their generous and essential help to individual staff members are found in the notes to the chapters in Appendix 2. The research staff here thanks collectively all the colleagues in the greater Boston academic community who gave ongoing guidance, support, and criticism.

As a body, the Commission is grateful to many other particularly knowledgeable people who smoothed our way, clarified our thinking, pointed to problems, and raised our confidence that we were addressing the right issues in meaningful ways.

Clark Kerr occupies a special place in the study of American higher education, both as a man and as an intellectual leader. Much of the systematic knowledge that exists, and that we needed, was brought together between 1967 and 1980 under his direction of the Carnegie Commission on Higher Education and the Carnegie Council on Policy Studies in Higher Education. His work has influenced everyone in the field and, in particular, two members of our Commission who earlier were members of his.

The Washington offices of the higher education associations were patient, interested, and helpful in providing information, comment, and forums for discussion of work in progress. We want especially to thank Thomas Bartlett, Newton Cattell, Russell Edgerton, Richard Humphrey, Allen Ostar, Jack Peltason, John Phillips, and George Rainsford.

For the first year of our meetings around the country, invited representatives of a wide range of institutions addressed the Commission. We had the benefit of careful, candid, and thoughtful discussions with Elias Blake, Derek Bok, Ernest Boyer, John Cooper, M.D., Sidney Drell, Hugh Gloster, Winfred Godwin, Harold C. Howe II, Howard Jordan, Walter Leonard, Robert Marshak, Samuel Nabrit, William Nirenberg, James Perkins, David Saxon, Donald Stewart, and Jerome Wiesner. In every case, we learned from the encounter in ways reflected in the report.

It was a special pleasure to be able to involve students in the research work. Because of the advantage of location, we could draw on the resources of the undergraduate and professional schools of Boston University, Harvard, and M.I.T. Our faith in higher education was reinforced by the always energetic, always questioning efforts and zeal of our young helpers: John Bartenstein, David Garvin, David Levine, Lawrence Lustberg, Martha McPhee-Taft, Elizabeth Nelson, Stephen Scotch, Steven Sulski, Richard Stafford, Sally Spears, and Richard Yurko.

Fred Hapgood helped to make academese more readable and at various stages Calvin Kytle, Mark Plattner, and John Walsh contributed in this way. Annette Neutra brought unity and clarity to the final text.

Linda Yowaiski, as librarian and copy editor, presided over the movement of paper in and out of the Cambridge office with grace and efficiency. She shared the more routine but indispensable operating and secretarial responsibilities with Beatrice Haines, Renia Platt, Jean Wharton, and others who kept us going cheerfully and intelligently.

Notes on Members
of the Commission

JEAN ALLARD is a lawyer practicing in Chicago, a partner in Sonnenschein Carlin Nath & Rosenthal since 1976. She was at the University of Chicago from 1953–58 as Research Associate and Assistant Dean in its Law School, and as Vice President for Business and Finance, 1972–75. She is a trustee of Culver-Stockton College.

JOHN D. BALDESCHWIELER, Professor of Chemistry and Chairman of the Division of Chemistry and Chemical Engineering, California Institute of Technology, is an active scientific advisor to the federal government and has served on many of its boards including the President's Scientific Advisory Committee. He was Deputy Director of the Office of Science and Technology, 1971–73.

LOUIS W. CABOT, Chairman of the Cabot Corporation, Boston, is vice chairman of the Brookings Institution and a former chairman of the Federal Reserve Bank of Boston. His interest in higher education is long-standing: he is a member of the Massachusetts Institute of Technology Corporation, Northeastern University, and a former member of the Board of Overseers at Harvard.

JAMES A. CAMPBELL, M.D., President of Rush-Presbyterian-St. Luke's Medical Center in Chicago, and Professor of Medicine at Rush Medical College since 1971, was Planning Director for Education in Health Fields of the Illinois Board of Higher Education from 1964 to 1968, while serving as Professor of Medicine at the University of Illinois. He is a trustee of Knox College.

EDWARD W. CARTER, Chairman of Carter Hawley Hale Stores, Inc., was its Chief Executive Officer 1946–77. Since 1952, he has served on the Board of Regents of the University of California, and is now its senior member. He is also a trustee of Occidental College, the Brookings Institution, and the National Humanities Center.

PETER B. CLARK is now publisher of *The Detroit News.* Before joining the *News* in 1961, he taught political science briefly at the University of Chicago and at Yale. He is chairman of the Federal Reserve Bank of Chicago, serves on the advisory council of the Woodrow Wilson International Center for Scholars and is a trustee of Kenyon College.

RALPH A. DUNGAN is U.S. Executive Director of the Inter-American Development Bank, Washington, D.C. He was Chancellor of Higher Education, State of New Jersey, 1967–77, Ambassador to Chile 1964–67, and Special Assistant to Presidents Kennedy and Johnson.

MURRAY H. FINLEY is President of the Amalgamated Clothing and Textile Workers Union, having served as President of the Amalgamated Clothing Workers from 1972. He is a lawyer who began his association with the Union as its attorney in Chicago in 1949. He is on the boards of the A. Philip Randolph Institute and the United Nations Association Business and Labor Economic Council.

NORMAN C. FRANCIS has been President of Xavier University in New Orleans since 1968. Now chairman of the College Entrance Examination Board and a director of the National Merit Scholarship Corporation, he serves on several other boards. He was on the Advisory Council on Developing Institutions, DHEW. He is a member of the Vatican's Pontifical Commission on Justice and Peace.

WILLIAM C. FRIDAY has been President of the University of North Carolina, Chapel Hill since 1956. He was chairman of President Johnson's Task Force on Education, president of the Association of American Universities and chairman of the American Council on Education. A trustee of Howard University, he is also on the Boards of Davidson and Meredith Colleges.

THOMAS S. GATES, former Chairman of the Board of Morgan Guaranty Trust Company and since 1977 a member of its Directors Advisory Council, has had careers both in public service and in finance. Among other posts, he has been Secretary of the Navy, Secretary of Defense, and Head of the U.S. Liaison Mission to the People's Republic of China, 1976–77. He is a life trustee of the University of Pennsylvania.

ROBERT J. GLASER, M.D. is President of the Henry J. Kaiser Family Foundation in Palo Alto. From 1965 to 1970 he was at Stanford as Vice President for Medical Affairs, Dean, and Professor at the School of Medicine. He is a charter member of the Institute of Medicine of the National Academy of Sciences, a trustee of Washington University in St. Louis, and a member of various national advisory boards.

A. LEON HIGGINBOTHAM, Jr., is Judge of the U.S. Court of Appeals, Third Circuit, Philadelphia. His long government career includes service as Special Deputy Attorney General for Pennsylvania, 1956–62, and Federal Trade Commissioner, 1962–64. He was vice chairman of the National Commission on the Causes and Prevention of Violence. He is a trustee of Thomas Jefferson University, and the University of Pennsylvania (life).

CARLA HILLS practices law in Washington, D.C. as a partner of Latham, Watkins & Hills. She was Secretary of Housing and Urban Development, 1975–77. In 1974 she was Assistant Attorney General, Civil Division of the Department of Justice. She serves as trustee of Pomona College, the University of Southern California, and is on advisory councils of Yale and its Law School.

ROBERT S. INGERSOLL is now Deputy Chairman of the Board of Trustees of the University of Chicago. For many years he was Chairman and Chief Executive Officer of the Borg-Warner Corporation. He has extensive government service: Ambassador to Japan, 1972–74, and Deputy Secretary of State, 1974–76. He is a trustee of the California Institute of Technology.

CARL KAYSEN, now Professor of Political Economy at Massachusetts Institute of Technology, from 1966 to 1976 was Director of the Institute for Advanced Study, Princeton. Between 1947 and 1966 he was at Harvard and was Lucius N. Littauer Professor of Political Economy. He was Special Assistant to President Kennedy.

JAMES R. KILLIAN, Jr., was President of Massachusetts Institute of Technology from 1948 to 1959, Chairman of its Corporation from 1959–71 and is now Honorary Chairman. As the first presidential science advisor, he was President Eisenhower's Special Assistant for Science and Technology, 1957–59. He has participated in many national commissions on government and education and served as trustee of Washington University and Mount Holyoke College.

SAMUEL D. PROCTOR is the Martin Luther King Memorial Professor in the Graduate School of Education, Rutgers University. He is also Senior Minister in the Abyssinian Baptist Church, New York. From 1964–69 he held administrative posts in the Peace Corps and the Office of Economic Opportunity. He is a trustee of the United Negro College Fund and Meharry Medical College.

WILLIAM M. ROTH is President of Roth Properties and of Ghiradelli Square, San Francisco. From 1963–69, he was U.S. Special Representative and Ambassador for Trade Negotiations in Geneva. A former member of the Board of Regents of the University of California, he is a trustee of the Johns Hopkins School of International Affairs and of the Carnegie Institution of Washington.

HARRIET W. SHERIDAN is now Dean of the College at Brown University. From 1953 to 1979 she was at Carleton College where she was Andrew W. Mellon Professor of Humanities, Dean, and Acting President. She is on advisory boards of the National Endowment for the Humanities and the Danforth Foundation Fellowships.

ROBERT L. SPROULL has been President of the University of Rochester since 1970. A physicist, he was earlier on the Cornell faculty and Vice President for Academic Affairs 1965–68. An active scientific advisor to the federal government, he was Chairman of the Defense Science Board and Director of Advanced Research Projects Agency, Department of Defense. He has been a trustee of Deep Springs College and of Cornell University.

DANIEL YANKELOVICH is President of Yankelovich, Skelly and White, Inc., a national survey organization on public attitudes. He is also Research Professor of Psychology at New York University and visiting Professor on the graduate faculty of the New School for Social Research. He is President and founder of the Public Agenda Foundation.

ALBERT W. BOWKER, Chancellor of the University of California at Berkeley, participated in many Commission meetings but not in the report.